Foundation Expression Blend 3 with Silverlight

Victor Gaudioso

DESIGNER TO DESIGNER™

an Apress® company

Foundation Expression Blend 3 with Silverlight

ISBN-13 (pbk): 978-1-4302-1950-7

ISBN-13 (electronic): 978-1-4302-1951-4

Distributed to the book trade worldwide by Springer-Verlag New York, Inc., 233 Spring Street, 6th Floor, New York, NY 10013. Phone 1-800-SPRINGER, fax 201-348-4505, e-mail orders-ny@springer-sbm.com, or visit www.springeronline.com.

For information on translations, please contact Apress directly at 2855 Telegraph Avenue, Suite 600, Berkeley, CA 94705. Phone 510-549-5930, fax 510-549-5939, e-mail info@apress.com, or visit www.apress.com.

Apress and friends of ED books may be purchased in bulk for academic, corporate, or promotional use. eBook versions and licenses are also available for most titles. For more information, reference our Special Bulk Sales–eBook Licensing web page at www.apress.com/info/bulksales.

The information in this book is distributed on an "as is" basis, without warranty. Although every precaution has been taken in the preparation of this work, neither the author(s) nor Apress shall have any liability to any person or entity with respect to any loss or damage caused or alleged to be caused directly or indirectly by the information contained in this work.

The source code for this book is freely available to readers at www.friendsofed.com in the Downloads section.

Credits

I would like to dedicate this book to my absolutely amazing and loving family: my beautiful, wonderful, and gorgeous wife, Shay; my awesome and so full-of-life kids, Brianna, Tristan, and little Luke; and my so dedicated and very essential parents, Ralph and Elfreide.

CONTENTS AT A GLANCE

CONTENTS

Chapter 3 **C#, XAML, and Object-Oriented Programming** **49**

Chapter 4 **Controls** **71**

ABOUT THE AUTHOR

Victor Gaudioso is an independent Windows Presentation Foundation and Silverlight developer. Victor has worked on some of the most cutting-edge WPF and Silverlight applications that have been developed to date, including the Surface Winebar CES demo and Surface Air Hockey with simulated physics, which debuted at PDC in 2008. Victor was also part of the team that launched the Silverlight Entertainment Tonight Emmy minisite, one of the very first Silverlight applications to market, which made live streaming video directly from the red carpet available to the site's visitors. In his spare time, Victor continues to write books under the friends of ED flagship Foundation series in hopes of presenting the powerful new Microsoft technologies of WPF and Silverlight to developers around the globe. It would appear that he is succeeding, as his first book, *Foundation Expression Blend 2*, is required reading in most courses on interactive web media development, and is available in university libraries around the world—from Germany to the Philippines to the United States. Along with development and writing books, Victor reaches out to the community, for which he teaches a course on WPF and Silverlight at Almer/Blank's Rich Media Institute in Venice, California. Victor is also active in the Flash community and often makes appearances at Flash events such as Flash in the Can (FiTC) and Flashapalooza.

ABOUT THE TECHNICAL REVIEWER

Jason Cook is a software engineer and user interface designer based in Hollywood, California. He has a highly decorated background in developing rich media applications, winning more than a dozen coveted industry awards over the last ten years. Jason has built a number of groundbreaking applications for industry-leading entertainment and consumer products clients such as ABC, NBC/Universal, Disney, Mattel, MTV, VH1, Honda, New Line Cinema, Sony Computer Entertainment America, Sony Pictures, and Touchstone Pictures. Jason has led seminars, conducted professional training programs, and offered personalized consulting for Fortune 500 software companies.

ABOUT THE COVER IMAGE DESIGNER

Corné van Dooren designed the front cover image for this book. Having been given a brief by friends of ED to create a new design for the Foundation series, he was inspired to create this new setup combining technology and organic forms.

With a colorful background as an avid cartoonist, Corné discovered the infinite world of multimedia at the age of 17—a journey of discovery that hasn't stopped since. His mantra has always been "The only limit to multimedia is the imagination," a mantra that is keeping him moving forward constantly.

After enjoying success after success over the past years—working for many international clients, as well as being featured in multimedia magazines, testing software, and working on many other friends of ED books—Corné decided it was time to take another step in his career by launching his own company, *Project 79*, in March 2005.

You can see more of his work and contact him through www.cornevandooren.com or www.project79.com.

If you like his work, be sure to check out his chapter in *New Masters of Photoshop: Volume 2* (friends of ED, 2004).

ACKNOWLEDGMENTS

First, I would like to dedicate this book to be to the readers. I created a special e-mail address for my last book, *Foundation Expression Blend 2: Building Applications in WPF and Silverlight*: wpfauthor@gmail.com. The overwhelmingly positive and numerous responses I received from you all made me appreciate each and every one of you so very much. Further, your dedication to learning this new technology inspired me to make the second book even better than the first. So this book is dedicated to readers of both books I have written, from my young computer genius buddy Lloyd Humphreys in Wales, to Lukas Ruebbelke, to Ariel Leroux, who wrote an entire blog (www.facingblend.com) about her experience reading and working through my first book. She even took me to task when I mentioned in the book that I would help you out if you got stuck. She e-mailed me with her problem, and we *did* figure it out together. I wish I could mention you all by name, but there are so many of you that it is just not feasible. However, know that I appreciate and remember you all. I encourage readers that have contacted me before to do so again, and new readers to drop me an e-mail and say hello and show me what this book has helped you to create. Or, as I mentioned in the first book, let me help you out when you get stuck. This book is dedicated to *all* of you!

I would also like to acknowledge the people who helped to make this publication possible. First, I would like to acknowledge my good friend and mentor Andrew Whiddett, who took me under his wing. He has taught me ever-inventive ways to develop applications and how to embrace and not be afraid of complex design patterns such as DataFactories, MVC, and most recently MVVM. I would also like to mention my wonderful aunt, Zan Gaudioso, who helped me with a ton of authoring questions and has always told me I could, even when I thought I couldn't. Further, I would like to acknowledge the team at Apress/friends of ED: my go-getter (and sometimes whip-cracker) project manager whom I consider a friend and whose job it is to motivate me to write, Kylie Johnston; my editor, Ben Renow-Clarke, whom I overworked with my horrible punctuation and stream of consciousness style of writing; my copy editors, Damon Larson, Heather Lang, and Sharon Wilkey, with their incredible attention to detail and never-ending stream of inquires that I never know the answers to. I would also like to acknowledge my friends over at Electric Rain. And finally I'd like to give a special acknowledgment to my technical editor and very dear friend Jason Cook, who never hesitated to be very tough on me when I would make plain inaccurate statements in the book, but who also took the time to help me understand how some very complex pieces of code worked when I needed it.

INTRODUCTION

Welcome to *Foundation Expression Blend 3 with Silverlight*! I am very excited about this, my second book, as I love Silverlight and I have a burning passion for developing and teaching it! Throughout the course of the book, I am going to take you step by step from being a novice in Blend 3/Silverlight to being a skilled practitioner who can create your own dynamic rich media Internet applications with animation storyboards, stunning effects, and some pretty advanced coding constructs, such as the CLRInstance DataFactory, XML serialization to native Silverlight objects, and custom Silverlight panels. By the time you are done with this book, you will know how to create awesome user interfaces, custom UserControls, and amazing state transitions. Because this technology is so new, only a handful of people in the world know how to develop well in it, and those who can are compensated very well and are highly sought after. It's a rapidly expanding market, and more and more companies are looking for Silverlight developers—if you have those skills, then you'll be a developer in demand! Silverlight is a very hot topic, and there are many more companies out there looking for designers and developers who can use it well. If you follow along closely, then I can help you become that designer or developer. I cannot promise it will be easy, but I can promise that if you get stuck, you can e-mail me at wpfauthor@gmail.com, and I will e-mail you back and help you through your problem. I did it on my last book and I had a ton of fun doing it, so I am making this promise again.

Who this book is for

Throughout my career, I have purchased many technological publications just to realize that I was not part of the target audience for that particular book. In order to help potential readers avoid this situation, I will outline exactly who this book is for. This book is for you if you know the basics of object-oriented programming (OOP) and have some programming experience in languages such as JavaScript, ActionScript, C++, Visual Basic, Java, or C, but have not used Silverlight. If you understand even just a little about OOP, you can benefit from this book and start to develop in Silverlight; however, if you do not have any experience in any of these languages, I suggest you buy a beginner's guide on C# first. *Beginning C# 2008: From Novice to Professional*, by Christian Gross (Apress, 2007), is a good book and will give you far more information than you will need to make good use of this title. An extra added skill would be experience with XML (Extensible Markup Language), as it is what a large part of Silverlight is based upon, including XAML (Extensible Application Markup Language). However, this isn't essential, as in this book I assume you know as little as possible, and I start off with the basics before leading you through more advanced tutorials.

What this book will teach you

Following is a list of exactly what this book will teach you so that you know what you will be able to accomplish in Silverlight and Blend once you have completed the book. You will

- Understand the typical Silverlight/Blend/Visual Studio workflow for creating Silverlight applications

- Understand the Blend 3 IDE—what tools are available and how to use them properly

- Understand XAML and C# basics, as well as some advanced C# constructs such as a CLRInstance of a DataFactory and a very popular user interface design pattern called Model-View-ViewModel (MVVM)

- Know the basic Silverlight content element controls

- Understand the very powerful Silverlight MediaElement and how to use it to create video and audio for your applications

- Learn how to create reusable styles and control templates

- Learn how to raise events and event handlers

- Learn how to quickly and easily create sample data in Blend 3

- Learn how to create an interactive, design-free prototype of a web application called a sketchflow

- Learn about reusable Silverlight visual brushes and how to use them

- Understand the difference between timelines and storyboards, and learn how to use timelines to create compelling storyboard animations

- Put all of the new knowledge you learned together to create a Silverlight web application with a powerful paging system that allows for fast download time and saves on system memory, and that you will be able to reuse as a template as you continue to develop in Silverlight

What Silverlight/Blend 3, C#, and XAML are

Silverlight has a large number of framework elements and controls, including Button, Grid, and MediaElement. These are all written in XAML, an XML-based markup language. XAML also allows you to create storyboard animations. These user interface controls can be controlled partially in XAML by storyboards, but for the most part they are controlled with C#. This type of structure is very similar to HTML and JavaScript, as HTML displays the content, while JavaScript adds functionality to the interactive parts of the HTML, such as mouseover effects. Conversely, controls can be created in C#, but are most often created in XAML. XAML can also display assets such as images, audio, and video. C# is a very robust object-oriented programming language developed by Microsoft, and is part of the .NET 3.5 (and soon 4.0) Framework. I like to think of XAML as the pretty exterior of a cool car, and C# as the powerful engine under the hood. So the typical way that Silverlight creates and displays content goes like this:

1. XAML describes how the controls, images, video, and other assets are shown.

2. C# gives these assets their functionality.

3. The compiler then puts the XAML user interface and functionality together into an executable (EXE) file for a Silverlight desktop or web application.

4. The browser or desktop then displays the application.

The real power of Silverlight is the robustness of C# and the capability of using XAML to create the interface.

Using Visual Studio and Blend

C# is usually created and edited in Visual Studio 2008 (or soon Visual Studio 2010), and XAML can be edited in both Blend and Visual Studio 2008. Since Blend 3, though, you have the ability to create and edit C# in Blend as well as Visual Studio 2008. However, you may still want to edit or create your C# code in Visual Studio, because Visual Studio has tools to assist in writing code, such as IntelliSense (discussed later in the book).

Blend, on the other hand, is a new instrument that allows you to create and display Silverlight assets such as controls and images in code or visually. The Selection, Brush Transform, and various shape tools are just a few of the features that Blend offers the developer. I will go into these and other tools in Chapter 3, and you will master these development tools in later chapters.

What Silverlight is and how it differs from WPF

Silverlight, formerly known as Windows Presentation Foundation Everywhere (WPF/E), is a cross-platform version of WPF. Basically, it is a subset of WPF that can run on a Mac or PC. WPF can only run on Windows Vista or Windows XP with .NET 3.0 or later installed (Windows XP ships with .NET 2.0). There are other differences, but most important is that WPF can make use of 3D objects, while Silverlight can do some faking of 3D, but not true 3D. This is because WPF can make use of the host machine's graphics card, while Silverlight cannot, as it is difficult to port 3D hardware acceleration across different platforms. The final difference is that Silverlight integrates right into an HTML page by using the Silverlight browser plug-in, while WPF needs to be inserted into an iframe to mix with HTML content. Silverlight is still being developed, so the differences I have just explained may not exist in future Silverlight releases.

Online resources

Throughout this book, I will point you to online Silverlight examples I have created, as well as code snippets and video tutorials. In the Appendix, I will also point you to additional resources that can help you grow as a Silverlight/Blend developer. These resources include weblogs, online tutorials, code examples, and much more.

Layout conventions

To keep this book as clear and easy to follow as possible, the following text conventions are used throughout:

- Important words or concepts are normally highlighted on the first appearance in **bold type**.
- Code is presented in fixed-width font. New or changed code is presented in **bold fixed-width font**.
- Menu commands are written in the form Menu ➤ Submenu ➤ Submenu.
- Where I want to draw your attention to something, I've highlighted it like this:

> *Ahem, don't say I didn't warn you.*

Chapter 1

SETTING UP THE SILVERLIGHT DEVELOPMENT ENVIRONMENT

What this chapter covers:

- Downloading and installing Visual Studio 2008 SP1
- Downloading and installing Silverlight Tools for Visual Studio 2008 SP1
- Downloading and installing Blend 3
- Downloading and installing the Silverlight Runtime
- Creating a Silverlight test application in Visual Studio
- Creating very simple content in your Silverlight test application
- Compiling/running your Silverlight test application
- Opening your Silverlight test application in Blend 3

Before I put you through the trouble of downloading and installing all of the software you will need to create Silverlight applications, I would like to make certain that you have the hardware to handle all of this new software. This chapter assumes the following:

- You have a computer that is running either Windows XP with Service Pack 2 (SP2) installed, or any version of Windows Vista.
- Your system has at least 1 GB of RAM.
- Your hard drive has at least 5 GB of free space available.

- Your PC has a relatively fast CPU.

- Your system has a relatively good video card.

- You have Internet access (high speed is preferred).

- You know how to navigate the Internet.

- You know how to download, save, and install programs from the Internet.

- You have uninstalled all previous trial versions of Blend/Visual Studio/.NET 3.0 or higher.

If I have not scared you off, you can start downloading and installing the Silverlight development environment.

> *Because Silverlight is a very new technology, the development tools tend to change over time with newer, better versions being released by Microsoft. That being the case, the information presented here may be slightly outdated. I suggest you read my blog on Amazon.com, as I post updated information there. To find my blog, you can go to Amazon.com and search for "Victor Gaudioso."*

Until recently, installing the Silverlight development environment was very difficult to do. Microsoft has made it much easier these days by setting up a section on Silverlight.net dedicated to installing everything you need to get started. The section is even called "Get Started." The URL is http://silverlight.net/GetStarted/. With that, let's begin by installing the Visual Studio 2008 SP1 90-day trial version.

> *If you want to use Windows XP for Silverlight development, you need to have SP2 installed, as well as the .NET 3.5 Framework.*

Downloading and installing the Visual Studio SP1 2008 Professional trial version

Like I mentioned before, you can use Silverlight.net's "Get Started" section to find the URLs that you need to install the Visual Studio 2008 SP1 Professional trial version. Here's how:

1. Open your web browser.

2. In the address box, type in **http://silverlight.net/GetStarted/**, as shown in Figure 1-1.

Figure 1-1. Navigate to the "Get Started" section of the Silverlight.net website.

3. Next, click the Visual Studio 2008 SP1 link, as shown in Figure 1-2.

Figure 1-2. Click the Visual Studio 2008 SP1 link.

This link took me to http://www.microsoft.com/downloads/details.aspx?FamilyID=c7a809d8-8c9f-439f-8147-948bc6957812&displaylang=en, where I had to download nine different files to install the trial versions of Visual Studio 2008.

> Note that the installation process changes from time to time. While I have documented my experience here, it may be different by the time you try to install. If that is the case, just follow the posted instructions to install Visual Studio.

4. Download all of the files, and when that is complete, run the first EXE file to start the installation process. These downloads may take some time, so this may be a good time to walk the dog (or whatever it is you like to do when downloading large files).

5. Once the file downloads have completed, you are ready to start installing Visual Studio. To do so, navigate to where you downloaded the files, and double-click the file with an .exe extension.

The installer will run you through the installation process. It will be pretty straightforward, so I won't explain it any further than I already have. If by chance the install fails, it means that you probably have previous trial versions of Blend, Visual Studio, or .NET 3.0 (or higher) installed. If this is the case, exit the installer, open the Windows Control Panel, and double-click Programs and Features. Then uninstall all previous versions of Blend, Visual Studio, and any program that has .NET 3.0 or .NET 3.5 as part of its name. Then start the Visual Studio install process again.

Downloading and installing Silverlight Tools for Visual Studio 2008 SP1

Now that you have Visual Studio installed, you need to install Silverlight Tools for Visual Studio 2008 SP1 so that you can actually create Silverlight applications. Do that now:

1. In your web browser, navigate back to the "Get Started" section of Silverlight.net.

2. Click Silverlight Tools for Visual Studio 2008 SP1, as shown in Figure 1-3.

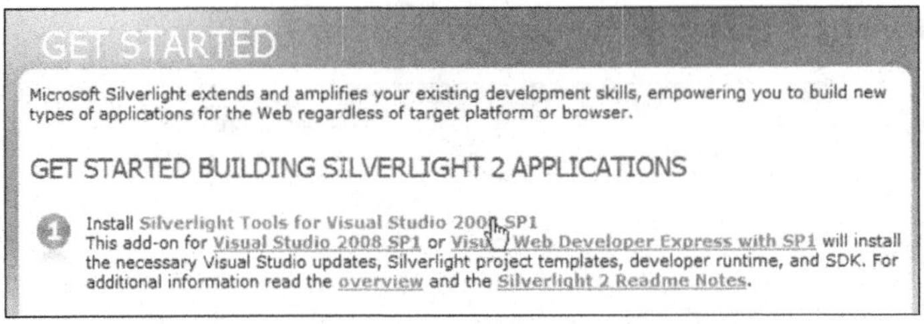

GET STARTED

Microsoft Silverlight extends and amplifies your existing development skills, empowering you to build new types of applications for the Web regardless of target platform or browser.

GET STARTED BUILDING SILVERLIGHT 2 APPLICATIONS

Install Silverlight Tools for Visual Studio 2008 SP1
This add-on for Visual Studio 2008 SP1 or Visual Web Developer Express with SP1 will install the necessary Visual Studio updates, Silverlight project templates, developer runtime, and SDK. For additional information read the overview and the Silverlight 2 Readme Notes.

Figure 1-3. Click the link to Silverlight Tools for Visual Studio 2008 SP1.

You will then be redirected to a page on Microsoft.com.

3. Click the Download button, save the file (Silverlight `_Tools.exe) to your local hard drive, and make a mental note of where you saved it.

4. Once it has downloaded, navigate to where you saved it and double-click it to start the installation process.

Once you have the Silverlight Tools installed, you are ready to go on and download Blend 3.

Downloading and installing Blend 3

You are almost done. Just one last program and you are ready to start developing in Silverlight!

1. In your web browser, navigate back to the "Get Started" section on Silverlight.net.

2. Click the Blend 3 link.

3. When prompted, save the file to your local hard drive, and again, make a mental note of the file name and location where you are saving it.

4. When the download is complete, navigate to where you saved it and double-click it.

The Blend 3 installer will run its course. Once it does, you'll have successfully installed the Silverlight development environment. Next, you need to install the Silverlight Runtime plug-in so you can see Silverlight applications in your web browser.

Installing the Silverlight Runtime plug-in

Now that you have all of the programs you need to develop in Silverlight, you need to be able to view your applications in a web browser. To do that, you are going to need to install the Silverlight Runtime plug-in. Do that now:

1. In a web browser, navigate back to the "Get Started" section of Silverlight.net.

2. Find the Install Silverlight box located on the right, and click Windows Runtime, as shown in Figure 1-4.

Figure 1-4. Install the Silverlight Windows Runtime.

> *At the time of writing Silverlight 3 was not yet released, but this book is 100% compatible with Silverlight 3. The current version of Blend only allows you to create Silverlight 3 applications.*

3. When prompted, save the executable file to your local hard drive. Again, make a mental note of the name of the file and the location in which you are saving it.

4. When the download is complete, navigate to where you saved the file on your local hard drive and double-click it.

The installation should be very fast—much faster than the previous versions of the Silverlight Runtime for certain. Now you are ready to start developing and running Silverlight applications. With that, let's get to it and create a Silverlight test application.

Creating a Silverlight test application

So, now you are ready to finally create your first Silverlight test application. To do that, complete the following procedure.

If you're running Visual Studio for the first time, it may take a while for it to start. Visual Studio will then ask you what type of developer you are; when it does, select the settings for a C# developer.

> *While Silverlight applications can be developed in many languages (including C#, Visual Basic, and Ruby, among others), this book will focus on development with C#, since this is the most common.*

Now you are ready to create a new Silverlight project. To do that, follow these steps:

1. Click File ➤ New ➤ Project, as shown in Figure 1-5.

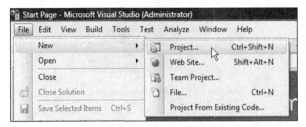

Figure 1-5. Creating a new project

2. When the New Project dialog box pops up, make sure that

- Silverlight is the selected project type
- Silverlight Application is the selected template
- The name of the project is SLTestApplication
- Make sure that you remember the location where this project is being saved (see Figure 1-6)

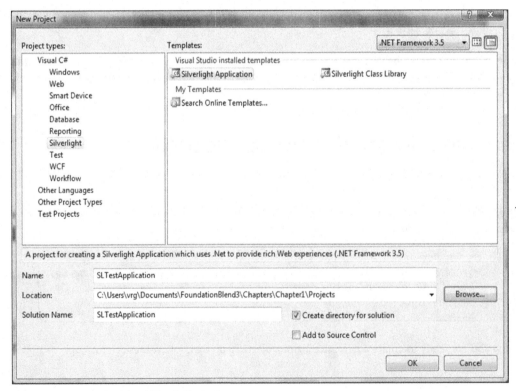

Figure 1-6. Your settings should be similar to these.

3. Now the Add Silverlight Application dialog box will pop up. On this dialog, check Automatically generate a test page to host Silverlight at build time, as shown in Figure 1-7, and click OK.

You're telling Visual Studio to create a test page at build time because you just want a simple Silverlight project, and you don't want to add an ASP.NET-based website to the project.

Figure 1-7. Tell Visual Studio to create a test page for you.

Visual Studio 2008 will then create the application for you. You will see Page1.xml with some default code. This is the code for the page that will first be displayed when your Silverlight application runs. You can now add a simple TextBlock so you will know that you have opened the correct application in Blend 3. Do that now:

> *Silverlight 2 will name your main XAML page (the page that is first displayed when the application is run)* Page1.xaml, *while Silverlight 3 will name the main page* MainPage.xaml. *Later you will only see applications with the main page named* MainPage.xaml.

1. Place your cursor between the opening and closing Grid nodes, and start to type the word TextBlock, as shown in Figure 1-8.

```
Page.xaml  Start Page
1 <UserControl x:Class="SilverlightApplication1.Page"
2     xmlns="http://schemas.microsoft.com/winfx/2006/xaml/presentation"
3     xmlns:x="http://schemas.microsoft.com/winfx/2006/xaml"
4     Width="400" Height="300">
5     <Grid x:Name="LayoutRoot" Background="White">
6         I
7     </Grid>
8 </UserControl>
9
```

Figure 1-8. Place your cursor between the opening and closing <Grid> tags.

2. When IntelliSense has figured out what you are trying to type, press Enter. Your code will look like the following:

```xml
<UserControl x:Class="SLTestApplication.Page"
    xmlns="http://schemas.microsoft.com/winfx/2006/xaml/presentation"
    xmlns:x="http://schemas.microsoft.com/winfx/2006/xaml"
    Width="400" Height="300">
    <Grid x:Name="LayoutRoot" Background="White">

        <TextBlock></TextBlock>
    </Grid>
</UserControl>
```

> *IntelliSense is a Visual Studio feature that attempts to figure out what you are trying to do, and then autocompletes your code for you. It is a very handy tool, and one that I use very often. I am sure you will too.*

So, now you have a TextBlock, but if you were to compile and run the application, you would not see anything because you have yet to specify what text you want the TextBlock to display. Fix that now:

3. Place your cursor in the TextBlock node and give it a Text property of Silverlight Test Application, so that your code looks like the following:

```xml
<UserControl x:Class="SLTestApplication.Page"
    xmlns="http://schemas.microsoft.com/winfx/2006/xaml/presentation"
    xmlns:x="http://schemas.microsoft.com/winfx/2006/xaml"
    Width="400" Height="300">
    <Grid x:Name="LayoutRoot" Background="White">

        <TextBlock Text="Silverlight Test Application"></TextBlock>
    </Grid>
</UserControl>
```

Now you can press F5 to compile and run the application. Visual Studio will show you your test application in your default web browser, complete with your TextBlock, as shown in Figure 1-9.

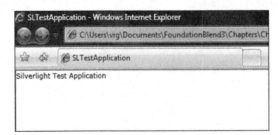

Figure 1-9. Your test application running in a browser

So, that's Visual Studio and Silverlight working. The only thing you have left to do is open your test application in Blend 3.

Opening the test application in Blend 3

In order to make certain that your Silverlight development environment is ready to rock and roll, open the SLTestApplicaton project in Blend 3. Blend 3 will then start. When it does, you will see the welcome screen. Click Open Project, as shown in Figure 1-10.

Figure 1-10. Click Open Project on Blend 3's welcome screen.

> When both Visual Studio 2008 and Blend 3 start, you will probably be asked to enter a license key or use the trial version. For now, just use the trial version. If you love Silverlight development after you are done with this book, then I suggest you buy licenses for both products.

Now navigate to where you saved your test application and double-click the SLN file. Blend will then show your test application complete with the TextBlock you created in the last section (see Figure 1-11).

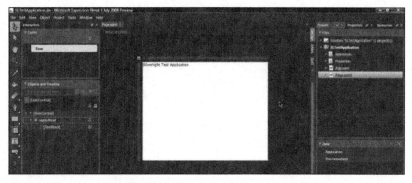

Figure 1-11. Your test application in Blend

Summary

Congratulations! You have successfully set up your Silverlight development environment by downloading and installing

- Visual Studio 2008 SP1
- Silverlight Tools for Visual Studio 2008 SP1
- Blend 3
- The Silverlight Runtime plug-in

You then tested out the development environment by

- Creating a Silverlight test application
- Adding simple content to it in the form of a TextBlock
- Compiling and running the application
- Opening the test application and viewing it in Blend

> *The installation process should be quite simple, but sometimes previously installed programs and features on your PC can make it very difficult. For that reason, it is possible that you may get stuck. If that is the case, I have set up a special e-mail so you can reach out to me if you need assistance. If this happens to be you, don't hesitate to shoot me an e-mail at wpfauthor@gmail.com. I will answer you within the day as long as I am not out of the United States.*

You are now ready to move on to developing some very cool Silverlight applications. But first I think it would be best if I showed you around Blend 3 and Visual Studio 2008. So let's move on to the next chapter where I'll do that.

Chapter 2

THE BLEND 3 INTEGRATED DEVELOPMENT ENVIRONMENT

What this chapter covers:

- The improved developer/designer workflow
- The Blend 3 toolbar
- The Objects and Timeline panel
- The Projects panel
- The Properties panel
- The Resources panel
- 3D objects that can be created in Blend 3

Now that you have your development environment set up, we can get to the basics, and discuss some of the major features of the Blend 3 integrated development environment (IDE). As we proceed, I will explain each major feature and then task you with little exercises that will help you to familiarize yourself with these tools and features. Some of these tools and features I will discuss briefly here and in more depth in later chapters. Before we get started, I want to provide you with a quick list of features brand new to Blend 3.

The improved developer/designer workflow

This feature is technically not new to Silverlight, but it is such an important part of the development cycle that it needs to be mentioned. Also, this workflow improves with every new version of Blend and Silverlight. With that, how does Silverlight improve the workflow between developer and designer? Microsoft has recognized some of the difficulties that crop up when designers and developers try to work together, and provided a better set of tools and workflow to allow them to interact more easily. Blend 3 is intended to be used by designers to visually manipulate the application user interface (UI)—they can control layout, create visual storyboard animations, add in assets such as graphics and video, and so on. Developers, on the other hand, can now use both Blend 3 and Visual Studio to interact with the application through code. This makes the workflow between designers and developers much simpler, more harmonious, and time efficient, and thus cost effective.

Before I started working in Silverlight, I was an ActionScript engineer for a large advertising firm in Los Angeles where we made large web sites for entertainment companies such as Disney, Universal, Mattel, and Warner Bros. Here I will describe a typical workflow between the developers, the designers, and myself, pointing out the limitations of that workflow along the way, and then describing how Silverlight addresses those problems.

1. First, the designers design the entire site, top to bottom, as a series of Photoshop mockups.
2. Once the mockups are agreed upon and signed off, the Photoshop PSD files are handed off to me and my team to "make work." This is a typical workflow not only for Flash development, but for other technologies as well (HTML, Java, etc.).
3. I use the Photoshop file as a guide and re-create an object, let's say something simple like a button. I re-create it in Flash, or sometimes if I'm lucky I can copy it from Adobe Illustrator as a vector graphic.
4. Then we plug the functionality into the newly created Flash objects—for example, the event handlers that handle the functionality for buttons.

This sounds pretty effective, so what then are the limitations? Let's say for some reason the client changes his mind and wants the button to look radically different. Being that I am not much of a designer, the job then falls upon the designers to make the change. They go back and make the required change to their Photoshop or Illustrator file. When they have completed the change, they then inform me that the files have been updated. I open up their Illustrator or Photoshop file and then either re-create the asset in Flash using the Photoshop file as a guide or copy the new vector graphic from Illustrator into Flash. This may not seem problematic, and in fact, it is not. It is, however, time consuming.

Microsoft's solution is to have the developers and the designers working on the same set of files in the same project, so that if the style of a Button changes, the designers can go into the same files that I, the developer, am working on and make the change. Further, Silverlight allows you to use something called **styles** to specify the way UI elements (UIElements) appear in your application. And these styles are 100% reusable, so that if I or the designer change the style (commonly defined in a ResourceDictionary, which we will get to later in the book) of, say, the navigation buttons, that change is then reflected in any Silverlight UIElements that make use of that style, which could be hundreds of buttons in a large application. As you can ascertain, this saves a good amount of time. Now, if you take into account that this type of scenario takes place many times during a project, the amount of time that is saved is dramatically increased. And as we all know, time is money, and money is what allows us to be able to pursue our hobby of developing rich Internet applications.

So, how does Silverlight create a harmonious workflow? To explain this, I think it would be a good idea to provide you with a real-world example. Recently, I was part of a team that was developing a complex web application. There was one developer on the project and two designers. The developer worked solely on the functionality of the application, in the C# code-behind files, while at the same time the two designers were creating the UI layer in the XAML files. Typically, as I explained before, the designers would finish the UI layer, usually in a separate program such as Photoshop, and then hand it off to the developer to "wire up." But now with Silverlight, the designers and developers could work on the application at the same time, thus saving vast amounts of time. This proved to be a much more effective and thus harmonious workflow.

New features in Blend 3

Microsoft has come a long way since Blend 2 by adding some very cool new features. Below is a list of features that are brand new to Blend 3:

- IntelliSense for XAML editing
- The ability to edit C# and Visual Basic code-behind files (no more having to jump into Visual Studio for quick code edits)
- A new Effects tab in the Asset Library
- The ability to create XML-based sample data
- The ability to import Adobe Illustrator (AI) and Photoshop (PSD) files
- Project template support
- A new Behaviors tab in the Asset Library that allows designers to drag snippets of code to the Timeline
- Improved object selection in the workspace
- A Brush Transform tool that is now separated into two tools
- Easier positioning of objects on the Objects and Timeline panel

The Blend 3 toolbar

If you are familiar with popular design/development products such as Adobe Photoshop, Flash, or Illustrator, the Blend 3 toolbar will be nothing new to you, as Microsoft has apparently attempted to make its toolbar functionally match that of the Adobe suite of design products. This, in my humble opinion, was a very smart move on the part of Microsoft, as it makes transition from an Adobe product to this new product quite easy. If, however, you are not familiar with the toolbar concept, this section will serve as a good introduction. The toolbar provides a set of tools that allow you to create and edit user interface (UI) content that the users of your Silverlight applications can interact with. The Blend 3 toolbar is located on the left side of the Blend 3 IDE, as shown in Figure 2-1.

Figure 2-1. The Blend IDE

Figure 2-2 shows an isolated view of the toolbar. I will cover some of the tools in more depth than others in this chapter, as I will discuss some of the others in greater depth in later chapters. To get started, go ahead and create a new Silverlight project:

1. Open Blend 3.
2. Click File ➤ New Project.
3. Select Silverlight 3 Website.
4. Name the project ExploringBlend.
5. Click OK.

Figure 2-2. The Blend 3 toolbar

The Selection tool

The Selection tool is the tool to use when you want to select objects (such as a MediaElement or an Image control) that the user of your Silverlight applications will interact with in the **workspace** (known as the **stage** in Flash). This tool allows you to select objects to change their properties, such as modifying their size or shape or changing their opacity or color (you will see how to do all of this later). This is probably the most used tool in all of Blend, so it would make sense for you to become very familiar with its location on the toolbar.

> *Most of the tools on the toolbar can be selected by using keyboard shortcuts. For example, to select the Selection tool, you can press the V key. You can see the keyboard shortcut in the tooltip.*

The Direct Selection tool

The Direct Selection tool, shown in Figure 2-3, is a tool that allows you to see and edit the different nodes that make up a custom shape known as a **path** (drawn using the Pen or Pencil tool). If you are not familiar with vector-drawing tools such as Illustrator, I probably just lost you. Because I don't want to lose you, I will jump ahead a little and show you how to use the Pen tool to create paths.

Figure 2-3.
The Direct
Selection tool

The Pen/Pencil tools

The Pen/Pencil tools (shown in Figure 2-4) allow you to create custom shapes or paths in Silverlight. By default, you will see the Pen tool in the Blend 3 toolbar. To get to the Pencil tool, you can click and hold or right-click the Pen tool until you see the option for the Pencil tool appear. The Pen tool basically allows you to create a series of points that can be manipulated with the Direct Selection tool. In order to demonstrate this, I will show you how to use the Pen tool to create a path.

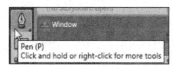

Figure 2-4. The Pen tool

1. Select the Pen tool from the Blend 3 toolbar.
2. Click to make a series of points.
3. Click the first point to close the shape.

The Pen tool cursor has features that help you understand the action that is about to be performed by the tool. For example, if you have created a series of points (see Figure 2-5), and you mouse over the first point, the Pen tool cursor shows a circle icon, indicating that if you click, you will close the path. Also, once you have created a path and mouse over a line on the path, a plus icon appears next to the Pen tool cursor, indicating that you are about to add a new point. Finally, if you mouse over a point in the path, you will see a minus icon appear next to the Pen tool cursor; this indicates that if you click, you will remove the point.

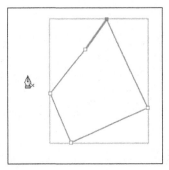

Figure 2-5. Use the Pen tool to
create points. Click the first point
to close the shape.

You have just created a custom path. Now you can select the Direct Selection tool and modify those points. You can also click and drag on a line segment of the path to move it.

4. To move a point, place your cursor directly over it, click once to select it, and then drag it. If you want to add a Bezier curve to a point, hold down the Alt key and then click and drag a point, as shown in Figure 2-6.

5. If you Alt-click a Bezier curve point, it will convert it back to an angle point.

6. Finally, dragging the handles on a Bezier curve will move them together, changing the shape of the curve. Alt-dragging a handle will reshape that side of the curve independently. Use this technique to create complex curved shapes.

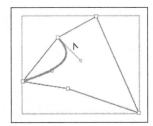

Figure 2-6. You can use the Direct Selection tool to modify your shape.

The Pencil tool allows you to create a shape by clicking and drawing in the workspace like you would on a piece of paper (see Figure 2-7).

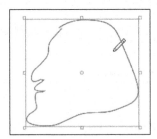

Figure 2-7. Using the Pencil tool, you can create shapes by drawing like you would on a piece of paper.

The Pen and Pencil tools in conjunction with the Direct Selection tool are very handy for creating shapes that are not symmetrical, as opposed to simple ellipses and rectangles.

The Pan tool

You should now have a better idea of paths and what the Direct Selection tool does, so let's jump back up the toolbar and carry on from where we left off. The Pan tool, shown in Figure 2-8, allows you to navigate around the workspace. This is very handy for large applications. When you select this tool, your cursor turns into a hand icon. If you click and drag your mouse, you can move your workspace. Manually selecting this tool, however, is impractical, because you can get the same result by holding down the spacebar and clicking and dragging your mouse. But there is something else that this tool is useful for: double-clicking it snaps into view the item that is currently selected in the workspace or the Objects and Timeline panel. Sometimes I find myself so far off of the workspace that I don't know where it has gone; at these times, I can just double-click the Pan tool and voilà, I have the object that I am working on right in the center of my view—very handy.

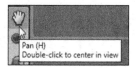

Figure 2-8. The Pan tool

The Zoom tool

The Zoom tool, shown in Figure 2-9, allows you to click the workspace to zoom in. You can also click and drag out the area you want to zoom in on. Further, if you hold down the Alt key and click, you will zoom out. Finally, if you double-click the Zoom tool, you will be shown your workspace at 100% with no zoom at all. I find this tool very handy for working with design details, such as creating complex buttons with many gradients.

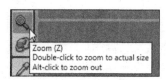

Figure 2-9. The Zoom tool

The Eyedropper tool

The Eyedropper tool, shown in Figure 2-10, is a very handy tool for selecting colors. The Eyedropper tool will select any color that is directly underneath it, whether it be a color of a vector shape or a bitmap image. I rarely use the Eyedropper tool from the toolbar, because the same tool can be found on the Brushes palette, which is much handier to use. I will discuss this more in later chapters, but for now just be aware that it exists.

Figure 2-10. The Eyedropper tool

The Paint Bucket tool

The Paint Bucket tool, shown in Figure 2-11, allows you to select an object and then click this tool. Blend 3 will copy attributes such as the fill color, and you can then click another object to apply these attributes.

Figure 2-11. The Paint Bucket tool

The Brush Transform and Gradient tools

The Brush Transform and Gradient tools, shown in Figure 2-12, are two of my personal favorites because they are so powerful. These tools allow you to manipulate an object's gradient.

> *A color gradient specifies a range of position-dependent colors, generally as an alternative to specifying a single color.*

Figure 2-12. The Gradient and Brush Transform tools

The Gradient Tool

To demonstrate these tools, the following exercise will show you how to create a Rectangle with a gradient, and then use the Brush Transform and Gradient tools to manipulate its gradient.

1. Select the Rectangle tool from the toolbar, as shown in Figure 2-13.

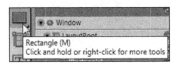

Figure 2-13. Selecting the Rectangle tool from the toolbar

2. Draw a Rectangle in the workspace, as shown in Figure 2-14.

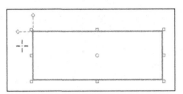

Figure 2-14. Drawing a Rectangle in the workspace

3. Activate the Selection tool (by pressing the V key) and click the Rectangle to select it.

4. In the Brushes section of the Properties panel, click the Fill property, as shown in Figure 2-15.

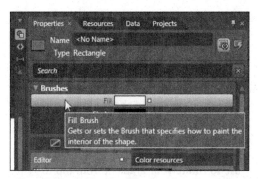

Figure 2-15. Clicking the Fill property in the Brushes section of the Properties panel

5. With the Fill property selected, click the Gradient brush button, as shown in Figure 2-16.

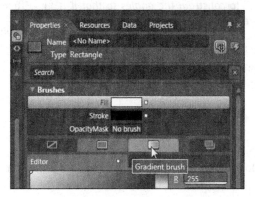

Figure 2-16. Clicking the Gradient brush button

Notice that your Rectangle now has a black-to-white color gradient, as shown in Figure 2-17.

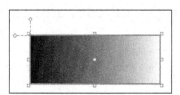

Figure 2-17. Your Rectangle now has a gradient that runs from left to right.

But say you want to change the gradient's direction. Well, as you might have guessed, you would use the Gradient tool. You'll do that now.

6. Click the Gradient tool (shown previously in Figure 2-12).

Notice that your Rectangle now has an arrow over it running in the same direction as your gradient (starting at the left and pointing right), as you see in Figure 2-18. You can now use this arrow to manipulate your gradient.

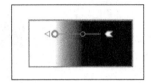

Figure 2-18. The gradient arrow

> **7.** Place your cursor over the arrow until it turns into a hand—when it does, click and drag your mouse to change the size of the gradient.
>
> **8.** Next, move your cursor around the tip of the arrow until your cursor turns into a curved, two-headed arrow; you can now click and hold the mouse to rotate your gradient from top to bottom, as in Figure 2-19.

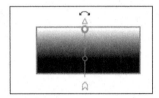

Figure 2-19. When your cursor turns into a double-headed arrow, you can then rotate your gradient from top to bottom.

> *When rotating your gradient using the Gradient tool, you can hold down the Shift key to constrain the angles so that it is easier to get a perfect up-to-down gradient.*

Notice there are two circles on the Brush Transform arrow. You can use those to reposition the color stops.

The Brush Transform Tool

You can select the Brush Transform tool by clicking and holding the Gradient tool until the Brush Transform tool appears. When it does, select it. Basically, this tool allows you to transform the gradient brush, while the Gradient tool allows you to manipulate the gradient brush's properties, such as start and stop points.

We will get into gradients in much more depth in later chapters, but this provides the gist of the Gradient and Brush Transform tools. With that, you can move forward.

The shape tools: Rectangle, Ellipse, and Line

There are three shape tools. The one that shows by default is the Rectangle tool (see Figure 2-20). If you hold down your mouse over the Rectangle tool or right-click it, you will see the icons for the Ellipse and Line tools, which you can then select. Since you have already seen how the Rectangle tool works, let's move on to the other shape tools.

> **1.** Click and hold on the Rectangle tool, and when you see the option for the Ellipse tool, select it.

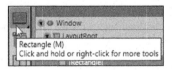

Figure 2-20. The Rectangle shape tool

2. With the Ellipse tool selected, draw an Ellipse in the workspace, as shown in Figure 2-21.

> *If you hold down the Shift key while drawing a shape (specifically a Rectangle or Ellipse), your shape will be perfectly symmetrical. Also, if you hold down the Alt key, the shape will be drawn from the center rather than the corner.*

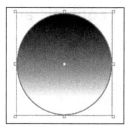

Figure 2-21. Draw an Ellipse in the workspace using the Ellipse shape tool.

Notice how Blend drew out the Ellipse with the same gradient that you used on the Rectangle earlier. This is a pretty cool feature and can save some time when making objects that are meant to look exactly alike.

Now try out the Line tool:

1. Hold down the Ellipse tool on the toolbar until the Line tool becomes visible, and select it.

2. Now draw a line in the workspace, as in Figure 2-22.

> *If you hold down the Shift key while drawing a line, your line's angle will be constrained so that it is easier to make a line that is perfectly vertical or horizontal.*

Figure 2-22. Using the Line shape tool to draw a line in the workspace

The shape tools, as you will see in later chapters, allow you to make very cool objects, such as custom buttons.

Layout controls

Next, we'll look at the layout controls (shown in Figure 2-23). The default layout control shown when Blend first starts is the Grid. That is because the Grid is by far the most common layout control. In fact, when you create a new Silverlight project, the default layout control that is placed in your workspace is a Grid named LayoutRoot. Basically, layout controls are the controls that handle the size and positioning of elements inside of them in a Silverlight application; that is, they are the containers that house your Silverlight objects.

Figure 2-23. If you click and hold the Grid tool on the toolbar, all nine layout controls will appear.

There are many different layout controls, and they are all used at different times to accomplish different goals because they each display their content differently. I will go into these controls in depth later on in the book, but for now just be aware that there are five: the Grid, the Canvas, the StackPanel, the ScrollViewer, and finally the Border. Again, don't worry about what these are and what they do now, because I am going to really break them down for you and work through exercises on them in Chapter 4.

Text controls and text input controls

The next tool on the toolbar is the TextBlock tool. If you click and hold on this tool, other controls will appear (see Figure 2-24). These are controls that allow you to add text to your applications, as well as text input controls such as a TextBox (a text input field) and a PasswordBox. I will discuss these controls in depth later in the book.

Figure 2-24. If you click and hold the TextBlock tool, the other text and text input controls will appear.

Input controls

The next tool on the toolbar is the Button tool. If you hold down this tool, you will see the other input controls available to you (see Figure 2-25).

These controls are essential because they allow your application to interact with the user. Probably the most common of these input controls is the Button control. If you have done any web development, most of these controls will already be familiar to you. We will use most of these controls later on in the book.

The Asset Library Last Used tool

Figure 2-25. If you click and hold the Button tool, the other input controls will appear.

The next tool on the Blend 3 toolbar is the Asset Library Last Used tool. This is a handy little feature that will turn into the last control you have used from the Asset Library. Say, for example, you select the CheckBox tool from the Asset Library to create a check box. The Asset Library Last Used tool will turn into a CheckBox control. What is the Asset Library, you ask? Find out in the next section.

The Asset Library

The next button you will find on the toolbar is a very handy one called the Asset Library. This is a collection of every control available to you in Silverlight (see Figure 2-26).

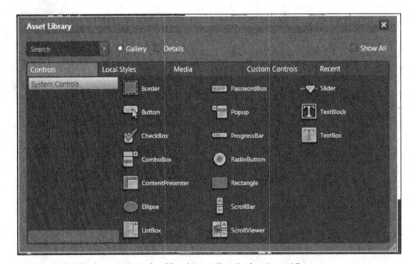

Figure 2-26. The last tool on the Blend 3 toolbar is the Asset Library.

This tool is great for a few reasons. First, it has a search feature that will filter out the controls you see. For example, if you type B in the search field, all controls that have the letter *B* in them will appear. If you continue to type the word Button, all controls with the word *Button* in them will appear. Currently, there are five controls with the word *Button* in them . . . I know that not because I am a genius, but because I tried the search I just mentioned while writing this chapter. Which brings up a good point: oftentimes we Silverlight developers forget the names of controls. When we do, the Asset Library is a great place to come to browse through them.

The other reason this is a great tool is because if you make a custom UserControl (we will do this in a later chapter), it will show up here under the Custom Controls tab. This makes it easy to implement the custom UserControl that you have made. But for now, you are just going to have to take my word for it, until you get to the custom UserControl tutorial in Chapter 6.

The Objects and Timeline panel

Now that you are familiar with the toolbar, let's move on to the Objects and Timeline panel of the Interaction panel, located on the left side of the Blend IDE, just to the right of the toolbar, as shown in Figure 2-27.

Figure 2-27. The Objects and Timeline panel is located just to the left of the toolbar in the Blend 3 IDE.

If you place an object in your workspace—say, a Button—it will show up here as an object because it now becomes part of your **visual tree**. The visual tree is a list of any objects in your website or application that show the hierarchy of the controls, much like a family tree shows ancestry. As you can see in Figure 2-28, the visual tree consists of a [UserControl]. Inside that [UserControl], you can see the LayoutRoot Grid (this is created automatically when the project is created). Inside of that is a series of Buttons. That is my visual tree, and if I want to select an item—say, a Button—I can just click it here in the Objects and Timeline panel. Oftentimes I prefer to select items here because it can be difficult to select an item in the workspace when there are a lot of things going on. For example, say I want to select a Button I have in the workspace, but it is being covered by a StackPanel. It would be very tricky to select the Button without moving items around. In this case, it would be much easier to simply select the Button from the Objects and Timeline panel.

Figure 2-28. An easy way to select items is through the Objects and Timeline panel.

Another thing you should know about this panel are the little eyeball icons for each object in the visual tree (again, shown in Figure 2-28). If you were to click the eyeball icon of a Button layer, your Button would become invisible in the workspace, and the eyeball icon would be replaced by a small blank circle icon. To reveal the item again, just click the blank circle icon, and it will reappear. Also, if there are any items in that object (as is the case of the LayoutRoot Grid), they and their eyeball icons would be invisible as well. This is because they are children of the LayoutRoot Grid. Keep in mind it hasn't been deleted, it's just hidden. And it is only hidden in the IDE, so if you were to run the application, you would see the LayoutRoot Grid and all of its children again. If you actually wanted to make it invisible to the user, you would have to change its visibility in the Properties panel—but we will get to that a little later.

If you look again at Figure 2-28, you will see that the LayoutRoot Grid object has a little circle icon next to its eyeball icon. If you click the circle icon, it will change into a padlock icon, effectively locking the object and all of its children. This is helpful because when you get an object designed and positioned perfectly, you can lock it so that nothing accidentally changes that object while you are working on other objects.

I have now covered the basics of the objects part of the Objects and Timeline panel, but I have yet to address the timeline aspect of it. I will do so in Chapter 11, which covers storyboards and animation, as that's where you'll actually put the timeline feature to use.

The Projects panel

The Projects panel (see Figure 2-29) shows you all of the assets that make up your application.

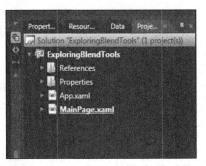

Figure 2-29. The Projects panel shows all of the resources of the current application.

The first thing you see is the name of your project solution. The project solution name in Figure 2-29 is ExploringBlendTools. Below that is a directory called References. This folder holds references to other DLLs that make the application work. You will not need to worry about that directory for the purposes of this book. But, just so you know, the References folder allows you to add references to other Silverlight projects and have all of the resources available in that project available to your new project.

Below that is a directory called Properties. I won't go into details about this folder, since it's not necessary for the purposes of this chapter. Next, you see App.xaml, which is a file that holds information about your application or website. Below that is AssemblyInfo.cs, which is a file that is automatically maintained by Visual Studio and Blend. There is no need to edit it manually.

Now you finally come to MainPage.xaml. This is the file that you have been working with when creating shapes. I will talk about XAML and C# in depth in the next chapter, but it is worth mentioning here that XAML is the UI layer. Visual objects are most often contained here, but they can also be added via code-behind files. Notice there is an arrow next to this file. If you click the arrow icon, it will expand and you will see MainPage.xaml.cs. This is called a **code-behind** page. Most every XAML page has a code-behind page. This code-behind page is written in C#. Code-behind files can be written in C#,

Visual Basic, and Ruby, among others, but C# is often the most popular choice. Code-behind pages can now be edited in Blend 3, but it is still recommended to edit them in Visual Studio 2008. But again, we will talk in depth about this in the next chapter.

The Projects panel is important because it allows you to easily navigate to any file you want by double-clicking it. Also, you can add items to a project solution in the Projects panel. Via a context menu command, you can navigate to your assets (images, video, audio, XML, etc.). Blend then makes a copy of whatever item you select and places it in the project in the folder you specify. To put an asset into a new folder you've created, follow these steps:

1. In the Projects panel right-click on the ExploringBlendTools project (not the Solution).
2. Left-click Add New Folder.
3. Name the new Folder Images.
4. Right-click that new folder.
5. Click Add Existing Item.
6. Navigate to an item—say, an image on your hard drive—and double-click it.

> A new feature that was added to Blend 3 allows you to actually drag and drop images from your hard drive right into the Projects panel.

The Properties panel

This Properties panel, shown in Figure 2-30, is where you set the properties for controls in your workspace. It has sections, also knows as **buckets**, that help to make it easier to navigate. For example, the Brushes bucket describes how objects are shown (fill color, stroke, etc.), and the Appearance bucket describes how objects are laid out in the application (height, width, visibility, etc.). You can get from the Projects panel to the Properties panel by clicking the tab that reads Properties.

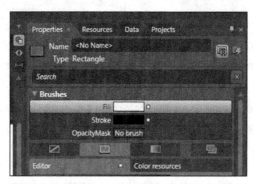

Figure 2-30. The Properties panel

The Properties panel is important and you will use it often, so now is a good time to start some hands-on work with Blend 3 to demonstrate its use.

Brushes

We've already taken a brief look at the Brushes bucket of the Properties panel, but let's take a closer look at it now, and set up a very simple project that you'll use to view the effects of some of the other panels.

1. Create a new project in Blend, and call it PropertiesPanel.

2. Select the Rectangle tool and draw a Rectangle in the workspace. Make it any size you wish, as you will change it later.

3. Make certain that the Rectangle is selected.

4. Find the Brushes bucket of the Properties panel. If it is collapsed, click the arrow icon next to the word *Brushes* to expand it—do so now so that you have something that looks like Figure 2-31.

First, take a look at the Fill property. Notice that this property is currently set to a solid color (see Figure 2-32).

Figure 2-31. The Brushes section of the Properties panel

Figure 2-32. The Fill property of your Rectangle is set to a solid color of white.

5. Change the color from white to another color. You can do this a few different ways:

   a. You can just click the color palette, and the color will change to whatever color you click (number 1 in Figure 2-33).

   b. You can adjust the RGBA values individually (number 2 in Figure 2-33).

   c. You can change the color by setting the hexadecimal value (number 3 in Figure 2-33).

   d. You can change the color value by using the Eyedropper (number 4 in Figure 2-33). The Eyedropper will pick up any color that is underneath it. This goes for your workspace or the Blend application as well.

   e. You can change the color by making use of a color resource (number 5 in Figure 2-33). You will create a color resource and apply it to another object a little later in this section.

Figure 2-33. Numbers 1 through 5 indicate
the different ways you can change the solid
fill of an object.

You can also choose a gradient for your object by selecting the Gradient brush option, as shown in
Figure 2-34. Let's take a look at gradients in a little more detail.

Figure 2-34. With your Rectangle selected,
you can also fill it with a gradient by choosing
a gradient fill.

Once you choose a gradient fill, your object will by default have a white-to-black gradient across it. This can be changed much like it is changed in popular design programs such as Adobe Flash and Photoshop. To change one of the gradient colors, follow these steps:

1. Select the color handle for the gradient color you want to change (as shown by the arrow in Figure 2-35), and then change the color by any method described in the previous exercise.

2. Drag the color slider (number 1 in Figure 2-35) to pick a hue, and then select a suitable color from the color palette (number 2 in Figure 2-35).

Figure 2-35. Changing one of the colors that make up your gradient

To add more color handles, and therefore more colors to the gradient, simply click in the gradient bar and a new handle will appear below where you clicked. To remove a handle, click it and drag it down off of the gradient bar.

This is a good time to talk about color resources. Say you have a gradient or even a color that appears in many different places in your application. As you may know, designers are very particular about maintaining their designs, and any deviation from the developer can cause problems. Because of this, developers in the past had to be meticulous and re-create the gradient or color for every object. But now you can create a color or gradient once and then turn it into a color resource so it can be applied to any object. But it goes much further than just color resources. Any property can be saved as a resource (e.g., a fill, the source of a MediaElement, the angle of an object—almost anything). Other objects can then use these resources. If the resource changes, all of the objects using that resource will automatically be updated throughout the project.

Back to the gradient example; assume your new gradient is exactly to the designer specifications.

1. Click the little white box next to the Fill property and click Convert to New Resource, shown in Figure 2-36, to create a Brush resource.

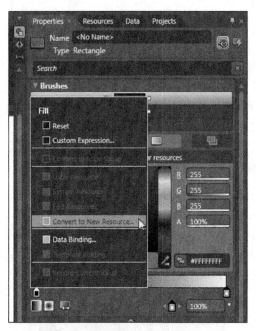

Figure 2-36. The +Brush button allows you to turn your gradient into a color resource that you can use again throughout your application.

A dialog box will pop up and ask you a few questions about your new color resource (see Figure 2-37).

2. The Name (Key) field is where you specify what name you would like for your new resource. The default name of Brush1 is fine for this demonstration, so you can leave it as is.

3. In the Define in area, Blend is asking you if you would like this new resource to be available to the entire application, the current document only, or a ResourceDictionary (we'll cover this in a minute). For your single-page application, select This document to make the resource available only to the current document.

4. Once you have set both the parameters in the dialog box, click OK.

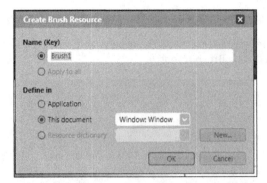

Figure 2-37. The Create Brush Resource dialog box

Since you know that any property can be set as a resource, I'll show you how to do that here as well. Here are the steps to create a resource for the source of a MediaElement:

1. In the Asset Library, select MediaElement.

2. Draw a MediaElement in the workspace.

3. In the Media bucket on the Properties panel, click the Source button.

4. When the Add Existing Item dialog box appears, navigate to an image or video on your local hard drive, and double-click the file.

5. Now click the Advanced property options button, as shown in Figure 2-38.

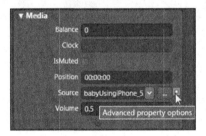

Figure 2-38. The Advanced property options button

6. Click Convert to new resource.

7. In the Create Resource dialog box, give the resource a name of VideoSource and click OK.

You have now created a resource out of your MediaElement Source property. Now that you've created a resource, you might be asking how to use it. Well, let me show you how to do that now:

8. Draw another MediaElement in the workspace.

9. With the new MediaElement selected, go to the Media bucket and click the Advanced property options button for the Source property, like you did earlier.

10. This time, instead of clicking Convert to new resource, click Local Resource, and you will see the VideoSource resource you created. Click it.

Notice that right away both MediaElements now have the same video source. This is handy because if you change the resource to, say, a different video, all MediaElements in the application that are using the resource will be updated.

This is a good time to talk about what a ResourceDictionary is. You can define a custom ResourceDictionary that holds reusable templates such as gradients. It is a good way to keep your custom resources organized. Also, resources in a ResourceDictionary are available to files across your entire project. Resources defined in MainWindow.xaml, however, are only available to MainWindow. xaml. So, go ahead and create one by following these steps:

1. Create a new Rectangle in the workspace.

2. Give it a gradient fill of your choice. I left mine with the default of Brush1.

3. Click the +Brush button in the Brushes bucket of the Properties panel.

4. In the Create Color Resource dialog box, give the new brush resource a name of your choice.

5. Click the New button near the grayed-out Resource Dictionary radio button at the bottom of the Create Color Resource dialog box.

6. Blend will now pop up a dialog box that will ask you what name you want to give your new ResourceDictionary. Just use the default, and click OK.

7. Then click OK in the Create Brush Resource dialog box. Notice now that Blend switches over to the last tab in the Brushes bucket of the Properties panel (as shown by the arrow in Figure 2-39), and displays a list of brush resources. By default, your new brush is selected. Blend also creates a new XAML file called ResourceDictionary1.xaml. That file holds the information for your new gradient.

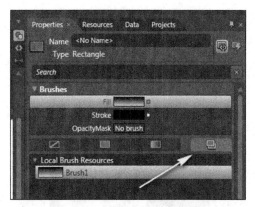

Figure 2-39. Blend switches your color over to the Color Resources option and selectes your new brush gradient.

> Remember earlier in the chapter that I said that most XAML files have code-behind files? A ResourceDictionary is an example of a XAML file that does not have a code-behind file.

Next, let's see how you can apply your new brush resource:

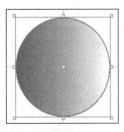

1. Select the Ellipse tool.

2. Create an Ellipse in the workspace.

3. Make sure your new Ellipse is selected.

4. In the Brushes bucket of the Properties panel, click the Brush Resources button.

5. Select your new brush, which should be named Brush1.

Figure 2-40. The Brush1 resource gradient applied to the Ellipse

Your Ellipse should now have the same gradient fill as your Rectangle (see Figure 2-40).

> It is possible that Blend remembered the last gradient you created and made your Ellipse that color by default. If that occurred, select your Ellipse, and in the Brushes section, give it a solid default color of black, and then follow steps 3 through 5 earlier.

You also have the option of editing the alpha of either one of the colors in a gradient or the entire color in a solid fill. The slider for this is right under the RGBA sliders in the Brushes section of the Properties panel. This is useful, but what if you want more control over which parts of an object can be seen through? In such cases, you can use an OpacityMask (shown in Figure 2-41). An OpacityMask allows you to apply different opacity levels to different parts of an element (as opposed to simple *opacity*, which is applied to an entire element in an all-or-nothing manner).

Figure 2-41. An OpacityMask allows you to apply various opacity levels to different parts of an object.

For example, you can use an OpacityMask if you want an object to fade from opaque on one side to transparent on the other, as in a reflection. The following exercise will show you how to do this with the Rectangle you created earlier.

1. Select the Rectangle, and copy it by pressing Ctrl+C.

2. Paste in a new Rectangle by pressing Ctrl+V.

3. Move your new Rectangle directly beneath the original one.

4. Move your cursor over the top-right handle of the new Rectangle, and rotate it 180 degrees so that it appears to be a mirror image of the original Rectangle, as shown in Figure 2-42.

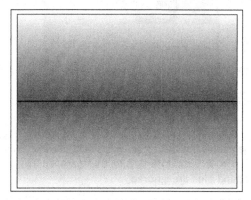

Figure 2-42. Create a duplicate copy of your Rectangle, move it below your original, and rotate it 180 degrees.

5. Now select your new Rectangle.

6. Click OpacityMask, as shown in Figure 2-43.

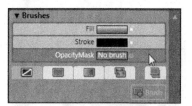

Figure 2-43. With your bottom Rectangle selected, click OpacityMask.

7. Select Gradient brush, as shown in Figure 2-44.

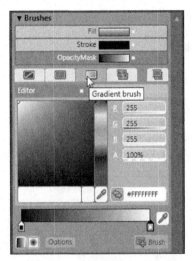

Figure 2-44. Select Gradient brush for the fill of your OpacityMask.

Here, it is important to understand that the colors you select are irrelevant in an OpacityMask. The only important part of a brush in an OpacityMask is its transparency. The value of alpha is calculated, but the values for red, green, and blue are ignored.

8. Set the alpha of one of the colors to 0%, as shown in Figure 2-45.

Figure 2-45. Set the alpha of one of the gradient colors to 0%.

Notice that half of your Rectangle is now invisible. But it doesn't look like a reflection, as the gradient for the OpacityMask is going the wrong way (left to right instead of top to bottom) (see Figure 2-46).

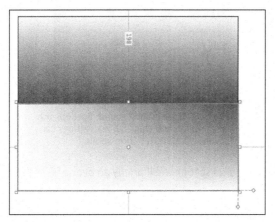

Figure 2-46. Your OpacityMask is working, but the gradient is going the wrong way.

9. Select the Brush Transform tool, rotate the gradient, and size it until it runs from top to bottom and looks something like Figure 2-47.

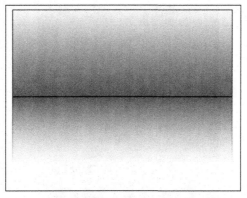

Figure 2-47. With the OpacityMask gradient adjusted properly using the Brush Transform tool, you get the reflection effect you are looking for.

Let's go through the other options in the Brushes bucket of the Properties panel very quickly:

- The BorderBrush option allows you to set the border color of an object.
- The Foreground option allows you to set the color of text in the foreground. This is most commonly used for text controls.
- The No Brush option allows you to give brushes (such as Stroke, Fill, and OpacityMask) no color at all. In Figure 2-48, the black arrow is pointing at the No Brush button.

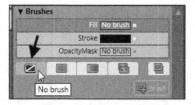

Figure 2-48. The Background, BorderBrush, Foreground, and OpacityMask settings can have the No Brush option applied.

Now that we've explored the Brushes section, we'll briefly go over a few other sections in the Properties panel.

Appearance

The Appearance bucket of the Properties panel, shown in Figure 2-49, controls how the object will appear. Click the little arrow at the bottom of the Appearance bucket to see all of the properties that can be set. You do things such as set an object's opacity and visibility, and give it bitmap effects. Let's look at that now.

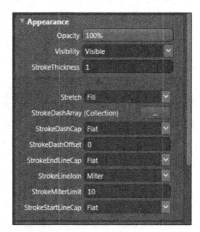

Figure 2-49. The Appearance bucket of the Properties panel

Layout

Moving along, you come next to the Layout bucket of the Properties panel, as shown in Figure 2-50. This section allows you to set how the object is laid out in the workspace. You can

- Set an object's height and width to a specific number, or let Blend do it for you by setting one or both to Auto.
- Set the row and column of an object that resides in a Grid.
- Set the row span and column span if the object is in a Grid. These options allow you to span rows across columns and columns across rows, much like HTML tables.

- Set the horizontal and vertical alignment of an object.
- Set the margin of an object, which describes in numbers how far an object is from the top, bottom, left, and right of its parent object (Grid, StackPanel, etc.).
- Set the z-index of an object—that is, whether it is on top of or under other objects. (A higher z-index will place the object higher in the stack. For example, an object with a z-index of 1 will appear in front of an object with a z-index of 0.)
- See advanced properties by clicking the collapse arrow at the bottom of the section.
- Set advanced properties such as whether an object has horizontal or vertical scrollbars.

There are other advanced layout properties, but I won't go into them at this time.

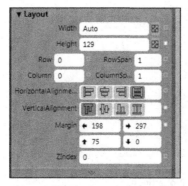

Figure 2-50. The Layout section of the Properties panel

Common Properties

The Common Properties bucket of the Properties panel, shown in Figure 2-51, contains properties common to all UI elements or controls. Here you can set properties such as

- What cursor an object will display when the mouse is over it (by specifying a value in the Cursor field)
- Whether the object can detect hits (by enabling the IsHitTestVisible option)
- Whether the object will display a tooltip and what it will read (by specifying text in the ToolTip field)

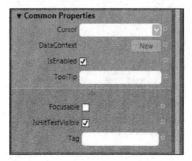

Figure 2-51. The Common Properties bucket of the Properties panel

One thing I want to cover in more depth is the Cursor property. In Silverlight, no control by default shows the hand cursor when you mouse over it—not even the Button control. However, the hand cursor creates a very good call to action for users; when they see the hand cursor, they know that they can click the object and something will happen. So, for any clickable object in my applications, I always set the Cursor property to Hand. You can set different cursor options (e.g., the arrow and the stylus, which are quite useful when creating interfaces), so I suggest you investigate them.

Text

The Text bucket of the Properties panel, shown in Figure 2-52, will only appear when controls that have text are selected. This bucket has properties for font, paragraph, line indent, and lists. These settings are all pretty self-explanatory, and I encourage you to play around with them.

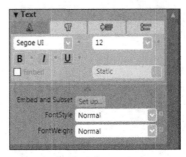

Figure 2-52. The Text bucket of the Properties panel

Transform

The Transform bucket of the Properties panel, shown in Figure 2-53, allows you to transform objects. You can perform render transformations (rotate, skew, etc.) here, or directly on the object, like you did when you rotated your Rectangle. I usually like to make my transformations directly on the object in the workspace. However, this panel is useful for making exact render transformations, or for making sure that a group of objects are transformed in the same way.

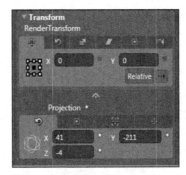

Figure 2-53. The Transform bucket of the Properties panel

If you click the arrow at the bottom of the Transform bucket, you will see that there is an advanced transform called a projection transform. This allows you to project your object along the x, y, and z axes. This essentially mimics 3D in Silverlight by making your control appear to be on a 3D plane. In Figure 2-54, you can see a Silverlight Button control that has a projection transform of 55 on the x coordinate, –45 on the y axis, and 15 on the z axis.

Figure 2-54. A Button with a projection transform applied

Miscellaneous

The Miscellaneous bucket of the Properties panel (see Figure 2-55) contains any properties that don't fit into the previously described buckets.

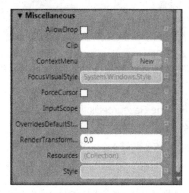

Figure 2-55. The Miscellaneous bucket of the Properties panel

Search

The final Properties panel feature that I will discuss is the Search feature, shown in Figure 2-56. This is a very handy and time-saving feature that I use regularly. Because the Properties panel is very large and has many properties for any given control, it is sometimes difficult to remember where exactly a property is located. Say, for example, you want to change the Cursor property, but you can't remember where it is located in the Properties panel. You can just start to type the word cursor into the search field, and Blend will locate it for you, as shown in Figure 2-56. To clear the Search panel so you can see all of the properties again, just click the X button at the right of the search field.

Figure 2-56. The Search feature of the Properties panel

The Resources panel

The Resources panel, shown in Figure 2-57, contains a list of all resources of your application. Remember the ResourceDictionary1.xaml file you created? It shows up in this list, and inside of it, the Brush1 resource color gradient you created is shown. You can use the Resources panel to actually apply the resources, which you'll do now by following these steps:

1. Select the Rectangle tool and create a Rectangle in the workspace.

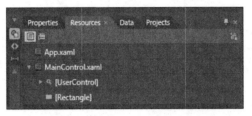

Figure 2-57. The Resources panel, which contains all resources available to your project, including the ResourceDictionary you created earlier

2. On the Resources panel, click the ResourceDictionary1 arrow so that the Brush1 custom gradient is shown, as in Figure 2-57.

3. Click and drag Brush1 to your new Rectangle in the workspace, and let go.

4. Blend will now ask you what property you want to apply Brush1 to; click Fill.

The Brush1 gradient will now be applied to your Rectangle.

The Data panel

The Data panel allows you to quickly and easily do the following:

- Add sample data to your applications for testing. You have the option of setting the data to show when the application is run.

- Import data from XML.

- Define a new object data source from data in your application.`

Blend development views and workspaces

Previously, Blend had two different development views. With the release of Blend 3, there are now three. At some point, you as a developer will have to work in all three, so you need to be familiar with each. I will discuss them briefly here and in depth in later chapters.

Design view

Blend's real power is its Design view. You can get to Design view by clicking the Design button, as shown in Figure 2-58. Visual Studio 2008 also has a Design view, but it is not nearly as powerful as Blend's, which can visually represent complex applications.

Figure 2-58. You can access Design view by clicking the Design button.

Design view allows you to basically do what you have been doing in these exercises—that is, drawing controls in the workspace visually instead of with code. What you may or may not know is that Blend 3 is actually creating the code for you in the XAML. You could (and at one time had to) write the XAML code manually, but that becomes cumbersome and takes quite a bit of time.

Another advantage of Design view is that you can easily tweak UI controls and see the effects immediately. Remember a while back when you were making your Rectangle reflection, and it looked all wrong until you adjusted the stroke with the Brush Transform tool? You were able to do that visually and keep tweaking it until it looked the way you wanted it to look. Imagine now if you wanted to tweak that gradient in the code. To better illustrate this point, let me show you the code that Blend created for you due to your adjustments:

```
<Rectangle.OpacityMask>
  <LinearGradientBrush EndPoint="0.487,0.236" StartPoint="0.487,1.387">
    <GradientStop Color="#FF000000" Offset="0"/>
    <GradientStop Color="#00FFFFFF" Offset="1"/>
  </LinearGradientBrush>
</Rectangle.OpacityMask>
```

See what I mean? This would have been much more difficult if you had to come to this exact code by trial and error. This provides a good segue into the next development view, XAML view.

XAML view

XAML view can be turned on by clicking the XAML button, as shown in Figure 2-59. This view reveals the code that is generated by Design view. You can add UI controls in XAML view, but it's better to add them using Visual Studio, for a couple of reasons. First, Visual Studio has collapsible code. That is, you can collapse a huge chunk of code so that it is not visible, save for a couple of lines. This allows you to ignore large blocks of XAML and focus on the block you are currently working on. Another good reason is that Visual Studio will format your XAML markup for you. This is very helpful in that it makes XAML more readable and just makes your markup cleaner in general.

Figure 2-59. You can access XAML view by clicking the XAML button.

Split view

Split view is a feature in Blend 3 that allows you to view half of the screen in Design view and half in XAML view. If you have ever played around with Adobe Dreamweaver, this concept should be nothing new to you. I think it is a real blast to draw out a control—say, a Rectangle—in the workspace, and then instantly see the XAML be created.

> *You can split the screen horizontally by clicking* View ➤ Split View Orientation ➤ Split View Horizontally.

Workspaces

Now that you know about views, it's important to understand what workspaces are. The Blend 3 IDE provides you with two distinct workspaces: the **Design workspace** and the **Animation workspace**. In each of the two workspaces, the Blend 3 IDE will change to allow you to focus on different aspects of development, namely design and animation.

The Design workspace

You are already familiar with the Design workspace, as that is what you have been working in. The Design workspace focuses on the visual tree of your application. Some panels are not visible in this workspace (e.g., the Timeline panel). This allows the developer more room to see the application, and thus makes it easier to design. By default, Blend 3 opens in the Design workspace. If you are in the Animation workspace, you can click Window ➤ Workspaces ➤ Design to get back to the Design workspace. Conversely, if you are in the Design workspace, you can click Window ➤ Workspaces ➤ Animation to get to the Animation workspace.

> *You can view the* Timeline *and* Interaction *panels in the Design workspace, but they are docked to the right and are very narrow, and thus not very easy to work with.*

The Animation workspace

The Animation workspace is a place where you can create storyboard animations in the Objects and Timeline panel, and create EventTriggers in the Interaction panel. Both of these panels are docked along the bottom of the IDE, which gives you more vertical space to work with. This lends itself very well to creating storyboards, as it allows you to see more of the timeline.

In the following exercise, you'll create an animation that will run when your page is loaded:

1. Delete everything from the workspace except your Rectangle and its reflection.

2. Select the Rectangle, hold down the Shift key, and click the reflection.

3. Select Object ➤ Group Into ➤ StackPanel, as shown in Figure 2-60.

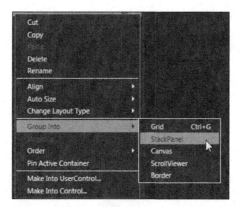

Figure 2-60. Create a StackPanel.

4. Give your new StackPanel a name of ReflectionSP, as shown in Figure 2-61.

Figure 2-61. Give your new StackPanel a name of ReflectionSP.

5. Center your new StackPanel in the workspace, and move it just below the workspace so that when the application starts, it will not be visible, as shown in Figure 2-62.

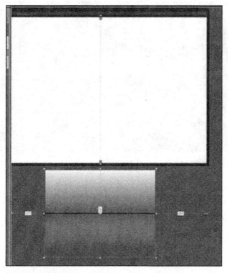

Figure 2-62. Place the Rectangle and its reflection in the ReflectionSP StackPanel.

6. Press F7 to view the Animation workspace.

7. With the StackPanel selected, click the New Storyboard button, as shown in Figure 2-63.

Figure 2-63. Click the New Storyboard button.

8. When the Create Storyboard Resource dialog box appears, leave the default name and click OK. A new timeline will appear, as shown in Figure 2-64, allowing you to create a new storyboard resource.

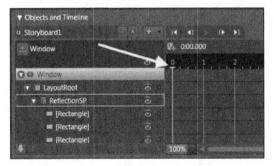

Figure 2-64. A new timeline appears.

9. Move the playhead out to 1 second, as shown in Figure 2-65.

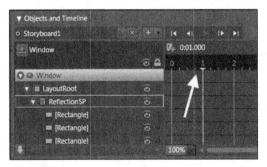

Figure 2-65. Move the playhead out.

10. Move the StackPanel to the center of the workspace.

11. Click the Close Storyboard button, as shown in Figure 2-66.

Figure 2-66. Close the storyboard.

12. Press F6 to go back to the Design workspace.

13. Press F5 to run the application, and you will see that the Rectangle StackPanel will animate into the application.

Easy, right? We will get into more complex animations later in the book, but for now you should be comfortable with the basics of both the Design and Animation workspaces.

Summary

In this chapter, you learned all about the Blend 3 IDE and how to make use of the toolbar and all the tools that Blend makes available to you. You also learned about the different layout controls that allow you to house controls in the workspace. Finally, you learned about the Design and Animation workspaces. In the next chapter, I will cover XAML and C# in greater detail.

Chapter 3

C#, XAML, AND OBJECT-ORIENTED PROGRAMMING

What this chapter covers:

- C# and the .NET Framework
- The basics of XAML

In this chapter, I am going to give an overview of the programming languages C# and XAML (Extensible Application Markup Language). I will give you a little bit of background on the origins of each language, and then explain in more detail how they interact to create Silverlight applications. Finally, I am going to have you create a new Silverlight application, and you are going to do a little bit of basic object-oriented programming (OOP). So with that, let's get started and discuss the very robust language known as C# (pronounced *see-sharp*).

C# and the .NET Framework

C# is a very robust OOP language based on the C++ syntax developed by Microsoft. C# is designed to use the tools in the .NET Framework efficiently. The .NET Framework is a series of technologies and products also developed by Microsoft. It has continued to evolve, beginning with the .NET 1.0 release in 2002, and continuing on with 1.1 and 2.0, and most recently 3.0 and 3.5 (version 4.0 is set to be released soon). The .NET Framework is shipped as part of the Microsoft Windows operating system. It was created to be an easy-to-use programming solution to many common programming needs including, but not limited to, web application development (.aspx and the older .asp pages), database connectivity, network communications, user interface (UI) components, and numeric algorithms. The .NET Framework allows for programmers to use methods of its class library in conjunction with their own code to create robust applications—in this case, Silverlight applications.

The .NET CLR

The .NET common language runtime (CLR) ships as part of the .NET Framework. It is an important part of the .NET Framework and worth giving a quick mention. The CLR is a **virtual machine**—similar to Adobe's Flash Player—that interprets code and translates it into a language that the computer can understand. The main purpose of this layer of abstraction between the programmer and the computer is to simplify management of memory, exceptions, threads, garbage collection, and security. The second purpose of the CLR is to allow the developer to write code in any CLR-supported language and know that it will execute the same way once compiled. This allows for Silverlight applications to be developed in C#, as well as Visual Basic, JScript, JavaScript, Python, Ruby, and other languages (although C# and Visual Basic are by far the most common).

In case you don't know, exception handling is a programming mechanism whose job it is to handle exceptional occurrences, also known as **errors**, in a programming routine of an application. In the .NET environment of Visual Studio 2008, every time an exception is thrown (i.e., there is an error in your code), the development environment will record debugging information known as **stack** and **heap** values. This debugging information is then given to you so that you can tell exactly what the exception thrown was. The debugging values can seem at times to be very cryptic and not at all intuitive as to what the error was.

You may also not be familiar with memory management, so I will take a few moments and explain that now. Memory management is simply the act of managing computer memory by allocating chunks of a computer's memory to programs that are running. For our purposes, this is an adequate description of the .NET CLR.

> *I find it useful to take exception errors and do a web search on them, because chances are very good that any problem you run into has been encountered by another programmer in the past. Also, the MSDN forums are a great place to post questions about exceptions.*

Why C#?

C# is a very popular OOP development language in both online and offline development communities. What makes OOP so special, you ask? OOP uses **objects** to create applications. An example of an object would be a built-in Silverlight Button control (you will learn more about this control and many others as you work your way through the book). Objects are important because they have the following characteristics.

Encapsulation

Any complex software system may have hundreds or even thousands of individual "moving parts"—each one with its particular responsibilities. Encapsulation is a principle that states that each part is responsible for itself and its duties, and knows as little as possible about the other parts. This leads to more stable, easier-to-understand code because making a change to one part is less likely to affect the rest of the system.

Classes

In OOP, objects get their instructions, or details of how they will function, from classes. Classes include two very important things: **properties** and **methods** (collectively known as class members). If objects are like nouns, the "things" in an application, properties are the adjectives that describe objects, like their color or position. Properties can be built in or custom made. Using a sample Silverlight "Hello World" application as an example, MainPage.xaml has a code-behind page called MainPage. xaml.cs. This page has in it a class called MainPage. MainPage has built-in properties such as a Background property. You can create your own custom properties in a class. The following code is the entire code for MainPage.xaml.cs. I have modified it so that it creates a Boolean (true or false variable) called thisBookRocks, sets it to true, and then prints out the result in the Output window, as shown in Figure 3-1.

```
using System;
using System.Collections.Generic;
using System.Text;
using System.Windows;
using System.Windows.Controls;
using System.Windows.Data;
using System.Windows.Documents;
using System.Windows.Input;
using System.Windows.Media;
using System.Windows.Media.Imaging;
using System.Windows.Navigation;
using System.Windows.Shapes;
using System.Diagnostics;

namespace HelloWorldSample
{
    public partial class MainPage : System.Windows.Controls.Page
    {
        Boolean thisBookRocks = true;
        public MainPage()
        {
            InitializeComponent();
            Debug.WriteLine
("thisBookRocks = " +
thisBookRocks.ToString());
        }

    }
}
```

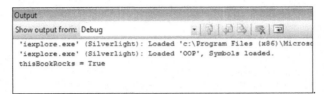

Figure 3-1. The Output window in Visual Studio shows the value of the thisBookRocks Boolean variable.

Methods are an object's verbs—the things an object can do. Classes come with a built-in method called a **constructor**. A constructor is a method that is named the same as the class and will run every time the object is instantiated (i.e., every time the object is placed on the workspace, either physically or by code). You can see the constructor in the following code as well; it is called MainPage. If you are new to classes, properties, methods, and constructors, fear not—I will be showing you how to work with them in great detail later on in the book.

The final thing I would like to mention about classes is that, just like custom properties and methods, there can be custom classes. For example, you can use a built-in .NET class called the Button class to create a button in your Silverlight application. You could, however, also make a custom class called MyCoolButtonClass. A good question for you to be asking might be "If I build this new custom button class, would I have to build into it all of the functionality of the .NET built-in Button class in order for them to act the same?" That's a good question, and the simple answer is yes, but .NET has provided a very good solution to this in the form of **inheritance**. So, if you want your new custom MyCoolButtonClass to act the same way as a .NET Button control, all you have to do is make your custom class *inherit* all of the methods and properties of the .NET Button class. That way, you can just add features to it, or even override (change) the features it currently has to make it your own. Inheritance is one of the key characteristics of OOP, so we'll look at it next.

Inheritance

Inheritance actually belongs to classes, but I want to give it its own section because it is a very important part of OOP. A class can be a child of another class and have child classes of its own. Basically, a class "inherits" all of the traits of its parent. I will use a classic example that I see in nearly every OOP book: imagine you have a class called Fruit. Fruit is the parent class or superclass. Fruit has some child classes—say Apple, Orange, and Peach. All three of the subclasses Apple, Orange, and Peach inherit from their parent class of Fruit. So they all know they are a fruit and have all of the traits of the Fruit class (i.e., they are edible containers for the seed of a plant).

So what is the advantage of inheritance? Imagine if you didn't have inheritance. In the preceding example, you would have to tell Apple, Orange, and Peach via code that they are all edible containers for the seed of a plant. That would mean you would have to write the code three times, once for each class. That is a big waste of time, and most importantly, prone to errors, because if you type a block of code once, you have one chance of getting it wrong; type it three times, you have three chances of getting it wrong. With inheritance, your classes can all share the code of a superclass, and this saves you a lot of time because it will generate fewer errors—maybe not for this fruit example, but certainly for large applications with hundreds of thousands of lines of code.

Modularity

OOP encompasses the concept of modularity, which was first presented by Information & Systems Institute, Inc., at the National Symposium on Modular Programming in 1968. Modularity basically means that large applications should be built-in modules that each has its own specific purpose. Further, these modules act independently within the application. The advantage to this type of programming is that modules can be reused in other applications or duplicated and used more than once in the same application. Another big advantage to this type of programming is that if you change the functionality of one module, you will not affect the functionality of any other module, as they have the ability to function independently of one another. Silverlight takes full advantage of this concept with classes and UserControls, which I will cover in depth later in this book.

Maintainability

Because OOP makes use of objects in its applications, and because these objects use classes that are built to be modular, the code is much easier to maintain than that of a traditional, procedural application. Say, for instance, you have a class called Foo. Foo has some complex functionality (exactly what is not important for this example). Foo has total encapsulation and is completely modular. So, if you go in and change Foo to give it some additional functionality, you know that you will not break the application, because no other object needs Foo in order to do its job. In procedural programming (i.e., non-OOP languages like C whereby the code is read line by line from top to bottom), it was very common for changes in one line of code in your application to cause some other part of your code to fail, because it was dependent on the line of code you changed, and thus the application would break.

I think that is a pretty adequate outline of why OOP is worth using. But I still have yet to finish telling you why C# is a great programming language. Let's continue.

Automatic garbage collection

Automatic garbage collection is basically memory management. And it does exactly what the name implies: it takes out the garbage for you. (I wish I had one of these in real life—just ask my wife, Shay). OK, let's break it down: objects take up memory when they are instantiated (another fancy name for "created"). Eventually, some instantiated objects will no longer be necessary. The garbage collector will automatically find and dispose of them, freeing precious memory. You can imagine how powerful this is in an application with hundreds (or even hundreds of thousands) of objects. It is worth noting here that some languages, such as C++, don't have automatic collection of garbage, so the programmer has to manually manage his/her garbage, and this can get quite cumbersome and have devastating performance effects if not done or not done properly.

Language Integrated Query

Language Integrated Query (LINQ) is a feature new to .NET 3.0 and allows for context-sensitive keywords such as from, select, and where. This allows the programmer to use similar syntax for managing databases, data collections, and even XML (Extensible Markup Language).

XML documentation

C# now allows programmers to embed XML comments right into their source files. This is done by putting /// before any line of code. C# will then treat that code as XML, and can even export it to a separate XML file. This is very handy when you have many developers working on the same application, and documentation is needed to explain to the next developer how to make use of the source file.

C# possesses many more powerful features, but for the scope of this book, I think I have adequately discussed some of the major ones. After all, this is a hands-on book, and I don't want to bore you with theory, but rather brush over this stuff so you can get to some real development. I think at this point it would be beneficial to go over XAML.

XAML

XAML is an XML-based declarative language developed by Microsoft. XAML is basically, as I described before, the UI language of Silverlight that defines objects and their properties. I say that XAML in its basic form describes how the application looks, but it can do much more than that. The number one advantage of XAML is its speed and efficiency—often, a single line of XAML can represent dozens of lines of equivalent C#. Further, with only a few lines of XAML, any Silverlight object can be hooked up to C# code-behind classes that can contain complex functionality. It is also worth mentioning that anything that can be done in XAML can also be done in C#, but usually with many more lines of code.

XAML objects are written in XML-based form and describe how the user sees the object or framework element, by setting properties in the XML. A typical XAML control looks like this:

```
<Button
  x:Name="spinBtn"
  HorizontalAlignment="Right"
  Margin="0,0,19.8,42.5"
  VerticalAlignment="Bottom"
  Width="186.25"
  Height="80"
  Background="Blue"
  Foreground="White"
  Content="Spin"/>
```

The preceding code creates a Button control. The Button is able to be referenced by C# code because it has an x:Name property set to spinBtn.

As you can see, it also has other properties, such as the following:

- HorizontalAlignment: Controls how the Button will be aligned in the application
- Margin: Determines where in the parent grid the control will be placed
- VerticalAlignment: Controls how the Button will be aligned in the application
- Width: Sets the width of the Button
- Height: Sets the height of the Button
- Background: Sets the background color of the Button
- Foreground: Sets the color of the content (text) of the Button
- Content: Controls what the text on the Button will be

Following is the C# code that would create the exact same Button:

```
Button button = new Button();
button.Name = "spinBtn";
button.HorizontalAlignment = HorizontalAlignment.Right;
button.Margin = new Thickness(0, 0, 19.8, 42.5);
button.Width = 186.25;
button.Height = 80;
button.Background = new SolidColorBrush
(Color.FromArgb(255, 0, 0, 255));
button.Foreground = new SolidColorBrush
(Color.FromARgb(255, 255, 255, 255));
button.Content = "Spin";
LayoutRoot.Children.Add(button);
```

As you can see, it is a bit more work in that you have to first create an object called button of the Button type. You then have to set each margin separately for Top, Left, Bottom, and Right. Finally, you then have to add the object as a child of the LayoutRoot (a Grid control in most cases).

XAML is great because it helps to separate the design of the application from the C# development. This allows for faster development by increasing the efficiency between designers and developers, as discussed in Chapter 2. To reiterate, this is done by separating the design layer (XAML) from the logic layer (C#).

Another advantage to Silverlight is its native support of vector graphics in addition to standard bitmap graphics. What is the difference, you ask? Vector graphics are created with mathematical coordinates and have no actual pixels like bitmaps do. This allows you to scale a vector graphic to any size and still retain perfect clarity of the graphic. If you scale up a bitmap, the quality of it reduces significantly, and it will pixelate (become blocky).

XAML has one very awesome functionality feature called **binding**. That means that an object can have one of its properties "bound" to the properties of another. For example, you can bind the property of a Rectangle's Width to the value of a Slider. Therefore, when you slide the slider up, the button grows in size, and conversely, when you slide the slider down, the button size will decrease. Binding is very powerful, and I think you will understand that when we get into it later in Chapter 7.

It is important to note that any object can be created in the C# code-behind file and added to the workspace. Also, binding can be done in C# as well because a XAML file and its C# code-behind file are both partial classes, connected to each other with the InitializeComponent method run in the code-behind's constructor method. They are different parts of the same object, whether it is a Page, Button, UserControl, or any other class; as such, at different times it may be more appropriate to write code for that object in the XAML file or the C# code-behind file.

XAML also allows you to define resources for the application. Resources can include Silverlight objects such as Storyboard, ControlTemplate, and DataSource. We will go over these in depth later on as well.

While XAML is very powerful, there is not much more to say about it on a background level, so at this point it will be better for you to learn about XAML through hands-on exercises, which is what you will start to do in the following chapters.

OOP project

While this book is primarily about Blend 3, it is also very much about Silverlight, and Silverlight makes use of OOP. That being the case, I thought it would be good to go over some basic OOP principles and constructs in a hands-on manner. In this section, you are going to learn about

- Creating custom classes
- Instantiating objects
- Adding properties to objects
- Encapsulating fields
- Superclasses
- Inheritance
- Extending classes
- Abstract classes
- Abstract methods
- Overriding methods
- Interfaces
- Extracting interfaces
- Enums

So let's get to it. First, carry out the following steps:

1. Open Visual Studio.
2. Click File ➤ New Project.
3. Select Silverlight as the project type.
4. Select Silverlight Application as the template.
5. Name the project OOP, as shown in Figure 3-2.
6. Click OK.

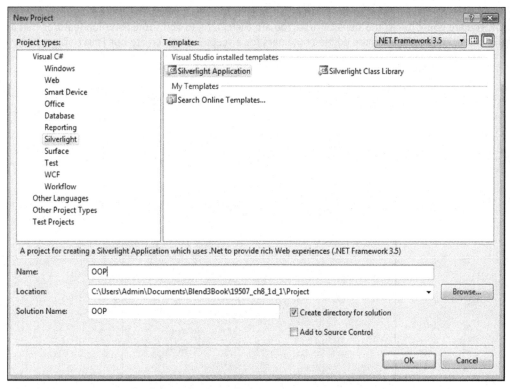

Figure 3-2. Create a new Silverlight application called OOP.

7. When the New Silverlight Application **dialog box appears, uncheck** Host the Silverlight application in a new Web site, **as shown in Figure 3-3, and then click** OK.

Figure 3-3. Uncheck the Host the Silverlight application in a new Web site check box.

The first thing you are going to do is create an object. In keeping with the preceding discussion on OOP, you are going to call this object Fruit. You are then going to add some common features that all fruits share. That is, all fruits are edible containers for a seed. So, let's create our Fruit object now:

1. In Visual Studio's Solution Explorer, right-click the OOP project.

2. Click Add ➤ Class, as shown in Figure 3-4.

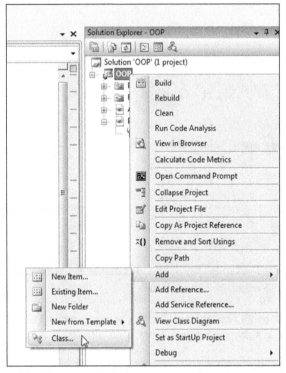

Figure 3-4. Add a new class.

3. When the Add New Item dialog box appears, name the new class Fruit, and click Add.

Now you can start adding your properties. You will make two Boolean properties—IsEdible and HasSeed—and set them both to true.

4. Inside the class, type private bool _IsEdible = true, as shown in Figure 3-5.

5. Next, right-click the new property, click Refactor ➤ Encapsulate Field, and then click OK.

6. When the Preview dialog box shows up, click Add.

```
namespace OOP
{
    public class Fruit
    {
        private bool _IsEdible = true;
    }
}
```

Figure 3-5. The _IsEdible class

What this does is turn your private variable into a public variable, and also creates getters and setters for it, as shown in the following code:

```
namespace OOP
{
    public class Fruit
    {
        private bool _IsEdible = true;

        public bool IsEdible
        {
            get { return _IsEdible; }
            set { _IsEdible = value; }
        }
    }
}
```

The problem now becomes this: a fruit is always edible, and therefore, no other object can ever set the IsEdible property to false. So, to fix this, what you will do is remove the setter. Then other objects will be able to read the IsEdible property, but not to set it. So, now your code should look like this:

```
namespace OOP
{
    public class Fruit
    {
        private bool _IsEdible = true;

        public bool IsEdible
        {
            get { return _IsEdible; }
        }
    }
}
```

Now that you have your Fruit superclass, you need to create a child for it. Let's create the Apple class.

7. Follow the same steps as you did previously to create a new class, but name this one Apple.

8. When the new class's code appears, enter " : Fruit" after the class declaration of public class Apple, as shown here:

```
namespace OOP
{
    public class Apple : Fruit
    {

    }
}
```

This means that the Apple class extends the Fruit class, and thus is one of its children. And as you know from the discussion on inheritance, Apple will inherit everything that Fruit contains, namely IsEdible. You can prove this by going to MainPage.xaml.cs and instantiating (creating) an instance of Apple.

9. In MainPage.xaml.cs, instantiate an Apple object called apple (all lowercase) under the InitializeComponent(); line, as shown here:

```
namespace OOP
{
    public partial class Page : UserControl
    {
        public Page()
        {
            InitializeComponent();
            Apple apple = new Apple();
        }
    }
}
```

Now you can write some code that proves that Apple really is a child of Fruit.

10. Write a conditional statement that will tell you if the Apple class's IsEdible property is true, as shown here:

```
namespace OOP
{
    public partial class Page : UserControl
    {
        public Page()
        {
            InitializeComponent();
            Apple apple = new Apple();
            if (apple.IsEdible == true)
            {
                MessageBox.Show("apple IsEdible is True");
            }
        }
    }
}
```

11. You could actually stop here, because when you typed apple and then a period, IntelliSense showed you that one of the properties of apple is IsEdible. Since you have not even written any code in Apple, there is no way it could have this property if it weren't a child of Fruit. But to be complete, press F5 to compile and run the application, and you will see the message box shown in Figure 3-6.

Figure 3-6. The message box showing the value of IsEdible

12. Now let's create a new class called Orange. Follow the preceding steps to create the Orange class, and make it extend Fruit. Your code should look like the following:

```
namespace OOP
{
    public class Orange : Fruit
    {

    }
}
```

13. Now go back to MainPage.xaml.cs and instantiate an instance of the Orange class, as shown here:

```
namespace OOP
{
    public partial class MainPage : UserControl
    {
        public MainPage()
        {
            InitializeComponent();

            Apple apple = new Apple();
            if (apple.IsEdible == true)
            {
                MessageBox.Show("apple IsEdible is True");
            }

            Orange orange = new Orange();

        }
    }
}
```

Now, you know full well that the new orange object is going to have an IsEdible property, and that property is set to true, so let's do something a little more fun. What I want to do is to have each Fruit have its own color. I could easily go into the superclass and make a public string variable called color and set it to, say, Green. I would also put a setter on it so each fruit could either accept the default color of green, change its color property itself, or have some other object change it. But say I want to set the default color in the Fruit superclass to Empty or None, and I want to demand that the children of this class define a color for themselves. I could use something called an **interface** to do exactly that. Let's do that now:

1. The very first thing you need to do is go into the Fruit class and change it to an abstract class. This means that Fruit will never be instantiated itself; only its children will be instantiated. I will explain why this is done in a moment. First, enter the following code:

```
namespace OOP
{
    public abstract class Fruit
    {
        private bool _IsEdible = true;
```

```
        public bool IsEdible
        {
            get { return _IsEdible; }
        }
    }
}
```

2. The next thing you need to do is declare a public abstract method called SetMyColor in Fruit:

```
namespace OOP
{
    public abstract class Fruit : OOP.IColor
    {
        private bool _IsEdible = true;

        public bool IsEdible
        {
            get { return _IsEdible; }
        }

        public abstract void SetMyColor();
    }
}
```

Notice how SetMyColor has no curly brackets after it. This is because the method will never be fired from here. Instead, the children of Fruit are going to be forced to implement this method, and they will need to have curly brackets. Let's extract the interface for this method now:

3. Right-click SetMyColor and click Refactor ➤ Extract Interface, as shown in Figure 3-7.

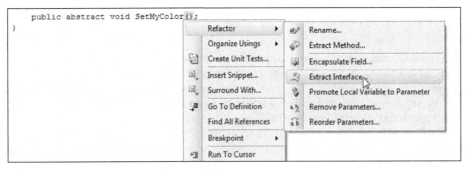

Figure 3-7. Extract the interface from SetMyColor.

4. When the Extract Interface dialog box appears, change the interface name to IColor, check the SetMyColor method, and click OK, as shown in Figure 3-8.

Figure 3-8. Set the properties for the new interface.

Notice that Visual Studio creates a new interface file for us called IColor.cs. This file has only one method in it, called—yep, you guessed it—SetMyColor (see the following code):

```
namespace OOP
{
    interface IColor
    {
        void SetMyColor();
    }
}
```

Now here is the fun part. Press Control+Shift+B to compile the Silverlight application, and notice you get two build errors saying that Orange and Apple do not implement Fruit.SetMyColor. This is exactly what we had hoped for because it means that Orange and Apple are now required to implement SetMyColor, but they have not done so. Let's have them implement SetMyColor now:

5. Open Orange.cs and place your mouse over the fruit.

6. Press Control+. (period), and IntelliSense will ask you if you want to implement the abstract class Fruit (see Figure 3-9).

Figure 3-9. IntelliSense wants to implement the abstract class for you.

7. Press the Enter key and notice from the following code that Visual Studio actually implemented the override for SetMyColor (and notice to that it *does* have curly brackets).

```
namespace OOP
{
    public class Orange : Fruit
    {

        public override void SetMyColor()
        {
            throw new NotImplementedException();
        }
    }
}
```

So now go ahead and open Apple.cs and do the same thing. Once you have done that, you need a property for Color for both Apple and Orange. But wait, didn't I say that if they have anything in common, it should be part of the superclass? Yes, I did. So if you create a MyColor property in Fruit, then both Apple and Orange will automatically inherit it. But what if the children want to make their color property something impossible, like turquoise? (As far as I know there is no such fruit with this color.) You could implement something called an **enum** (an enumerable list) of allowed colors. Then the children would only be able to select from that select group of colors. Let's implement this now:

8. Open Fruit.

9. Create a public enum called FruitColor:

```
namespace OOP
{
    public abstract class Fruit : OOP.IColor
    {
        private bool _IsEdible = true;
        public bool IsEdible
        {
            get { return _IsEdible; }
        }

        public enum FruitColor
        {
            None,
            Green,
            Red,
            Yellow
        }

        public abstract void SetMyColor();
    }
}
```

10. Now you need to create a private variable called _MyFruitColor and set it to FruitColor. None:

```
namespace OOP
{
    public abstract class Fruit : OOP.IColor
    {
        private bool _IsEdible = true;
        public bool IsEdible
        {
            get { return _IsEdible; }
        }

        private FruitColor _MyFruitColor = FruitColor.None;

        public enum FruitColor
        {
            None,
            Green,
            Red,
            Yellow
        }

        public abstract void SetMyColor();
    }
}
```

11. Now right-click _MyFruitColor and click Refactor ➤ Encapsulate Field.

12. Press the Enter key twice and you should see something like the following:

```
namespace OOP
{
    public abstract class Fruit : OOP.IColor
    {
        private bool _IsEdible = true;
        public bool IsEdible
        {
            get { return _IsEdible; }
        }

        private FruitColor _MyFruitColor = FruitColor.None;

        public FruitColor MyFruitColor
        {
            get { return _MyFruitColor; }
            set { _MyFruitColor = value; }
        }
```

```
        public enum FruitColor
        {
            None,
            Green,
            Red,
            Yellow
        }

        public abstract void SetMyColor();
    }
}
```

13. Now you can go into both Apple and Orange's SetMyColor override method and set their color.

Apple:

```
namespace OOP
{
    public class Apple : Fruit
    {

        public override void SetMyColor()
        {
            MyFruitColor = FruitColor.Green;
        }
    }
}
```

Orange:

```
namespace OOP
{
    public class Orange : Fruit
    {

        public override void SetMyColor()
        {
            MyFruitColor = FruitColor.Red;
        }
    }
}
```

14. Now you can go back to MainPage.xaml.cs and code your message box to show what color each fruit is:

```
namespace OOP
{
    public partial class Page : UserControl
    {
        public Page()
        {
```

```
            InitializeComponent();

            Apple apple = new Apple();
            Orange orange = new Orange();

            MessageBox.Show
("apple | IsEdible: "+apple.IsEdible+" Color: "
+apple.MyFruitColor+" orange | IsEdible: "
+orange.IsEdible+" Color: "
+orange.MyFruitColor);

        }
    }
}
```

15. Now press F5 to run this, and you should see the message box shown in Figure 3-10.

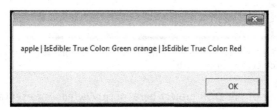

Figure 3-10. The message box is showing the properties for apple and orange.

Wait a minute. Didn't we set those properties in the SetMyColor override methods? Yes, actually we did. But think about an abstract method requirement: the child classes are mandated to implement the methods, *not* to actually fire them. In order for them to fire them, you need to tell each class to do so. This is accomplished with the following code:

```
namespace OOP
{
    public partial class Page : UserControl
    {
        public Page()
        {
            InitializeComponent();

            Apple apple = new Apple();
            apple.SetMyColor();

            Orange orange = new Orange();
            orange.SetMyColor();

            MessageBox.Show
("apple | IsEdible: "
+ apple.IsEdible + " Color: "
+ apple.MyFruitColor +
```

```
                              " orange | IsEdible: "
    + orange.IsEdible + " Color: "
    + orange.MyFruitColor);

            }
        }

    }
```

16. Now press F5 to run the application again, and you should see the message box shown in Figure 3-11.

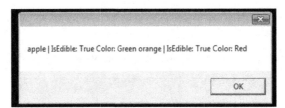

Figure 3-11. You now see the correct values for each object's color property.

You can download a copy of this OOP project here: http://windowspresentationfoundation.com/Blend3Book/OOP.zip.

Summary

In this chapter, you learned about C# and the .NET Framework. I went over some advantages of using C#, and delved into the basics of classes and OOP and some advantages of both. I also covered the basics of XAML—what it is, what it can do—and some powerful features such as data binding. Finally, I took you through a hands-on tutorial on how to do some basic tasks in OOP. In the next chapter, I am going to talk about the layout controls that allow you to place content into your Silverlight applications.

Chapter 4

CONTROLS

What this chapter covers:

- Layout elements
- Item controls
- User interaction controls

As I have already discussed, Silverlight uses XAML to create the user interface (UI) layer that provides the "face" of any Silverlight application. In other words, XAML allows the developer to create the interface that users will see when they use your application. Silverlight uses **layout elements** in order to arrange your content (e.g., a Grid, Canvas, or StackPanel control), and any other UI FrameWork elements. I tend to think of layout elements much like tables in HTML. Of course, as you may have already guessed, Silverlight controls are a lot more complex than HTML tables, but the comparison should help provide you with a starting point regarding what layout elements are. Further, Silverlight has controls known as **item controls** that allow you to easily arrange items such as data objects in a collection. An example of this type of control would be a ListBox. Finally, Silverlight has controls that collect information about what the user of your applications is doing, such as text input controls or button controls. These controls are known as **user interaction** controls. In this chapter, I will discuss all of the most popular controls by talking about what makes them unique and when it is appropriate to use each one. I will also walk you through creating a new project that uses each one.

Layout elements

As discussed in the previous section, layout elements are a very important part of Silverlight, allowing us to arrange our content in our applications. Here we are going to go over the most popular ones and the properties that make them unique.

The Grid

Undoubtedly the most popular and most used Silverlight layout element is the Grid. In fact, when you first create a new Silverlight application, Visual Studio 2008 automatically puts in a Grid layout element for you. You can see the code here:

```
<UserControl x:Class="LayoutControlsProject.MainPage"
    xmlns="http://schemas.microsoft.com/winfx/2006/xaml/presentation"
    xmlns:x="http://schemas.microsoft.com/winfx/2006/xaml"
    Width="400" Height="300">
    <Grid x:Name="LayoutRoot" Background="White">

    </Grid>
</UserControl>
```

This does not mean that you cannot add other layout elements; in fact, layout elements are meant to have other layout elements placed inside of them. Which one you choose depends on how you want to display your content. A Grid is very much like an HTML table in that you can define rows and columns and then place content inside of those rows and columns. This is a good time to create a new Silverlight Application project in Visual Studio 2008. To do that, first open Visual Studio 2008, create a new Silverlight Application project, and call it LayoutControlsProject, as shown in Figure 4-1. Click OK.

Notice in the XAML that Visual Studio 2008 has created a Grid by default.

Leave Visual Studio 2008 open. Go ahead and start Blend 3, open LayoutControlsProject, and look at it in Design view. Notice around your main Grid there is a blue bar at the top and on the left. These are where you add RowDefinitions and ColumnDefinitions. When you place your cursor over the top bar, notice that a yellow line is drawn from the top of your Grid to the bottom. If you click the blue bar, the line becomes blue, and does not go away when you move your mouse off of it, because you have just created a new ColumnDefinition (see Figure 4-2).

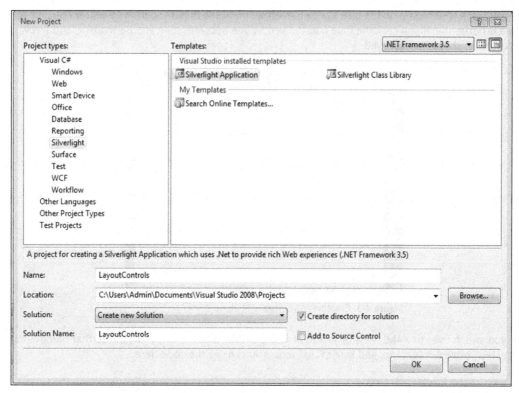

Figure 4-1. Creating a new Silverlight application in Visual Studio 2008

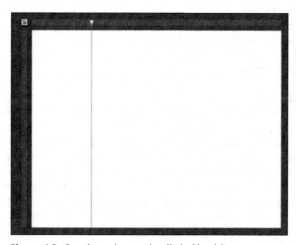

Figure 4-2. Creating columns visually in Blend 3

If you place your mouse on the blue bar to the left, you will see that it too draws a yellow line, but this line is horizontal. If you click the blue bar, the yellow line becomes blue and permanent, and a row is created, as shown in Figure 4-3.

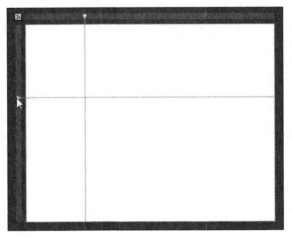

Figure 4-3. Creating rows visually in Blend 3

If you switch over to XAML view or just look at the XAML in Split view, you can see that Blend 3 has created ColumnDefinitions and RowDefinitions. You can see the code here:

```
<Grid.RowDefinitions>
  <RowDefinition Height="0.37*"/>
  <RowDefinition Height="0.63*"/>
</Grid.RowDefinitions>
<Grid.ColumnDefinitions>
  <ColumnDefinition Width="0.24*"/>
  <ColumnDefinition Width="0.76*"/>
</Grid.ColumnDefinitions>
```

Notice that the columns and rows have Height and Width values. If you hard-code the Height and Width values, it means that your Grid cannot scale to accommodate for content placed inside of it. For this reason, it is good practice to not hard-code these values, and instead take full advantage of the way Silverlight's powerful layout engine can position objects automatically. Blend 3 has placed Height and Width values in for you because your Grid is in Canvas Layout mode as opposed to Grid Layout mode. The Blend team created Canvas Layout mode to make it easier for designers not experienced with layout panels to get started. Fortunately for you, you are getting started with me, and I am going to teach you about the slightly more complex Grid Layout mode. At the very top left of the Grid, you can see a little button that if clicked will change the Grid's mode to Grid Layout mode, as shown in Figure 4-4.

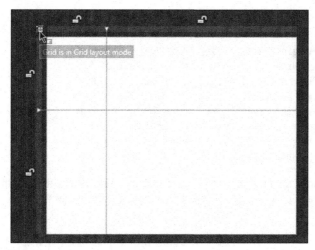

Figure 4-4. The main Grid in Grid Layout mode

Now you will see little lock icons appear where the blue row and column lines are. These little lock icons allow you to lock the height of a row or the width of a column; click one of the lock icons so that it turns to a "locked" state. If you look at the XAML code, you will see that the RowDefinitions and ColumnDefinitions still have Height and Width values with an asterisk after them. If the row or column's lock icon is not locked, these values can change depending on the size of the content that they display or by the size of the application window. If you lock one of the icons by clicking it, you will notice that the asterisk disappears and the lock icon appears locked. Now if the content dynamically changes or the size of the application window changes, the locked column or row will not change.

Now that you have rows and columns, what can you do with them? Well, you can add controls into the Grid and then specify in the XAML what row and column they should be in. Here's how:

1. Select the TextBlock tool from the toolbar.
2. Draw a TextBlock on the workspace.
3. Set the text to be Row 0 Column 0.

Now if you look at the XAML, you will see something that looks like this:

```
<TextBlock Margin="23,37,21.072,51.112" Text="Row 0 Column 0"
TextWrapping="Wrap"/>
```

You can see that the control does not specify what row or column it is in. If you do not specify a column or row, Blend 3 will automatically place your content into row 0 and column 0. So, now you'll alter the code to hard-code the TextBlock to be in row 0 and column 0.

4. Change your code so that it resembles the following:

```
<TextBlock Margin="23,37,21,51" Text="Row 0 column 0"
TextWrapping="Wrap" Grid.Column="0" Grid.Row="0"/>
```

5. Now copy this XAML and paste it four times, and change the values for the text as well as the Grid.Column and Grid.Row so that your code looks like this:

```
<TextBlock Margin="23,37,21,51" Text="Row 0 Column 0"
TextWrapping="Wrap" Grid.Column="0" Grid.Row="0"/>
<TextBlock Margin="23,37,21,51" Text="Row 0 Column 1"
 TextWrapping="Wrap" Grid.Column="1" Grid.Row="0"/>
<TextBlock Margin="23,37,21,51" Text="Row 1 Column 0"
TextWrapping="Wrap" Grid.Column="0" Grid.Row="1"/>
<TextBlock Margin="23,37,21,51" Text="Row 1 Column 1"
TextWrapping="Wrap" Grid.Column="1" Grid.Row="1"/>
```

6. Click the Design tab in Blend 3; you will see that your TextBlocks all place themselves into their correct rows and columns. Your project should look like the one shown in Figure 4-5.

> The rows and columns start with a value of 0, not 1.

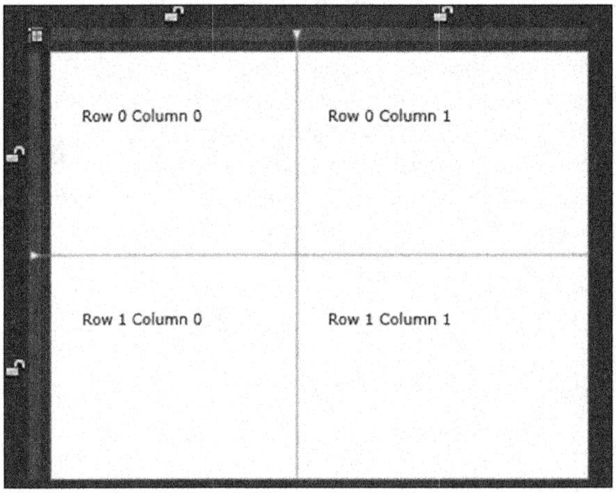

Figure 4-5. TextBlocks in different Grid rows and columns

Another interesting thing about the Grid is that it positions its content using **margins**. Basically, margins determine distance from the boundaries of the Grid, or the boundaries of the Grid cell if the element is inside a Grid cell.

Say, for example, you have a Rectangle control inside of a Grid, and its VerticalAlignment is set to Top and its HorizontalAlignment is set to Left. If you give the Rectangle control a Margin property of "10,10,0,0", the Rectangle will be 10 display units from the left and 10 display units from the top, as the values for Margin set the left, top, right, and bottom distances in that order. Conversely, if you set the Rectangle's HorizontalAlignment to Right and its VerticalAlignment to Bottom, and then give it a Margin property of "0,0,10,10", the Rectangle control will be 10 display units from the right and 10 display units from the bottom.

The Canvas

The next layout element I am going to talk about is the Canvas. This is one of my personal favorites because it allows the user to specify *absolute positioning of its children*. The Canvas will never change the position of child elements in it, and I find this very useful. To see how the Canvas works, you have to make some changes to the project:

1. In Blend 3, change the XAML so that MainPage is now 600×600 (to give you some breathing room).

2. Change each of the TextBlocks to have a Width of 150 and a Height of 20.

3. Move each of the TextBlocks up to the top left of its cell.

Your project should look something like Figure 4-6.

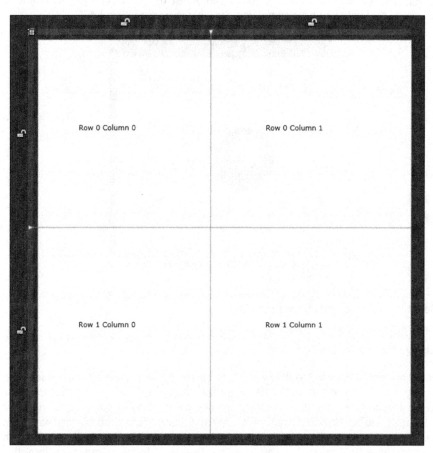

Figure 4-6. The TextBlocks are now in different cells of the parent Grid.

4. Click and hold down the Grid tool on the toolbar until the other layout element options become visible, and select the Canvas layout element.

5. In the Row 0 Column 1 cell, draw a Canvas. With the Selection tool, click the new Canvas in the Objects and Timeline panel so that it has a blue line around it indicating it is selected.

Now you can add some content to your Canvas because when a layout control has a blue line around it, anything drawn in the workspace will go into it. Add some content now by following these steps:

1. Select the Ellipse tool from the toolbar.

2. Hold down Shift and draw an Ellipse in the Row 0 Column 1 cell.

3. With the new Ellipse selected, change the Background to a gradient in the Brushes section of the Properties panel.

4. Change the gradient to a radial gradient and adjust the colors and gradient with the Brush Transform tool until you have something like what you see in Figure 4-7.

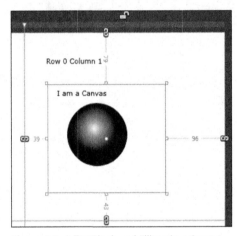

Figure 4-7. A TextBlock and Ellipse in a Canvas in your main Grid

5. Select the TextBlock tool from the toolbar.

6. Draw out a TextBlock in your new Canvas.

7. Change the text to read I am a Canvas.

If you look at the XAML, you will see the new Canvas inside of your main Grid, and inside of the Canvas you will see the Ellipse and the TextBlock. The interesting thing to see here is that the Canvas itself has a Margin property, and thus its positioning can be controlled by its parent Grid. However, notice that the Ellipse and TextBlock do not have any Margin properties—rather, they have Canvas.Top and Canvas.Left properties. This means that they are overriding the AttachedProperty of their parent Canvas and essentially telling the Canvas where they want to be placed. Therefore, the Canvas cannot implicitly change the position of its child objects, nor can the Grid.

You may at this point be asking what an AttachedProperty is. An AttachedProperty is a property that is exposed by the parent element and can be set by the child. In the preceding example, the

AttachedProperty of Canvas.Left is exposed by the parent Canvas and can be set by the child (in the preceding case, the Rectangle).

Let's now move on to another very useful layout element called the StackPanel.

The StackPanel

A StackPanel is another layout element, and its claim to fame is that it will position content inside of it for you in a stacking manner (horizontally or vertically). This is different from the Grid or Canvas, which rely on the developer to set the relative or absolute positioning of child objects. Here you'll create a StackPanel and see exactly how it does this:

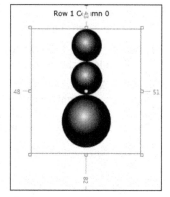

Figure 4-8. A StackPanel will position its child content horizontally or vertically.

1. Select the StackPanel tool from the toolbar.

2. In Row 1 Column 0, draw out a StackPanel.

3. Select the Ellipse tool again from the toolbar.

4. Draw three Ellipses in the newly created StackPanel.

Notice that the StackPanel arranges your three Ellipses vertically inside of it (see Figure 4-8).

You can override the way the StackPanel stacks its content by changing values in the XAML or by changing the Orientation property from Vertical to Horizontal in the Layout section of the Properties panel. Do that now, and you will see that the StackPanel changes from displaying its content from vertically to horizontally, as shown in Figure 4-9.

> *I set each Ellipse to have a HorizontalAlignment of Center. If I hadn't done this, they would have been aligned to the left by default.*

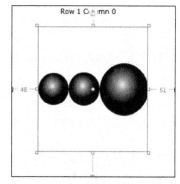

Figure 4-9. A StackPanel can position its child content automatically.

Let's keep going and explore the next layout element in WPF, the Border.

The Border

The Border is a very simple layout element that allows you to draw a Stroke around another element and then give it a Background or an actual border. The Border layout element can only have one child element, and that content can be either left, right, top, bottom, or center aligned. These properties can be set manually in the XAML, or in Blend 3 in the Layout section of the Properties panel. Try making a Border element now:

1. Select the Border tool from the toolbar.

2. In Row 0 Column 1, draw a Border.

3. Copy the red Ellipse inside of your Canvas into the new Border.

4. Change the HorizontalAlignment property in the Layout section of the Properties panel to see how the child object is affected.

5. Change the VerticalAlignment property in the Layout section of the Properties panel to see how the child object is affected.

6. Change the Background of the border to a gradient in the Brushes section of the Properties panel.

7. Use the Brush Transform tool to adjust the gradient to go from top to bottom.

8. Select the BorderBrush property in the Brushes section of the Properties panel and select a solid color; I chose green.

9. In the Appearance section of the Properties panel, give the Border a BorderThickness of 3 for the left and right and 1 for the top and bottom.

Your Border should look something like that shown in Figure 4-10.

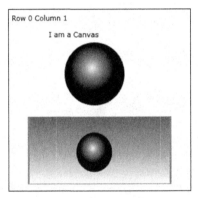

Figure 4-10. The Border content control allows you to draw a stroke and background around an element.

Item controls

Oftentimes in Silverlight we have collections of data that need to be displayed. For example, we could have a collection of strings (a string of characters such as "Hello," "World," and "Silverlight"). In order to better demonstrate this, I am going to show you how to do the following:

- Create a new Silverlight project called ListBoxSample.
- Create sample data in Blend 3.
- Populate the sample data.
- Add a ListBox item control to the project.
- Bind the ListBox to the sample data.

With that, let's forge ahead and create the new Silverlight project:

1. In Blend 3, create a new project by clicking File ➤ New Project.

2. Select Silverlight 3 Application.

3. Name the project ListBoxSample.

4. Click OK.

5. Click the Data tab and click the Add Sample Data button, as shown in Figure 4-11.

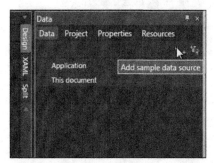

Figure 4-11. Add sample data to the project.

6. Click Define New Sample Data.

7. When the Define New Sample Data dialog box pops up, give the data source a name of LBDataSource, and then click OK, as shown in Figure 4-12.

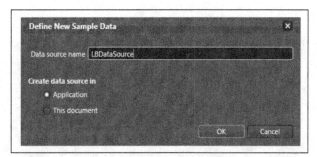

Figure 4-12. Name the data source LBDataSource.

8. On the Data tab, click the little arrow next to LBDataSource, and then click Collection.

9. Click the Edit sample values button, as shown in Figure 4-13.

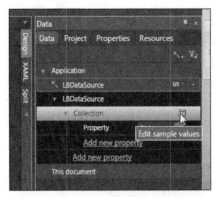

Figure 4-13. Edit the sample data.

10. When the Edit Sample Values dialog box appears, change the number of records to 4, as shown in Figure 4-14.

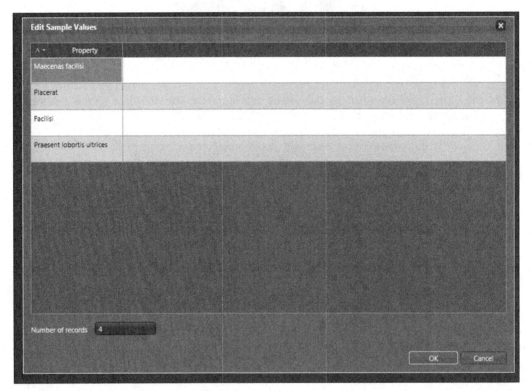

Figure 4-14. Change the number of records to 4.

11. Now double-click each sample value, change them to "Hello," "World," "Silverlight," and "Rocks," as shown in Figure 4-15, and then click OK.

Figure 4-15. Change the value of the sample data.

At this point, you have a collection of strings. Now all you need to do is bind this collection to an item control. Luckily, Blend 3 has made this very easy to do. Let's do it now:

1. On the Data tab, make sure the arrow icon next to the LBDataSource is facing downward. Click and hold Collection and start to drag it, as shown in Figure 4-16.

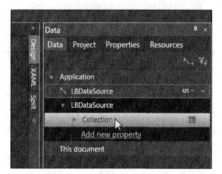

Figure 4-16. Click-hold and drag Collection.

2. Drag the collection to the Objects and Timeline panel and drop it onto LayoutRoot, as shown in Figure 4-17.

Figure 4-17. Add the collection to LayoutRoot.

Notice how when you drag it over the LayoutRoot in the Objects and Timeline panel, you get a message telling you that Blend 3 is going to add a ListBox with an ItemsSource set to your collection. Also notice that when you drop the collection onto the LayoutRoot, it automatically creates a ListBox in the workspace and sets its ItemsSource to your collection. You should have what is shown in Figure 4-18.

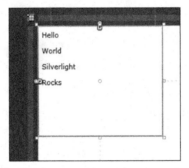

Figure 4-18. A ListBox with an ItemsSource of the LBDataSource collection

At this point, you should adequately understand item controls. So with that, let's move ahead and discuss the final controls that we'll explore in this chapter: input controls.

Input controls

Software applications by default are developed to interact with their users. HTML applications, for example, have user input controls such as text fields, buttons, radio buttons, and check boxes, just to name a few. Silverlight is no different in that it, too, has user input controls that have the ability to gather information from the user. In fact, all of the HTML controls that I just named are included in Silverlight. You may recall that I mentioned in the preceding section that a ListBox is an item control. Interestingly, a ListBox is also an input control as well. If you were to run the ListBox application you created in the last section, you would notice that you can click any of the items (Hello, World, etc.), and they would become highlighted. The code-behind could then react to your selection, thus making it an input control. So, let's make a new sample Silverlight application and make some input controls:

Figure 4-19. A list of all of the Silverlight input controls

1. In Blend 3, create a new Silverlight 3 application called InputControlProject.

2. On the toolbar, hold down the Button tool until you see a list of the other input controls, as shown in Figure 4-19.

3. Start by adding the most common of all input controls, the Button control.

4. Once you have selected the Button control, draw a button in the workspace, as shown in Figure 4-20.

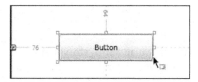

Figure 4-20. A Button control

Repeat this process for the CheckBox, RadioButton, and Slider controls so that you have something that looks like Figure 4-21.

Figure 4-21. Button, CheckBox, RadioButton, and Slider controls

Now you have made four user input controls that can react to user interaction. We are going to be seeing a lot more of these and other input controls as we progress through the book, so we won't wire them up at this stage. Just know that these are a few of the built-in Silverlight input controls and that they can alter the application when interacted with.

Summary

Content or layout controls allow you to easily place content into your applications. You have gone through each of the major layout elements and actually created them with hands-on exercises. You also learned that each layout element has its own special ability:

- The Grid allows you to declare rows and columns so that you can then position objects precisely within that Grid.
- The Canvas allows you to specify where the content inside of it is placed by using the Margin property.
- The StackPanel positions its content automatically, but you can specify whether the content is stacked horizontally or vertically.
- The Border simply allows you to draw a Stroke around the content placed inside of it, as well as a Background.

You also learned about item controls such as a ListBox. You even learned how to create sample data and then bind a ListBox's ItemsSource to it. This will prove very handy for testing when you start making your own data-driven Silverlight applications.

Finally, you learned about a few key input controls that allow your application to react to the actions of the application's users.

In the next chapter, I am going to teach you all about storyboards and how to use them to create cool and fun animations that can really send your Silverlight applications to the next level. I am also going to show you how to use Blend 3 to create storyboards in XAML, and then we are going to jump over to Visual Studio and create a storyboard by hand in the code-behind. Finally, I am going to teach you to make a very handy little StoryboardHelper class that you will find helpful in just about every one of your own Silverlight applications. Excited? Me too! Let's get to it!

Chapter 5

STORYBOARDS

What this chapter covers:

- Understanding Silverlight storyboards
- Creating storyboards visually using the Visual State Manager
- Wiring up states in Visual Studio
- Creating storyboards in code-behind with Visual Studio
- Creating a Storyboard helper class

A Silverlight storyboard is basically a timeline tree that acts as a container for timeline animations. The storyboard timeline tree can combine many different types of timeline animations that allow the developer to target properties of objects in the visual tree. This allows for better organization of timelines, and the net effect is more complex, perfectly timed animations. A simple example of a storyboard would be the animation of a Silverlight Button control. Say, for instance, that you want the button to change color when the mouse is over it, to shrink by 20% when the mouse is down (click), to grow by 15% when the mouse is up, and to change back to its original color when the mouse moves off of it. In this instance, a storyboard would be a perfect solution. Storyboards can be created visually in Blend 3, or by hand with code-behind in both Blend 3 and Visual Studio. In this chapter, I am going to show you how to do both. As an added bonus, I am going to show you how to create a Storyboard helper class that will allow you to create storyboards quickly and easily in code-behind. So, let's get started.

> *Prior to Blend 3, you could not edit code-behind files in Blend. Even though that's now possible, it is still more practical to edit code-behind files in Visual Studio, because of features such as autoformat and IntelliSense (an autocomplete feature in Visual Studio).*

Creating storyboards visually in Blend 3

To get started, open Blend 3, and create a new project called StoryboardProject. You can see my settings in Figure 5-1.

> *Make certain to remember where your new application is being saved, as you will be opening it up in Visual Studio later in the chapter.*

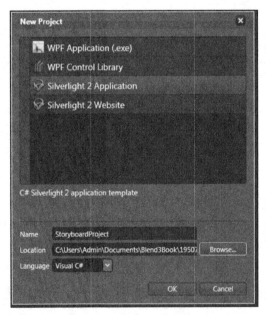

Figure 5-1. Create a new project in Blend 3.

Once Blend 3 creates the new Silverlight application, you are going to need to put some visuals into your workspace so you have something to animate.

1. Select the Rectangle tool from the toolbar and draw a Rectangle in the workspace.

2. Give it a blue fill, and center it in the workspace, as shown in Figure 5-2.

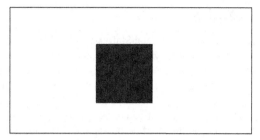

Figure 5-2. Draw a Rectangle in the workspace.

> *Storyboards are a framework-level feature and thus can only animate objects that are part of the visual tree, such as FrameworkElements.*

Now that you have a visual in the form of a Rectangle in your application, it is time to create a storyboard animation. Before doing that, though, we have to decide what we want the animation to consist of. So, let's say we want the Rectangle to change to yellow when the mouse is over it (called the MouseEnter event) and change back to blue when the mouse moves off of it (called the MouseLeave event). Further, when we click the Rectangle (called the MouseDown event for FrameworkElements that are not derived from the Button class), we want it to grow by 20% in a time span of .3 seconds and then shrink back down to its original size in a time span of .5 seconds. That sounds simple enough, but we need to first give the Rectangle a name (called the x:Name property) so that we can code against it. So let's do that now:

3. Make certain the Selection tool is selected (this can be done using the keyboard shortcut V).

4. On the Properties tab, give the Rectangle a name of MyRectangle, as shown in Figure 5-3.

> *If you were to try and apply a storyboard to a FrameworkElement in Blend 3 without first assigning it a Name property, Blend would do it for you, but it is not best practice to do so.*

Figure 5-3. Name the Rectangle MyRectangle.

Creating states in Blend 3

Something relatively new to Silverlight is the Visual State Manager (VSM). This allows the developer to create custom states such as MyMouseEnter, MyMouseLeave, and MyMouseDown. When a state is created in a VisualStateGroup, everything that the developer does to any visual in the workspace is recorded into a storyboard timeline. These states can then be wired up in Visual Studio to native Silverlight events (such as MouseEnter, MouseLeave, and MouseDown). When a state is activated, the associated storyboard that was created will begin and start to change properties of visual elements in the workspace. Next, we are going to create a VisualStateGroup called MyMouseStateGroup. In that group, we are going to add four states:

- MyMouseEnterState: This will run a storyboard that changes the color of the Rectangle to yellow.

- MyMouseLeaveState: This will run a storyboard that will change the color of the Rectangle back to blue.

- MyMouseDownState: This will run a storyboard that will increase the size of the Rectangle by 20%.

- MyMouseUpState: This will run a storyboard that will change the size of the Rectangle back to its original size.

Let's go ahead and create the states and associated storyboards now:

1. In the States panel, click the Add state group button, as shown in Figure 5-4.

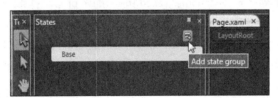

Figure 5-4. Add a new state group.

2. Next, name the new state group MyMouseStateGroup, as shown in Figure 5-5.

Figure 5-5. Name the new state group MyMouseStateGroup.

3. Change the default transition duration to .3 seconds (this is how long it will take each state to execute), as shown in Figure 5-6.

Figure 5-6. Change the default transition duration to .3 seconds.

4. Now click the Add state button, as shown in Figure 5-7.

Figure 5-7. Add a new state to the state group.

5. Name the new state MyMouseEnterState, as shown in Figure 5-8.

Figure 5-8. Name the new state MyMouseEnterState.

Notice now that there is a red line around the workspace. Also, in the top right of the workspace, you will see a message that reads "MyMouseEnterState state recording is on." This is informing you that any change you make to any part of the visual tree will be recorded into a storyboard.

Figure 5-9 shows the timeline that appears when the Show Timeline button is clicked.

Figure 5-9. The timeline of the MyMouseEnterState visual state

For our purposes, we will just use the default duration of .3 seconds. So let's change the color of the Rectangle to yellow now:

6. Make sure the MyRectangle Rectangle is selected.

7. On the Properties tab, change the Fill property in the Brushes bucket to yellow by clicking the yellow portion of the color palette, as shown in Figure 5-10.

Figure 5-10. Change the color of the Rectangle to yellow.

Notice that the Rectangle in the workspace has changed to yellow (see Figure 5-11). Now that we have created the enter state, let's move on and add the leave state.

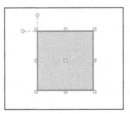

Figure 5-11. The Rectangle is now yellow.

Next, we need to add the MyMouseLeaveState state:

8. Click the Add state button.

9. Name the new state MyMouseLeaveState.

Notice that the Rectangle turns back to its original color of blue. This is the color we want when the mouse leaves the Rectangle, so all we have to do is record the keyframe. To record the keyframe, follow these steps:

10. In the Objects and Timeline panel, click the Show Timeline button, as shown in Figure 5-12.

Figure 5-12. Click the Show Timeline button.

11. Now click the Record Keyframe button, as shown in Figure 5-13.

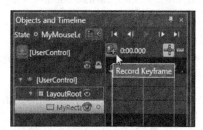

Figure 5-13. Click the Record Keyframe button.

Doing this will record all of the properties of the Rectangle, including the Fill property. Now, we need to add the final two states, MyMouseDown and MyMouseUp, which will scale the Rectangle.

12. Click the Add state button to add a new state.

13. Name this new state MyMouseDownState.

14. Select the Rectangle.

15. Hold down the Shift key (to keep the correct aspect ratio of the Rectangle) and the Alt key (to make the Rectangle scale from the center).

16. Use the scale handles, and make the Rectangle roughly 20% bigger, as shown in Figure 5-14.

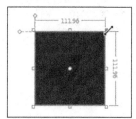

Figure 5-14. Scale up the Rectangle by roughly 20%.

17. Click the Add state button again, and name the new state MyMouseUpState.

18. Because the Rectangle is at its original size, all you need to do is record the keyframe by clicking the Record Keyframe button.

19. Click the Base button on the States panel to stop all recording, as shown in Figure 5-15. The Base state is simply how the application appears when not in any state.

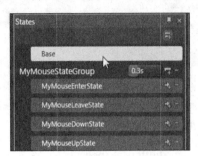

Figure 5-15. Click the Base button in the States panel to stop all recording.

At this stage, it is time for us to compile our project and then switch over to Visual Studio to wire up our states. But before we do, it would be good for you to see exactly what Blend 3 has done under the hood with regard to the storyboards and states.

If you click the XAML tab, as shown in Figure 5-16, you will see the XAML that Blend 3 has created for us. You can see that Blend 3 created a VSM for us with a VisualStateGroup called MyMouseStateGroup, and inside of that there are four states: MyMouseEnterState, MyMouseLeaveState, MyMouseDownState, and MyMouseUpState. See the following XAML:

```
<vsm:VisualStateManager.VisualStateGroups>
 <vsm:VisualStateGroup x:Name="MyMouseStateGroup">
 <vsm:VisualStateGroup.Transitions>
 <vsm:VisualTransition GeneratedDuration="00:00:00.3000000"/>
 </vsm:VisualStateGroup.Transitions>
 <vsm:VisualState x:Name="MyMouseEnterState">
 <Storyboard>
 <ColorAnimationUsingKeyFrames
 BeginTime="00:00:00" Duration="00:00:00.0010000"
Storyboard.TargetName="MyRectangle"
Storyboard.TargetProperty="(Shape.Fill).(SolidColorBrush.Color)">
 <SplineColorKeyFrame KeyTime="00:00:00" Value="#FFE0EC00"/>
 </ColorAnimationUsingKeyFrames>
 </Storyboard>
 </vsm:VisualState>
 <vsm:VisualState x:Name="MyMouseLeaveState">
 <Storyboard/>
 </vsm:VisualState>
```

```
<vsm:VisualState x:Name="MyMouseDownState">
<Storyboard>
<DoubleAnimationUsingKeyFrames
BeginTime="00:00:00" Duration="00:00:00.0010000"
Storyboard.TargetName="MyRectangle"
Storyboard.TargetProperty="(UIElement.RenderTransform)
.(TransformGroup.Children)[0].(ScaleTransform.ScaleX)">
<SplineDoubleKeyFrame KeyTime="00:00:00" Value="1.244"/>
</DoubleAnimationUsingKeyFrames>
<DoubleAnimationUsingKeyFrames
BeginTime="00:00:00" Duration="00:00:00.0010000"
Storyboard.TargetName="MyRectangle"
Storyboard.TargetProperty="(UIElement.RenderTransform)
.(TransformGroup.Children)[0].(ScaleTransform.ScaleY)">
<SplineDoubleKeyFrame KeyTime="00:00:00" Value="1.244"/>
</DoubleAnimationUsingKeyFrames>
</Storyboard>
</vsm:VisualState>
<vsm:VisualState x:Name="MyMouseUpState"/>
</vsm:VisualStateGroup>
</vsm:VisualStateManager.VisualStateGroups>
```

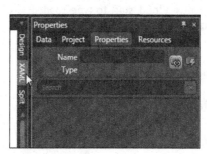

Figure 5-16. Click the XAML tab to see the XAML that Blend has created.

Wiring up the interaction in Visual Studio

Now that we have used Blend 3 to create our VisualStateGroup and our states, we need a way to tell the application when to activate these different states. This is typically much easier to do in Visual Studio, so let's do that now.

In Blend 3, press Ctrl+Shift+B to compile the application and fire up Visual Studio. Once Visual Studio opens, click File ➤ Open ➤ Project/Solution, navigate to where you saved your project, and double-click it to open it. Now you can start to wire up our states.

1. In Visual Studio's Solution Explorer, click the arrow next to Page.xaml to reveal Page.xaml.cs, and double-click to open it, as shown in Figure 5-17.

Figure 5-17. Open Page.xaml's code-behind file, Page.xaml.cs.

Now that we have the application open and the correct file open, we can raise and handle events. The first event we are going to raise and handle is the Loaded event, which occurs whenever the application is loaded. Then, in the Loaded event handler, we are going to wire up our mouse enter, leave, down, and up events.

2. In the InitializeComponent method, start to type loaded+=. When you do this, Visual Studio will realize you want to create a Loaded method (which will run when Page.xaml.cs is loaded). You can then press the Tab key twice, and Visual Studio will create the code that raises the event and also the code that handles the event. See my code, which follows:

```
namespace StoryboardProject
{
    public partial class Page : UserControl
    {
        public Page()
        {
            // Required to initialize variables
            InitializeComponent();
            Loaded += new RoutedEventHandler(Page_Loaded);
        }

        void Page_Loaded(object sender, RoutedEventArgs e)
        {
            throw new NotImplementedException();
        }
    }
}
```

Now you can delete the default code that reads throw new NotImplementedException();.

3. Place your cursor where the default code was, and create the MouseEnter event on the Rectangle by typing the name of the Rectangle (MyRectangle). Then type += and press the Tab key twice to finish raising the event and creating the event handler for it. The following code will be generated:

```
void Page_Loaded(object sender, RoutedEventArgs e)
        {
            MyRectangle.MouseEnter +=
new MouseEventHandler(MyRectangle_MouseEnter);
        }

        void MyRectangle_MouseEnter(object sender, MouseEventArgs e)
        {
            throw new NotImplementedException();
        }
```

4. Now, type the following code, which will execute the MyMouseEnterState state that we created earlier in Blend 3:

```
void MyRectangle_MouseEnter(object sender, MouseEventArgs e)
        {
            VisualStateManager.GoToState
(this, "MyMouseEnterState", true);
        }
```

If you press F5 to compile and run the application, you can place your mouse over the Rectangle, and it will change from blue to yellow. This means that your MyMouseEnterState has fired its associated storyboard. Now go ahead and wire up the remaining tasks (this is done almost exactly as before—type the name of the Rectangle and then the event, type +=, and press the Tab key twice).

5. Raise the MouseLeave event, and create the event handler.

6. Raise the MouseDown event, and create the event handler.

7. Raise the MouseUp event, and create the event handler.

8. Switch to the appropriate state in each event handler, as shown in the following code:

```
namespace StoryboardProject
{
    public partial class Page : UserControl
    {
        public Page()
        {
            // Required to initialize variables
            InitializeComponent();
            Loaded += new RoutedEventHandler(Page_Loaded);
        }

        void Page_Loaded(object sender, RoutedEventArgs e)
        {
            MyRectangle.MouseEnter += new
MouseEventHandler(MyRectangle_MouseEnter);
            MyRectangle.MouseLeave += new
MouseEventHandler(MyRectangle_MouseLeave);
            MyRectangle.MouseLeftButtonDown += new
MouseButtonEventHandler(MyRectangle_MouseLeftButtonDown);
            MyRectangle.MouseLeftButtonUp += new
```

```
        MouseButtonEventHandler(MyRectangle_MouseLeftButtonUp);
        }

        void MyRectangle_MouseLeftButtonUp(object sender,
    MouseButtonEventArgs e)
        {
            VisualStateManager.GoToState(this, "MyMouseUpState", true);
        }

        void MyRectangle_MouseLeftButtonDown
    (object sender, MouseButtonEventArgs e)
        {
            VisualStateManager.GoToState(this, "MyMouseDownState",
    true);
        }

        void MyRectangle_MouseLeave(object sender, MouseEventArgs e)
        {
            VisualStateManager.GoToState(this, "MyMouseLeaveState",
    true);
        }

        void MyRectangle_MouseEnter(object sender, MouseEventArgs e)
        {
            VisualStateManager.GoToState(this, "MyMouseEnterState",
    true);
        }
    }
}
```

Press F5 to compile and run the application, and all of the states should be firing their storyboards just as you would expect. Pretty cool, yes? Now, I'll show you how to create and run a storyboard from code-behind.

Creating storyboards in code-behind

Now that you have learned how to create storyboards in Blend using the VSM, it is time you learned how to write them in code-behind in Visual Studio. In order to do this, we need a visual that we can run the storyboard on. So let's go ahead and add an invisible (opacity of 0) TextBlock, and when the application starts, run a storyboard that will fade the new TextBlock in.

1. Switch back over to Blend 3.

2. Click the TextBlock tool from the toolbar.

3. Draw a TextBlock in the workspace.

4. Double-click the default text that reads TextBlock, and type "Developing in Silverlight is FUN!" as shown in Figure 5-18.

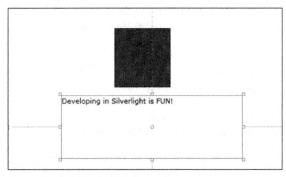

Figure 5-18. Add a TextBlock to the workspace.

5. In the Text bucket of the Properties panel, change the font size to 20.

6. In the Appearance bucket of the Properties panel, change the Opacity from 100% to 0% (this will make the TextBlock appear invisible).

7. Change the Name property to MyTextBlock in the Properties panel.

Now, we need to go into the Loaded event handler and create the new storyboard that will fade in the TextBlock. The following code shows how this is accomplished:

```
void Page_Loaded(object sender, RoutedEventArgs e)
    {
        MyRectangle.MouseEnter += new
MouseEventHandler(MyRectangle_MouseEnter);
        MyRectangle.MouseLeave += new
MouseEventHandler(MyRectangle_MouseLeave);
        MyRectangle.MouseLeftButtonDown += new
MouseButtonEventHandler(MyRectangle_MouseLeftButtonDown);
        MyRectangle.MouseLeftButtonUp += new
MouseButtonEventHandler(MyRectangle_MouseLeftButtonUp);

        // Create the animation
        DoubleAnimation FadeInTBAnimation = new DoubleAnimation();

        // Set the values that the animation starts and ends with
        FadeInTBAnimation.From = 0;
        FadeInTBAnimation.To = 1;

        // Set the time the animation is to begin
        //(3 seconds in this case)
        FadeInTBAnimation.BeginTime = TimeSpan.FromSeconds(3);

        // Set the duration of the animation
        //(3 seconds in this case)
        FadeInTBAnimation.Duration = new
Duration(TimeSpan.FromSeconds(3));
```

```
            // Set the target of the animation
            Storyboard.SetTarget(FadeInTBAnimation, MyTextBlock);

            // Set the property the animation is to affect
            Storyboard.SetTargetProperty(FadeInTBAnimation, new
    PropertyPath(FrameworkElement.OpacityProperty));

            // Create a new storyboard
            Storyboard FadeInTBSB = new Storyboard();

            // Add the animation to the storyboard
            FadeInTBSB.Children.Add(FadeInTBAnimation);

            // Begin the storyboard
            FadeInTBSB.Begin();
        }
```

Basically, the preceding code does the following:

1. Creates a DoubleAnimation called FadeInTBAnimation.

2. Sets the To and From values (1 and 0, respectively) for the animation. This means that the property will start at a value of 0 and go to a value of 1.

3. Sets how long it will take the animation to begin (3 seconds).

4. Sets how long the animation will take to complete (3 seconds).

5. Sets the target, or what visual the animation will act upon (MyTextBlock in this case).

6. Sets the property of the visual that the animation is to affect (Opacity in this case).

7. Creates a new storyboard called FadeInTBSB.

8. Adds the animation to the storyboard.

9. Begins the storyboard.

> *A DoubleAnimation is a type of Silverlight animation that animates a Double property.*

Now when you press F5 to compile and run the application, you will see that the storyboard runs after 3 seconds and takes 3 seconds until it completely fades in the TextBlock. Now, what if you had an application in which you had to do this over and over again? This is quite a bit of code to duplicate repeatedly. What if we had a helper class that we could just invoke to accomplish this for us? Well, this is exactly what I am going to show you how to create next.

Building a Storyboard helper class

Now let's build a helper class that you can use to fade in FrameworkElements (objects you can see in the visual tree).

1. In Visual Studio, right-click the project, and click Add ➤ Class, as shown in Figure 5-19.

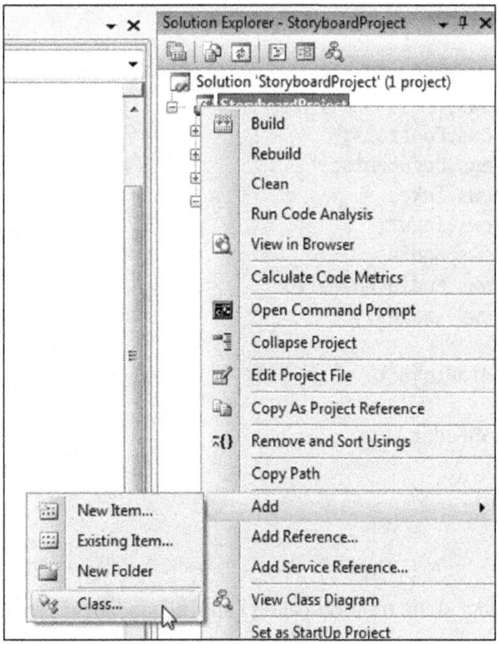

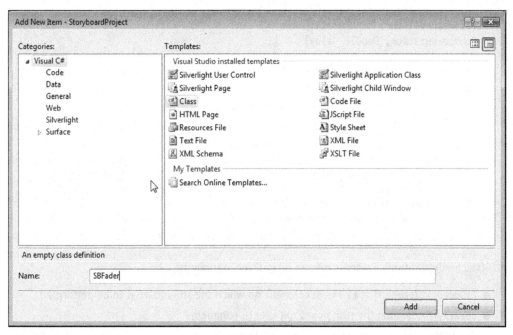

Figure 5-19. Add a new class to the project.

2. In the Add New Item dialog box, name the class SBFader, and click Add, as shown in Figure 5-20.

Figure 5-20. Name the class SBFader, and click Add.

Your new class's code will look like the following, as this is the default code that is created when you create a new class:

```
using System;
using System.Net;
using System.Windows;
using System.Windows.Controls;
using System.Windows.Documents;
using System.Windows.Ink;
using System.Windows.Input;
using System.Windows.Media;
using System.Windows.Media.Animation;
using System.Windows.Shapes;

namespace StoryboardProject
{
    public class SBFader
    {

    }
}
```

3. You now need to add a static method called FadeInFrameworkElement, as shown in the following code.

```
public class SBFader
    {

        public static Storyboard FadeInFrameworkElement
(FrameworkElement frameworkElement,
Double duration, Double delay)
        {
            Storyboard sRet = null;

            return sRet;
        }
    }
```

> A static method is a method that can be executed without creating an instance of the class, but just by calling it on the class directly. For example, the FadeInFrameworkElement method will be executed on the SBFader class like so: SBFader.FadeInFrameworkElement();.

This static method returns a storyboard and takes three arguments:

- FrameworkElement: The FrameworkElement on which the storyboard is to be performed
- duration: How long the storyboard will take to complete
- delay: How long before the storyboard will begin

Now, we can add our code to create the storyboard:

```
public static Storyboard FadeInFrameworkElement(FrameworkElement
 frameworkElement,
Double duration, Double delay)
        {
                Storyboard sRet = null;

                // Create the animation
                DoubleAnimation FadeInTBAnimation = new DoubleAnimation();

                // Set the values that the animation starts and ends with
                FadeInTBAnimation.From = 0;
                FadeInTBAnimation.To = 1;

                // Set the time the animation is to begin
                FadeInTBAnimation.BeginTime = TimeSpan.FromSeconds(delay);

                // Set the duration of the animation
                FadeInTBAnimation.Duration = new
Duration(TimeSpan.FromSeconds(duration));

                // Set the target of the animation
                Storyboard.SetTarget(FadeInTBAnimation, frameworkElement);

                // Set the property the animation is to affect
                Storyboard.SetTargetProperty(FadeInTBAnimation, new
PropertyPath(FrameworkElement.OpacityProperty));

                // Create a new storyboard
                Storyboard FadeInTBSB = new Storyboard();

                // Add the animation to the storyboard
                FadeInTBSB.Children.Add(FadeInTBAnimation);

                // Set return variable to the new storyboard
                        return FadeInTBSB ;
        }
```

We can go back to page.xaml.cs now and comment out our earlier code that created and began our storyboard; we'll use the newly created SBFader class to accomplish the same thing but with less code. See the following code:

```
void Page_Loaded(object sender, RoutedEventArgs e)
        {
                MyRectangle.MouseEnter += new
MouseEventHandler(MyRectangle_MouseEnter);
                MyRectangle.MouseLeave += new
MouseEventHandler(MyRectangle_MouseLeave);
                MyRectangle.MouseLeftButtonDown += new
```

```
              MouseButtonEventHandler
(MyRectangle_MouseLeftButtonDown);
              MyRectangle.MouseLeftButtonUp += new
MouseButtonEventHandler
(MyRectangle_MouseLeftButtonUp);

              //// Create the animation
              //DoubleAnimation FadeInTBAnimation =
new DoubleAnimation();
              //// Set the values that the animation starts and ends with
              //FadeInTBAnimation.From = 0;
              //FadeInTBAnimation.To = 1;
              //// Set the time the animation is to begin
              ///(3 seconds in this case)
              //FadeInTBAnimation.BeginTime = TimeSpan.FromSeconds(3);
              //// Set the duration of the animation
              ///(3 seconds in this case)
              //FadeInTBAnimation.Duration =
new Duration(TimeSpan.FromSeconds(3));
              //// Set the target of the animation
              //Storyboard.SetTarget(FadeInTBAnimation, MyTextBlock);
              //// Set the property the animation is to affect
              //Storyboard.SetTargetProperty(FadeInTBAnimation, new
  PropertyPath(FrameworkElement.OpacityProperty));

              //// Create a new storyboard
              //Storyboard FadeInTBSB = new Storyboard();
              //// Add the animation to the storyboard
              //FadeInTBSB.Children.Add(FadeInTBAnimation);
              //// Begin the storyboard
              //FadeInTBSB.Begin();

              // Create a new SB using SBFader
              // Arguments are FrameworkElement, Duration, and Delay
              Storyboard fadeInSB =
SBFader.FadeInFrameworkElement(MyTextBlock, 3, 3);
              // Make sure that fadeInSB is not null
              if (fadeInSB != null)
              {
                  // If the storyboard is not null then begin it
                  fadeInSB.Begin();
              }
          }
}
```

If you now press F5 to compile and run the application, you will see that it acts just as it did before, but SBFader is creating the storyboard instead of doing it manually every time. You may say, "What's the big deal? It took us just as long to create the SBFader class as it did to do it manually." You would be correct, but the difference is that if you want to use SBFader again, you only have to use one line of code (Storyboard fadeInSB = SBFader.FadeInFrameworkElement(MyTextBlock, 3, 3);), as opposed to the nine or so lines that it took to do it manually. This is a great little helper class and one that I use very often in almost every application I build.

My challenge to you is to edit SBFader, add a new static method called FadeOutFrameworkElement, and make it take the same arguments—with the only difference being, obviously, that it fades a FrameworkElement out rather than in. You can then set MyTextBlock to have an opacity of 1 and then use SBFader to fade it out. Good luck!

Summary

In this chapter, you learned all about storyboards: what they are, what they can do, and how they help keep timeline animations organized. You also learned how to build them using the Visual State Manager. You then learned how to raise native Silverlight events and wire up the states you created in the event handlers for those events. Next, you learned how to manually create and run a storyboard in code-behind. Finally, you learned how to make a Storyboard helper class that allows you to fade in a FrameworkElement with only one line of code. In the next chapter, you are going to learn about the powerful and fun Silverlight MediaElement and create a fun and interactive Silverlight video player.

Chapter 6

USING THE VSM AND BLEND 3'S STATES PANEL TO CREATE A SILVERLIGHT MEDIA PLAYER

What this chapter covers:

- Understanding the Visual State Manager (VSM)
- Understanding Blend 3's States panel
- Creating a Silverlight test project to show how to use VSM
- Creating a new Silverlight project
- Styling up a media player
- Adding Play, Pause, and Stop buttons
- Adding a MediaElement to the project
- Adding a source to the MediaElement
- Adding a ClipGeometry region to the MediaElement
- Creating VSM states with Blend 3's States panel to hide and show the Play, Pause, and Stop buttons
- Wiring up the states in Visual Studio 2008
- Wiring up the Play, Pause, and Stop buttons

Silverlight 3 saw the addition of something called the VSM, which enables you to easily add states to any UIElement such as a Button, Rectangle, Ellipse, or even an entire UserControl. As you may remember, a state allows you to easily switch between different views of an object or even the application by executing storyboards. For example, you can define and execute a state when your mouse is over a button. You can also define and execute another state when your mouse is not over the very same button. You can, of course, do all of this in code-behind, but it would be tedious. For that reason, Microsoft has introduced the States panel. The States panel enables you to very easily and quickly create states. Then all you need to do is go into the code-behind file and wire up those states.

In this chapter, I am first going to show you how to use VSM to create states for a simple button and wire up those states in Visual Studio 2008. I am then going to show you how to take what you have learned and create a very highly styled Silverlight media player that uses VSM to show and hide the navigation buttons (Play, Pause, Stop). If you are like me and have absolutely no patience, you can navigate the following URL and see what the final product will look like in action. Also, you should have a WMV movie ready, because you are going to obviously be adding a video to our video player. If you don't have your own WMV videos, Vista ships with three; just do a search on your hard drive for Bear.wmv to find it and make a mental note of where it is so you can get to it later. With that, let's get to it!

Silverlight media player:

```
http://windowspresentationfoundation.com/BookProjects/SLVSMMediaPlayer/
bin/Debug/Default.html
```

You can also see a screenshot of it here:

Using the VSM

Often when I explain VSM to developers, they get confused and mistake the VSM for Blend's States panel. That being the case, I thought it best to clear up the difference between the two right off the bat. The VSM is the code that actually contains the states (in code) and executes the different states. Blend's States panel (explained and shown in depth in the next section) is the tool you will use to create the visual states. The following is an example of VSM code in XAML:

```
<vsm:VisualStateManager.VisualStateGroups>
    <vsm:VisualStateGroup x:Name="MouseEnterLeaveStateGroup">
        <vsm:VisualStateGroup.Transitions>
            <vsm:VisualTransition GeneratedDuration=
"00:00:05. "/>
        </vsm:VisualStateGroup.Transitions>
        <vsm:VisualState x:Name="MouseEnter">
            <Storyboard/>
        </vsm:VisualState>
        <vsm:VisualState x:Name="MouseLeave">
            <Storyboard/>
        </vsm:VisualState>
    </vsm:VisualStateGroup>
</vsm:VisualStateManager.VisualStateGroups>
```

I will quickly run you through this code:

- A VisualStateManager.VisualStateGroups node is declared using the vsm namespace.
- A VisualStateGroup node is then declared and named MouseEnterLeaveStateGroup.
- A default transition time is declared and tells all VisualStates in this group to take 0.5 seconds to execute.
- A VisualState named MouseEnter is declared with an empty storyboard.
- Another VisualState, called MouseLeave, is declared with an empty storyboard.

The following code is the accompanying C# code-behind that will execute the MouseEnter state when a button named MyBtn is moused over:

```
void MyBtn_MouseEnter(object sender, MouseEventArgs e)
{
    VisualStateManager.GoToState("MouseEnter");
}
```

Seems pretty straightforward, right? Next I am going to explain and show you Blend's States panel.

Using Blend 3's States panel

As I stated before, Blend's States panel is how you create a VSM. You can see this panel in Figure 6-1.

Figure 6-1. Blend 3's States panel above the Objects and Timeline panel

As I have stated many times before, this is a hands-on book; so with that, let's roll up our sleeves. You'll create a new Silverlight application and use VSM and the States panel to create some states for a button.

A simple Silverlight project

To show you how to quickly use VSM, we are going to make a simple sample application and create a StateGroup with states. Let's get to it!

1. Open Blend 3 and click File ➤ New Project, as shown in Figure 6-2.

2. In the New Project dialog box, select Silverlight 3 Application + Website.

3. Name the project SimpleVSMProject.

4. Select the location where you want to save the project.

5. Make a mental note of where you are saving the project, because you will need to open it in Visual Studio 2008 later.

Figure 6-2. Create a new project in Blend 3.

6. Click OK (see Figure 6-3).

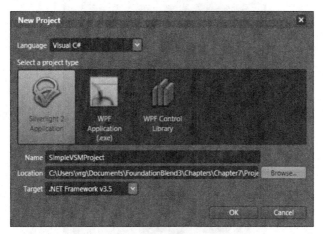

Figure 6-3. Make certain that your New Project dialog box is the same as what is shown here.

7. After Blend 3 has created the project, select the Rectangle tool from the toolbar, as shown in Figure 6-4.

8. Draw a Rectangle that will act as a button on the workspace, as I have done in Figure 6-5.

Figure 6-4. Select the Rectangle tool.

Figure 6-5. Draw a Rectangle control on the workspace.

9. Select the Rectangle and in the Properties panel give it a name of MyRectangle and give it a solid color fill of black. See Figure 6-6.

Figure 6-6. Name and color the rectangle.

Now you should have something like Figure 6-7.

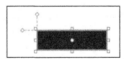

Figure 6-7. Your rectangle should look like this.

10. Now you have to go over to Blend's States panel and click the Add State Group, as I am about to do in Figure 6-8. Blend will then highlight the new state group so you can name it. Name the new state group MouseEnterLeaveStateGroup, as I have done in Figure 6-9.

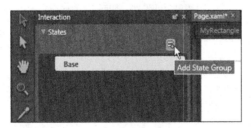

Figure 6-8. Add a new state group in the States panel.

Figure 6-9. Name the state group.

Notice that next to the state group name you can see 0s. This represents the amount of time in seconds it takes for the states (yet to be added) to complete.

11. You need to click this number and change it to 0.5s; this means your states will take 0.5 seconds to complete. Your States panel should look like Figure 6-10.

Figure 6-10. Your States panel should look like what I have here.

With the visual state group created, you can now add a state (called a VisualState in code).

12. To add a state, click the Add State button, as shown in Figure 6-11.

Figure 6-11. Add a state to your visual state group.

13. Name your new state MouseEnter. Click the Add State button once again and name the new state MouseLeave. Your States panel should look like Figure 6-12.

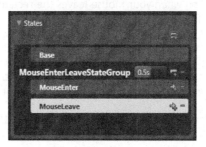

Figure 6-12. Your States panel should now have one state group and two states.

As you may have noticed, after you created a new state, Blend placed a red line around your workspace to indicate that any action you perform on any FrameworkElement on the workspace is being recorded. I didn't have you perform any actions because you can simply click on a state anytime to start recording your actions. So, go ahead and click on the MouseEnter state so the red line will appear around your workspace. Now change the fill color of your rectangle to red, as I have done in Figure 6-13.

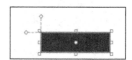

Figure 6-13. Change the rectangle to be red.

14. Click on the default Base state in the States panel so you are no longer recording your actions, as I have done in Figure 6-14.

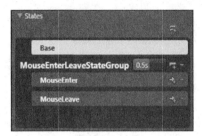

Figure 6-14. Click on the Base state.

Notice that the rectangle is now black again. This is because in the default Base state, the rectangle is its original color. Now you may be thinking that I am going to instruct you to click on the MouseLeave state and do something to your rectangle. I am not. Why, you ask? Well, let's think of the behavior we want:

- When the application starts, we want the rectangle to be its default color.
- When the rectangle has a mouse over it, we want it to turn red.
- When the mouse moves off the rectangle, we want it to turn back to its default color of black.

This being the case, your MouseLeave state is already correct because if you click on the MouseLeave state, you will see that the rectangle is already black. So you are probably asking yourself, why create a MouseLeave state if the default state of the rectangle is black? If you are, that is a good question and one I had to ask myself when writing this chapter. If you don't add the MouseLeave state (that has the rectangle with a fill of black), then when your mouse leaves the rectangle in the running application, it will stay red. So, you need to have the MouseLeave state.

So, now press Ctrl+Shift+B to compile (also called build) the application. When the build has completed, open Visual Studio 2008 and click File ➤ Open ➤ Project/Solution. Navigate to where you saved the project and open it. After it has opened, open the Page1.xaml.cs code-behind page. Now you are going to raise the MouseEnter and MouseLeave events and create event handlers for both events:

1. In the Constructor under the InitializeComponent call, start to type the name of the rectangle (MyButton).

2. After IntelliSense shows you the full name of the rectangle, press Enter.

3. Type a period and start to type MouseEnter. Press Enter when IntelliSense highlights MouseEnter.

4. Type += and press the Tab key twice.

Visual Studio will raise the event for you and create the event handler. See the following code.

```
public Page()
{
    // Required to initialize variables
    InitializeComponent();
```

```
        Loaded += new RoutedEventHandler(Page_Loaded);
}

void Page_Loaded(object sender, RoutedEventArgs e)
{
    MyRectangle.MouseEnter += new MouseEventHandler
(MyRectangle_MouseEnter);
}

void MyRectangle_MouseEnter(object sender, MouseEventArgs e)
{
    throw new NotImplementedException();
}
```

5. Now erase the default throw new... code and replace it with this code:

```
        void MyRectangle_MouseEnter(object sender, MouseEventArgs e)
        {
            VisualStateManager.GoToState(this, "MouseEnter", true);
        }
```

6. Repeat these steps, with the only difference being you are going to raise the MouseLeave event. Your code should look like the following:

```
namespace SimpleVSMProject
{
    public partial class Page : UserControl
    {
        public Page()
        {
            // Required to initialize variables
            InitializeComponent();
        Loaded += new RoutedEventHandler(Page_Loaded);
        }

        void Page_Loaded(object sender, RoutedEventArgs e)
        {
            MyRectangle.MouseEnter += new MouseEventHandler
(MyRectangle_MouseEnter);
            MyRectangle.MouseLeave += new MouseEventHandler
(MyRectangle_MouseLeave);
        }

        void MyRectangle_MouseLeave(object sender, MouseEventArgs e)
        {
            VisualStateManager.GoToState(this, "MouseLeave", true);
        }

        void MyRectangle_MouseEnter(object sender, MouseEventArgs e)
        {
            VisualStateManager.GoToState(this, "MouseEnter", true);
```

```
            }
          }
        }
```

7. Now press F5 to compile and run the application, and place your mouse over the rectangle and see how it turns red. Move your mouse off the rectangle and see how it turns black again.

At this point, I am willing to bet you are saying to yourself, "So, what's the big deal?" I wouldn't hold it against you if you are, because this is not an impressive implementation of VSM. So, I want to show you how you can take full advantage of the powerful VSM to make a cool application. Next you are going to build a very styled media player and then use VSM to show and hide the video controls (Play, Pause, and Stop).

Creating a media player by using VSM

Before we create a media player, I would like to give credit where credit is due. The design that I am going to show you how to implement is loosely based on the Deadline Advertising website (www.dead-line.com) designed by my talented friend and former colleague, Chris McCall (see Figure 6-15).

Figure 6-15. www.dead-line.com designed by Chris McCall

Creating the Silverlight project in Blend 3

The first thing you need to do is close the current project in Blend and create a new Silverlight application. Name it SLVSMMediaPlayer. Remember to make a mental note of where you save this project, as you will be opening it in Visual Studio later. Your New Project dialog box should look something like Figure 6-16.

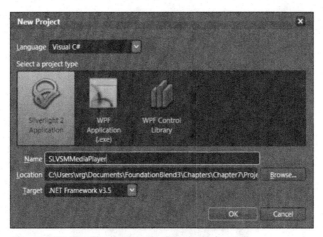

Figure 6-16. The Blend 3 New Project dialog box

Designing the navigation orbs

The next thing you need to do is to create the navigation orbs. This is going to be a series of ellipses, one on top of the next, with different gradients. After you have the series of ellipses the way we want them, you are going to group them into a canvas and then tell Blend 3 to turn them into a Silverlight Button control. Let's start now:

1. On the Blend toolbar, hold down the Rectangle tool until you see the option for the Ellipse tool.

2. Draw an ellipse roughly 60×60 display units on the workspace, as shown in Figure 6-17.

3. With the ellipse selected, give it a Gradient brush fill in the Properties panel, as I am about to do in Figure 6-18.

Figure 6-17. Draw an ellipse on the workspace.

Figure 6-18. Give the ellipse a gradient fill.

4. Adjust the color stops so that the gradient goes from gray to white (see Figure 6-19).

Figure 6-19. Adjust the gradient of the ellipse.

5. Select the Stroke property and click No brush, as I am about to do in Figure 6-20.

Figure 6-20. Remove the stroke from the ellipse.

6. In the Objects and Timeline panel, select the grid named LayoutRoot.

7. In the Properties panel, change the background color from white to black.

8. Now select the ellipse again and press Ctrl+C to copy it.

9. Press Ctrl+V to paste another ellipse on top of it.

10. Hold down Alt (to make the ellipse scale from the center).

11. Hold down Shift (to make the ellipse stay symmetrical).

12. With the Selection tool selected, grab one of the corner scale handles and move your mouse to make the top ellipse smaller than the first (see Figure 6-21).

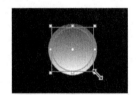

Figure 6-21. Scale the top ellipse so that it is smaller than the bottom ellipse.

13. Now change the top ellipse to a solid color fill of black (it should turn black by default when you select Solid Color). See Figure 6-22.

14. Select the topmost ellipse and press Ctrl+C to copy it.

15. Press Ctrl+V to paste in another ellipse.

16. Set the new top ellipse to have a linear gradient, as shown in Figure 6-23.

17. Change the color stops so that the gradient goes from white to white.

18. Select the right color stop.

19. Change the alpha (see the arrow in Figure 6-24) to be 0%.

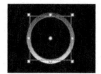

Figure 6-22. The top ellipse should now be black.

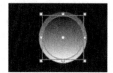

Figure 6-23. Add another ellipse.

Figure 6-24. Change the gradient to go from white to white, and give the right color an alpha of 0%.

You should now have something that looks like Figure 6-25.

Figure 6-25. This ellipse has a linear gradient that goes from white to white with the right color alpha of 0%.

20. Adjust the top ellipse so that it is smaller and a little oblong until you have what I have in Figure 6-26.

Figure 6-26. Your top ellipse should now look like this.

Looking at Chris's design, I see that the outer gray bezel, for lack of a better word, is smaller than what I have. So, follow these steps:

21. In the Objects and Timeline panel, select the ellipse that is at the top of the visual tree (you can tell which ellipse is at the top of the visual tree because it will be at the bottom of the stack of objects in the Objects and Timeline panel). See Figure 6-27.

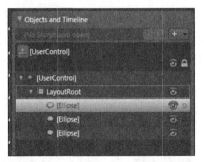

Figure 6-27. Select the topmost ellipse in the visual tree.

22. Hold down Shift+Alt and use the scale handles to adjust the size of the ellipse (see Figure 6-28).

Figure 6-28. Your orb should look like this now.

I think that looks pretty good now. At this point, you are ready to group all of your ellipses into a canvas and have Blend 3 turn them into a Silverlight Button control. Do that now:

23. With the Selection tool (the shortcut to select the Selection tool is the V key), draw a box around all of the ellipses so that they are all selected.

24. In the Objects and Timeline panel, right-click to bring up the context menu, and then click Group Into ➤ Canvas, as I am about to do in Figure 6-29.

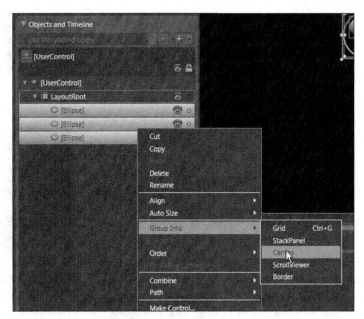

Figure 6-29. Group all ellipses into a canvas.

25. With the newly created canvas selected, click Tools ➤ Make Into Control (see Figure 6-30).

26. When the Make Into Control dialog box appears, make certain Button is selected and give it a Name (Key) of Style_OrbButton, as I am doing in Figure 6-31. Click OK.

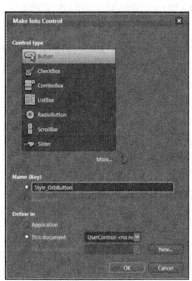

Figure 6-30. Make the new canvas a control.

Figure 6-31. Make certain that the control type is set to Button and give the new style a name of Style_OrbButton.

Now if you look in the Objects and Timeline panel, you will see that you are still editing your canvas with ellipses, but look above that and you will see that you are no longer in the LayoutRoot grid. You are now in a template. If you look above that in the Objects and Timeline panel, you see that you are actually in Style_OrbButton.

27. We are pretty much done with editing here, so click the little arrow icon next to Style_OrbButton and it will place us back in the LayoutRoot grid.

Notice that you are back in the LayoutRoot grid but you no longer see the canvas. It has been replaced with a Silverlight Button control that uses the Style_OrbButton style. Cool, huh?

Next, we need to tweak the Foreground property so that we can see the ContentPresenter (represented as the text that appears in the button).

28. Select the button in the LayoutRoot grid.

29. In the Properties panel in the Brushes bucket, give the button a foreground color of white and you should have something like Figure 6-32.

30. Now you need to select the button, and copy and paste it two times so that you have three orb buttons, as shown in Figure 6-33.

Now you need to name each button and give each the correct content in the ContentPresenter (so the buttons have the correct text).

31. Select the first orb and in the Properties panel name it PlayBtn.

32. In the Common Properties bucket of the Properties panel, give the button a Content property of Play.

33. Name the second button PauseBtn with a Content of Pause.

34. Name the third button StopBtn with a Content of Stop so that you have what I have in Figure 6-34.

Figure 6-32. Your new button should now look like this.

Figure 6-33. You should now have three orb buttons on the workspace.

Figure 6-34. Your buttons should all be named and have the correct content (text).

Creating the backplate for the MediaElement

So what you need to do now is create the background for your MediaElement. In looking at my project, I realized that I left the default size of the application, which Blend set to a width of 640 and a height of 480. Let's go ahead and change that to a bigger size to give us a little breathing room:

1. Select the UserControl in the Objects and Timeline panel, as I have done in Figure 6-35.

2. In the Layout bucket of the Properties panel, change the height to 600 and the width to 800.

Figure 6-35. Select the main UserControl
in the Objects and Timeline panel.

Now that you have a little more space to work with, let's go ahead and create the backplate for the
MediaElement:

1. Select the Ellipse tool from the toolbar.

2. Hold down the Shift+Alt keys and draw an ellipse on the workspace. Make it about the size I
   have in Figure 6-36.

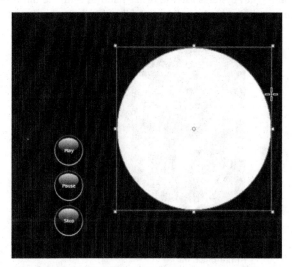

Figure 6-36. Draw an ellipse on the workspace roughly
400×400.

3. Give the ellipse a gradient fill and no stroke, as shown in Figure 6-37.

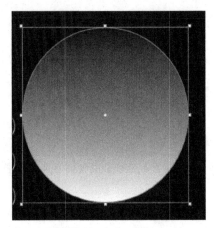

Figure 6-37. The backplate ellipse with no stroke and a linear gradient fill

4. Now copy and paste the backplate ellipse.

5. Hold down the Shift+Alt keys and use the resize handles to make the top ellipse a little smaller than the bottom one, and give it a solid color fill of black, as shown in Figure 6-38.

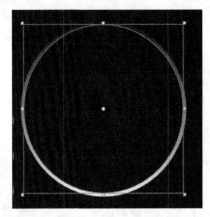

Figure 6-38. Copy and paste a new ellipse with a black fill.

It is starting to look good, but I think at this point it would look much better if we put a highlight effect on top of the backplate, the same as we did for the buttons. Let's do that now:

6. Copy and paste the ellipse with the black fill.

7. Give it a gradient fill.

8. Change the gradient to go from white to white.

9. Select the right color stop and change the Alpha value to 0%.

10. Use the resize handles and make the ellipse a little smaller and a little oblong so that you have something like Figure 6-39.

Figure 6-39. Give the topmost ellipse a
gradient and the right color stop an
alpha of 0%.

It's looking pretty good, but you need to tweak the gradient a bit to get the effect we are looking
for.

11. Select the Gradient tool, as shown in Figure 6-40.

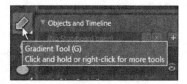

Figure 6-40. Select the Gradient tool.

12. Select the highlighted ellipse and use the Brush Transform handles to adjust the gradient so
that it looks like Figure 6-41.

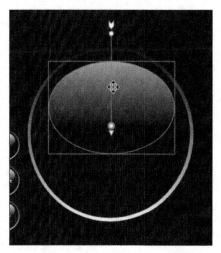

Figure 6-41. Adjust the gradient with the
Brush Transform tool.

The next thing I want you to do is to create another highlighted ellipse with a radial gradient fill. This one's a little trickier to conceptualize, so we'll do it a different way. This time, I'll give you the XAML so you can place it under the XAML of the last ellipse in your markup. After you've added the code, you can go ahead and use the Brush Transform tool to play around with the fill in Design mode to see how I accomplished this gradient.

The code for this final highlighted ellipse is as follows:

```
<Ellipse HorizontalAlignment="Stretch" Margin="371,273,125,116"
VerticalAlignment="Stretch" RenderTransformOrigin="0.5,0.5">
    Ellipse.Fill>
                                <RadialGradientBrush GradientOrigin=
"0.017,0.552">
                                <RadialGradientBrush.
RelativeTransform>
                                    <TransformGroup>
                                        <ScaleTransform
CenterX="0.5" CenterY="0.5" ScaleX="1.679" ScaleY="1.679"/>
                                        <SkewTransform
CenterX="0.5" CenterY="0.5"/>
                                        <RotateTransform
CenterX="0.5" CenterY="0.5"/>
                                        <TranslateTransform
X="0.144" Y="0.238"/>
                                    </TransformGroup>
                                </RadialGradientBrush.
RelativeTransform>
                                <RadialGradientBrush.
Transform>
                                    <MatrixTransform/>
                                </RadialGradientBrush.
Transform>
                                <GradientStop Color=
"#FFFFFFFF" Offset="0.90699899196624756"/>
                                <GradientStop Color=
"#00000000" Offset="0.78039344567249325"/>
                            </RadialGradientBrush>
                    </Ellipse.Fill>
                    <Ellipse.RenderTransform>
                        <TransformGroup>
                            <ScaleTransform/>
                            <SkewTransform/>
                            <RotateTransform Angle="180"/>
                            <TranslateTransform/>
                        </TransformGroup>
                    </Ellipse.RenderTransform>
            </Ellipse>
```

You may have to move the new highlighted ellipse in Design view to get it in the correct position so that you have something like Figure 6-42.

Figure 6-42. Your backplate should look like this.

The next thing you are going to do is to add some decorative ellipses and rectangles. Do that now:

13. Select the Ellipse tool, hold down the Shift+Alt keys, and draw an ellipse on the workspace, as I have done in Figure 6-43.

Figure 6-43. Draw a decorative ellipse on the workspace.

14. Give the new ellipse a gradient fill.

15. Add two new color stops to the center by clicking in the color bar twice, as I have done in Figure 6-44.

Figure 6-44. Add two color stops to the center of the gradient.

16. Change the leftmost color stop to a color of #FF0D0F35.

17. Change the color of the color stop to the right of the preceding one to #FF878787.

18. Change the next color stop to the right to #FF878787 as well.

19. Finally, change the rightmost color stop to #FF050620 so that you have what I have in Figure 6-45.

20. Now copy and paste the decorative ellipse.

21. Move the new ellipse down below the one you copied from.

22. Hold down the Shift+Alt keys and make the new ellipse a little smaller than the one you copied from.

23. Repeat the preceding steps until you have something like Figure 6-46.

Now you are going to want to add some decorative rectangles to the right of the media player:

24. Select the Rectangle tool from the toolbar.

25. Draw a rectangle.

26. Give the rectangle a gradient fill.

27. Leave the default gradient.

28. Copy the rectangle and make it smaller than the one you copied from.

29. Repeat steps 24 through 28 until you have something like Figure 6-47.

Figure 6-45. Your decorative ellipse should look something like this.

Figure 6-46. Decorative ellipses

Figure 6-47. Decorative rectangles

At this stage, your background should look something like Figure 6-48.

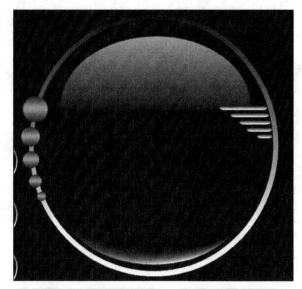

Figure 6-48. The media player backplate

30. In the Objects and Timeline panel, select all of the ellipses and rectangles that compose the backplate and group them into a canvas by holding down the Ctrl key and clicking each object.

31. In the Properties panel, name the newly created canvas Backplate.

Adding the MediaElement

The backplate looks pretty good at this stage, so I think you should add the MediaElement that will be the container for our video:

1. Click on the Asset Library.

2. In the search field, type MediaElement, as shown in Figure 6-49.

3. When the MediaElement appears, select it.

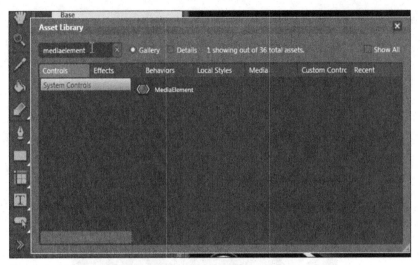

Figure 6-49. Find the MediaElement in the Asset Library.

4. Draw a `MediaElement` on the workspace, as I have done in Figure 6-50.

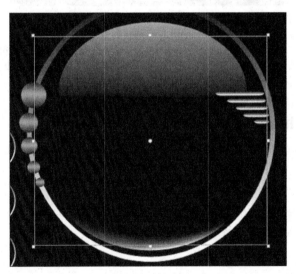

Figure 6-50. Draw a MediaElement on the workspace.

5. In the Media bucket of the Properties panel, click the Choose an Image button, as I am about to do in Figure 6-51.

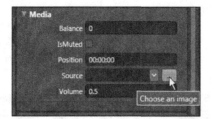

Figure 6-51. Click the Choose an Image button.

6. Navigate to a video on your hard drive that is in the WMV format.

7. Double-click the WMV video file.

8. Now select the MediaElement and name it MyME in the Properties panel.

You should see the MediaElement on the workspace populate with the first frame of your video file (see Figure 6-52). You are probably thinking to yourself that this looks really bad, because the MediaElement is covering up most of the backplate. You would be right to think such a thing. So to fix this problem, you can add a ClipGeometry. A ClipGeometry is simply a geometrical shape that will clip or hide certain regions of the object being clipped.

Figure 6-52. The MediaElement with a source video

Follow these steps to add the ClipGeometry:

9. Select the Ellipse tool from the toolbar.

10. Hold the Shift+Alt keys and draw an ellipse over the MediaElement, as I have done in Figure 6-53.

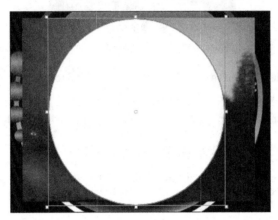

Figure 6-53. The MediaElement with an ellipse over it

11. Right-click the new ellipse to bring up a context menu.

12. Click Path ➤ Make Clipping Path, as shown in Figure 6-54.

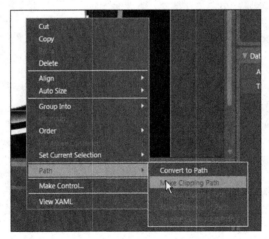

Figure 6-54. Turn the ellipse into a clipping path.

13. When the Make Clipping Path dialog box pops up, select MyME, as shown in Figure 6-55.

14. Click OK.

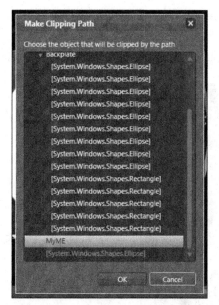

Figure 6-55. Select MyME from the dialog box.

Notice that the MediaElement named MyME is now clipped based on the shape of the ellipse and that the ellipse has disappeared. At this point, your MediaElement may need to be positioned to be in the center of the backplate. See Figure 6-56.

Figure 6-56. The MediaElement now has an ellipse ClipGeometry.

You may notice that the MediaElement is sitting above the highlights and a little bit of the decorative rectangles. To change that, you need to move MyME into the backplate canvas and just under the highlight ellipses.

1. Make sure the backplate canvas is expanded in the Objects and Timeline panel.

2. In the Objects and Timeline panel, select MyME.

3. Drag it to the correct place in the backplate canvas. See Figure 6-57.

Figure 6-57. Move MyME into the backplate and under the highlight ellipses.

Your MediaElement and backplate should look like Figure 6-58. You're now ready to position those navigation controls you created earlier so you can control the video.

Figure 6-58. The MediaElement in the backplate

Positioning the navigation buttons and the backplate

The navigation buttons and the background are in the wrong places on our layout. To correct this, I want you to put the navigation buttons on the right side of the backplate and then center the MediaElement on the backplate so that the video is playing in the very center (see Figure 6-59).

Figure 6-59. The correctly positioned backplate and navigation buttons

Adding a reflection

I promised you that this would be a highly styled media player, and what is any self-respecting styled application without reflections in this day and age? To accomplish that, we'll need to duplicate the background, flip it, and then add an opacity mask to it so that it appears that our media player has a slight reflection. Let's do that now:

1. Select the background in either the workspace or the Objects and Timeline panel.

2. Copy and paste another one into the workspace.

3. Name it backgroundReflection in the Properties panel.

4. From the File menu, choose Object ➤ Flip ➤ Vertical so the reflection looks like Figure 6-60.

Figure 6-60. Copy, flip, and rename the reflection backgroundReflection.

5. With backgroundReflection selected, go to the Properties panel and give it an opacity mask with a gradient, as I have done in Figure 6-61.

Figure 6-61. Give backgroundReflection an opacity mask.

6. Set both color stops to be white.

7. Set the left color stop to an alpha of 0%.

8. Set the right color stop to an alpha of 40%.

9. Use the Brush Transform tool and adjust the opacity mask so it looks like Figure 6-62.

Figure 6-62. The media player with a reflection

Adding the states

Well, I think it is finally time for you to add the states, because you have now completed the final design. I know it is not quite as intricate as the design by Chris McCall, but remember I did say that this design was loosely based on his. What we want to happen via the use of the VSM is for the navigation buttons and the design elements (ellipses on the left and bars on the right) to disappear in a very cool way when the mouse moves off the entire player and to do the opposite when the mouse moves over the player. With that, go ahead and add a state group:

1. In the States panel, click the Add State Group button.

2. Name the new state MouseEnterLeaveStateGroup.

3. Make the default transition time 0.5 seconds, as I have done in Figure 6-63.

Figure 6-63. Add a new state group in Blend's States panel.

4. Add two new states for MouseEnter and MouseLeave, as I have done in Figure 6-64.

Figure 6-64. Add the MouseEnter and MouseLeave states.

5. Now click the MouseEnter state and start recording what will occur when the mouse enters the media player. We're going to have the navigation buttons animate and disappear when we enter the media player, and then animate back again when the mouse leaves it. We'll also move the decorative elements off, then back on again.

6. Start by making the navigation buttons spin around a few times and then shrink. See Figure 6-65.

7. Make the opacity 0 in the Properties panel under the Appearance bucket.

8. Do this for all three navigation buttons.

9. Next move your decorative ellipses off the right of the media player, as I have done in Figure 6-66.

10. Set their opacity to 0 in the Appearance bucket of the Properties panel.

Figure 6-65. Spin, shrink, and make the navigation buttons have an opacity of 0 in the MouseEnter state.

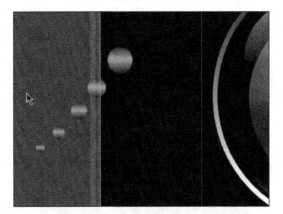

Figure 6-66. Move the decorative ellipses to the right of the media player and give them an opacity of 0.

11. Now scale the decorative rectangles to be very small, as I have done in Figure 6-67.

12. Give them an opacity of 0 in the Appearance bucket of the Properties panel.

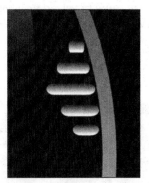

Figure 6-67. Scale down the decorative rectangles and give them an opacity of 0.

Your media player should now look like Figure 6-68.

Figure 6-68. Your media player should now look like this in the MouseEnter state.

Now click on the Base state, and your media player should be back to the default appearance, which is also how it appears in the MouseLeave state. Now we need to build the project and switch over to Visual Studio 2008 and wire up the states on MouseEnter and MouseLeave as well as the functionality of the navigation buttons. Do that now.

Wiring up the states and navigation buttons in Visual Studio 2008

In the current version of Blend, there is no way to tell a state when to activate, visually anyway, as you can now in code in Blend. So, you have to manually go into the code-behind and tell the states when they should activate. Let's do that now!

1. In Blend's Project panel, right-click on the project, and click Edit in Visual Studio, as I am doing in Figure 6-69.

Figure 6-69. Open the project in Visual Studio.

2. Open MainControl.xaml.cs.

3. In the constructor under the InitializeComponent, call and raise the Loaded event and create an event handler, as I have done here:

```
namespace SLVSMMediaPlayer
{
    public partial class Page : UserControl
    {
        public Page()
        {
            // Required to initialize variables
            InitializeComponent();
            Loaded += new RoutedEventHandler(Page_Loaded);
        }

        void Page_Loaded(object sender, RoutedEventArgs e)
        {
            throw new NotImplementedException();
        }
    }
}
```

4. Delete the default throw new... code and tell the application to go to the MouseLeave state when the application first starts, as I have done here:

```
void Page_Loaded(object sender, RoutedEventArgs e)
        {
            VisualStateManager.GoToState(this, "MouseLeave", true);
        }
```

5. In the Loaded event handler, raise the MouseEnter and MouseLeave events on the LayoutRoot grid and create the event handlers, as I have done in the following code:

```
void Page_Loaded(object sender, RoutedEventArgs e)
        {
            VisualStateManager.GoToState(this, "MouseLeave", true);
            LayoutRoot.MouseEnter += new MouseEventHandler
(LayoutRoot_MouseEnter);
            LayoutRoot.MouseLeave += new MouseEventHandler
(LayoutRoot_MouseLeave);
        }

        void LayoutRoot_MouseLeave(object sender, MouseEventArgs e)
        {
            throw new NotImplementedException();
        }

        void LayoutRoot_MouseEnter(object sender, MouseEventArgs e)
        {
            throw new NotImplementedException();
        }
```

6. Remove the default throw new... code, and in the MouseEnter event handler tell the VisualStateManager to go to the MouseEnter state.

7. Remove the default throw new... code, and in the MouseLeave event handler tell the VisualStateManager to go to the MouseLeave state, as I have done here:

```
        void LayoutRoot_MouseLeave(object sender, MouseEventArgs e)
        {
            VisualStateManager.GoToState(this, "MouseLeave", true);
        }

        void LayoutRoot_MouseEnter(object sender, MouseEventArgs e)
        {
            VisualStateManager.GoToState(this, "MouseEnter", true);
        }
```

Now for the fun part: press F5 to compile and run the application, and place your mouse over the application and then move it off. Notice how all of the controls morph away. Pretty snazzy looking, yes? Well, the last thing you need to do is raise the Click events and handle them appropriately. Do that now:

8. In the Loaded event handler, raise the Click event and create the event handlers for all three navigation buttons, as I have done here:

```
void Page_Loaded(object sender, RoutedEventArgs e)
{
    VisualStateManager.GoToState(this, "MouseLeave", true);
    LayoutRoot.MouseEnter += new MouseEventHandler
(LayoutRoot_MouseEnter);
    LayoutRoot.MouseLeave += new MouseEventHandler
(LayoutRoot_MouseLeave);
    PlayBtn.Click += new RoutedEventHandler(PlayBtn_Click);
    PauseBtn.Click += new RoutedEventHandler(PauseBtn_Click);
    StopBtn.Click += new RoutedEventHandler(StopBtn_Click);
}

void StopBtn_Click(object sender, RoutedEventArgs e)
{
    throw new NotImplementedException();
}

void PauseBtn_Click(object sender, RoutedEventArgs e)
{
    throw new NotImplementedException();
}

void PlayBtn_Click(object sender, RoutedEventArgs e)
{
    throw new NotImplementedException();
}
```

9. Now play the MediaElement in the PlayBtn event handler.

10. Pause the MediaElement in the PauseBtn event handler.

11. Stop the MediaElement in the StopBtn event handler, as I have done here:

```
void StopBtn_Click(object sender, RoutedEventArgs e)
{
    MyME.Stop();
}

void PauseBtn_Click(object sender, RoutedEventArgs e)
{
    MyME.Pause();
}

void PlayBtn_Click(object sender, RoutedEventArgs e)
{
    MyME.Play();
}
```

Now if you compile and run the application, you will see that the navigation buttons do in fact work. All you need to do is to finish up by adding some nice usability features.

Finishing it up

In web applications, web surfers are used to a call-to-action cursor. That is, the cursor will change to a hand cursor when something can be clicked. I think that we should have this functionality on our navigation buttons. We can do this in either C# or XAML. Because you are already in the code-behind, go ahead and add it in the Page_Loaded event handler, as I have done here:

```
void Page_Loaded(object sender, RoutedEventArgs e)
{
    VisualStateManager.GoToState(this, "MouseLeave", true);

    LayoutRoot.MouseEnter += new MouseEventHandler
(LayoutRoot_MouseEnter);
    LayoutRoot.MouseLeave += new MouseEventHandler
(LayoutRoot_MouseLeave);

    PlayBtn.Click += new RoutedEventHandler(PlayBtn_Click);
    PauseBtn.Click += new RoutedEventHandler(PauseBtn_Click);
    StopBtn.Click += new RoutedEventHandler(StopBtn_Click);

    PlayBtn.Cursor = Cursors.Hand;
    PauseBtn.Cursor = Cursors.Hand;
    StopBtn.Cursor = Cursors.Hand;
}
```

The next usability issue I would like to address is the fact that if you stop the video, it continues to show the frame that it was stopped on. I feel that if you stop a video, it should go away. So, I added functionality to hide the MediaElement on Stop and to make it visible again on Play. Add this code, as I have done here now:

```
void StopBtn_Click(object sender, RoutedEventArgs e)
{
    MyME.Stop();
    MyME.Visibility = Visibility.Collapsed;

}

void PauseBtn_Click(object sender, RoutedEventArgs e)
{
    MyME.Pause();
}

void PlayBtn_Click(object sender, RoutedEventArgs e)
{
    MyME.Visibility = Visibility.Visible;
    MyME.Play();
}
```

If you now compile and run the application, you will see that the media player disappears when stopped and reappears when played.

Summary

In this chapter, you learned all about the VSM and Blend 3's States panel. You created a simple Silverlight application and created a state group and two states to control how a simple Rectangle control behaved when the mouse was over it and when the mouse was not. You then created another Silverlight project and styled up a cool-looking media player. You also created a custom Silverlight Button control. You then switched over to Visual Studio and wired up the states. You also wired up the functionality for the navigation buttons. Finally, you added some additional functionality that provided for a better user experience. Nice job!

If you would like to e-mail me a link to your video project, I would love to have a look—especially if you were all creative and deviated from the design instructions provided in this chapter. You can e-mail me at wpfauthor@gmail.com.

Chapter 7

THE SILVERLIGHT MEDIAELEMENT

What this chapter covers:

- Defining the Silverlight MediaElement
- Comparing Silverlight versus Flash for video
- Building a Silverlight media player
- Parsing and serializing XML for application data
- Implementing drag-and-drop functionality
- Creating a singleton DataFactory
- Creating a custom UserControl

Because Silverlight was designed to develop rich Internet applications (RIAs) with lots of embedded media, such as video and audio, the MediaElement is a very important and useful tool, so I have decided to dedicate an entire chapter to it. The Silverlight MediaElement is a rectangular UserControl that can be used to play audio or video. In the current version of Silverlight, the MediaElement supports the following types of media:

- Advanced Stream Redirector (ASX) playlist file format
- Windows Media Audio 7 (WMA7)
- Windows Media Audio 8 (WMA8)

- Windows Media Audio 9 (WMA9)

- ISO/MPEG layer-3–compliant data stream input (MP3)

- Windows Media Video 7 (WMV1)

- Windows Media Video 8 (WMV2)

- Windows Media Video 9 (WMV3)

- Windows Media Video Advanced Profile, non-VC1 (WMVA)

- Windows Media Video Advanced Profile, VC1 (WMVC1)

In this chapter, I am going to compare the pros and cons of using Silverlight instead of Flash for video, and then I am going to show you how to build a very cool, Silverlight video player with interaction that is very different and more complicated than the video player we made in the previous chapter.

Choosing between Silverlight and Flash for video

If you have been paying any attention whatsoever to the world of RIA development over the last year, you have undoubtedly heard the Flash versus Silverlight debate. Staunch supporters of both technologies will recommend their preferred technology even in the face of clear evidence that one is better than the other, given the RIA requirements. Being a former Flash developer and a current Silverlight developer, I find it easy to objectively look at both Flash and Silverlight to determine which platform is better suited to handle the needs and requirements of the application that is to be developed. Now, you are probably wondering, "Well then, which one *is* better for video?" The answer is that it depends on the requirements of the application. For example, if you have an RIA that streams video, you may want to use Silverlight: you can save on costs by streaming less overall bandwidth because of higher compression ratios in Silverlight video.

Choosing Silverlight

Here are some advantages to using Silverlight for video:

- Silverlight has industry-leading content protection. Silverlight's DRM, powered by PlayReady Content Protection, enables protected in-browser experiences using Advanced Encryption Standard (AES) encryption or Windows Media DRM.

- It does not require additional video codecs to play industry-standard video formats.

- Silverlight provides built-in content access protection known as digital rights management (DRM).

- Silverlight has live and on-demand true HD Internet Information Services (IIS), formerly IIS Media Pack. As an integrated HTTP media delivery platform, it features smooth streaming, which dynamically detects and seamlessly switches, in real time, the video quality of a media file delivered to Silverlight based on local bandwidth and CPU conditions.

- Silverlight has more format choices. In addition to native support for VC-1/WMA, Silverlight 3 now offers users native support for MPEG-4–based H.264/AAC audio, enabling content distributors to deliver high-quality content to a wide variety of computers and devices.

- Silverlight has true HD playback in full-screen mode. Leveraging graphics processor unit (GPU) hardware acceleration, Silverlight experiences can now be delivered in true full-screen HD format.

- Silverlight has extensible media format support. With the new raw AV pipeline, Silverlight can easily support a wide variety of third-party codecs. Audio and video can be decoded outside the runtime and rendered in Silverlight, extending format support beyond the native codecs.

Choosing Flash

And these are some advantages to using Flash for video:

- Nearly all web users have the Flash Player plug-in.

- Flash video requires much less CPU power and bandwidth than Silverlight, so it runs better on older machines and in low-bandwidth scenarios like mobile phones.

- The Flash video encoder supports a wide range of video and animation formats that can be encoded into the FLV format. A list of supported video and animation formats follows:

  - Mobile Video (3G2)

  - GIF (Animated GIF)

  - DLX (Sony VDU File Format Importer, Windows only)

  - DV (in a MOV or AVI container or as a containerless DV stream)

  - Flash Video (FLV, F4V)

  - M2T (Sony HDV)

  - MOV (QuickTime, which in Windows requires the QuickTime player)

  - MP4 (XDCAM EX)

  - MPEG-1, MPEG-2, and MPEG-4 (MPEG, MPE, MPG, M2V, MPA, MP2, M2A, MPV, M2P, M2T, AC3, MP4, M4V, M4A)

  - MTS (AVCHD)

  - Media eXchange Format (MXF)

  - Netshow (ASF, Windows only)

  - QuickTime (MOV; 16 bpc, requires QuickTime)

  - Video for Windows (AVI, WAV; requires QuickTime on Mac OS)

  - WMV (WMV, WMA, ASF; Windows only)

So what does this all mean? Basically, it means that you, as the developer, must decide what tool you need, given the requirement of the RIA you are developing. In some cases, the tool will be Silverlight, and in others, the tool will be Flash.

Creating the Silverlight video player application

In staying with my philosophy that the best way to learn is by hands-on experience, I am now going to show you how to build a fun, interactive Silverlight video player. I have decided that this particular application would be a good time to show you how to do some very cool things in Silverlight, such as the following:

- Using XML for data
- Making user interface objects draggable
- Creating a singleton DataFactory
- Making user interface objects react when other user interface objects are dropped on them

To develop this application, you will need at least three videos in the WMV format as well as corresponding JPG thumbnail images for each (I made my thumbnail images about 100 pixels wide and tall). For simplicity, I named my videos video1.wmv, video2.wmv, and so on, and my corresponding thumbnails video1.jpg, video2.jpg, and so on.

> Windows Vista ships with sample WMV videos. These can usually be found in C:\
> Users\Public\Videos\Sample Videos. If you cannot find them there, do a search for
> *.wmv to find them.

With that, let's fire up Visual Studio, and create our Silverlight video player:

1. Open Visual Studio.
2. Click File ➤ New ➤ Project.
3. In the New Project dialog box, select Silverlight for the Project Type.
4. Select Silverlight Application for the Template.
5. Type SLVideoPlayer01 for the project Name.
6. Be sure to make a mental note where the project is being saved, so we can open it in Blend down the road (see Figure 7-1).
7. When the New Silverlight Application dialog box appears, check the box that reads Host the Silverlight application in a new Web site, as shown in Figure 7-2. We need to do this so Visual Studio will set up an intranet site for us. If we do not, when we run the application, we will merely open the application on our hard drive, and a video will never play.
8. Click OK.

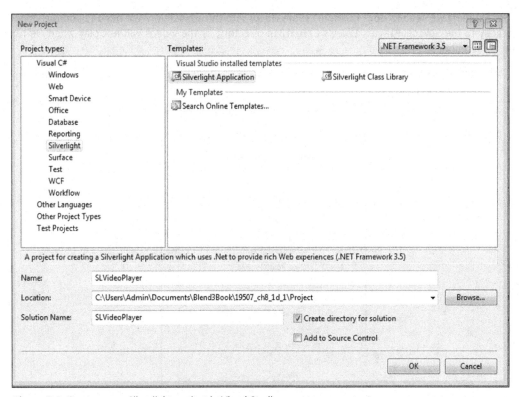

Figure 7-1. Create a new Silverlight project in Visual Studio.

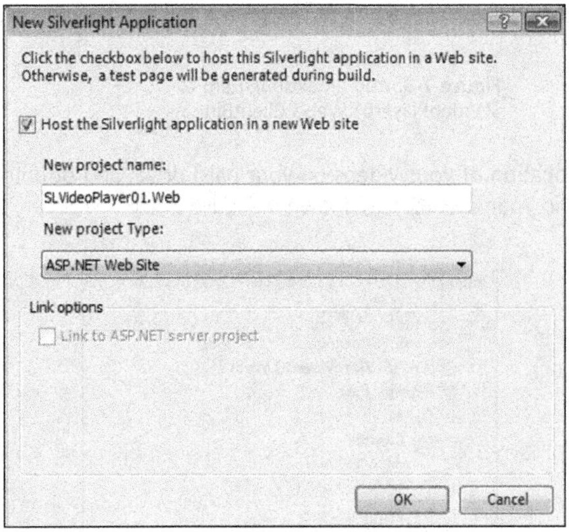

Figure 7-2. Opt to host the Silverlight application in a new web site.

The first thing we need to do is to import some videos into the application. We need to add the videos directly to the SLVideoPlayer01.Web's ClientBin directory, or the videos will not play when we run the application.

1. In Solution Explorer, right-click SLVideoPlayer01.Web's ClientBin, and choose Add Existing Item, as shown in Figure 7-3.

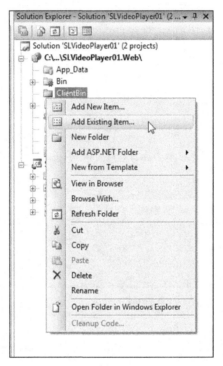

Figure 7-3. Add an existing item to SLVideoPlayer01.Web's ClientBin.

2. Navigate to the location of your videos on your hard drive, and double-click them so that you now have videos in your ClientBin, as shown in Figure 7-4.

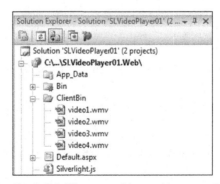

Figure 7-4. When you add your videos, your Solution Explorer should look something like this.

Now that we have our videos added, we need to add the thumbnails.

3. Right-click SLVideoPlayer01 (not SLVideoPlayer01.Web) in Solution Explorer, and select Add
➤ Existing Item, as shown in Figure 7-5.

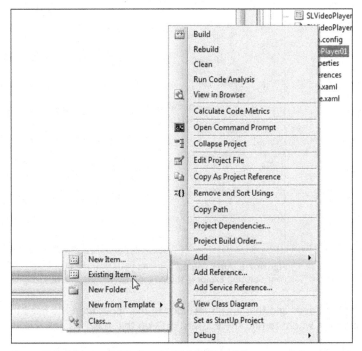

Figure 7-5. Add an existing item to SLVideoPlayer01.

4. Navigate to your thumbnail images on your hard drive, and select them.

Your Solution Explorer should look the one shown in Figure 7-6.

Figure 7-6. After you have added your thumbnails,
your Solution Explorer should look something like this.

Now that we have our videos and thumbnails included in the application, we need to create the XML that tells the application where to find these assets. Let's do that now:

5. In the SLVideoPlayer01.Web project, right-click ClientBin, and click Add New Item, as shown in Figure 7-7.

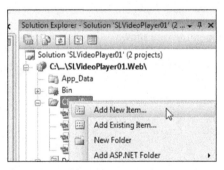

Figure 7-7. Add a New Item to the
SLVideoPlayer01.Web project.

6. In the Add New Item dialog box, select XML File for the template.

7. Name the new XML file videodata.xml.

8. Select Add, as shown in Figure 7-8.

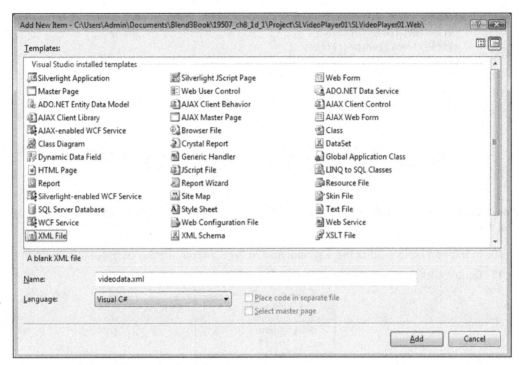

Figure 7-8. Add a new XML File to the application.

9. When the new file opens, change your code so it looks like the following (if you named your videos or thumbnails differently than I have, make sure your XML file reflects that):

```
<VideoData
  xmlns:xsd="http://www.w3.org/2001/XMLSchema"
  xmlns:xsi="http://www.w3.org/2001/XMLSchema-instance">

  <Video>
    <Url>video1.wmv</Url>
    <Title>Me Working</Title>
    <ThumbnailImage>video1.jpg</ThumbnailImage>
  </Video>

  <Video>
    <Url>video2.wmv</Url>
    <Title>Butterfly</Title>
    <ThumbnailImage>video2.jpg</ThumbnailImage>
  </Video>

  <Video>
    <Url>video3.wmv</Url>
    <Title>Bear</Title>
    <ThumbnailImage>video3.jpg</ThumbnailImage>
  </Video>
```

```
<Video>
  <Url>video4.wmv</Url>
  <Title>IdentityMine</Title>
  <ThumbnailImage>video4.jpg</ThumbnailImage>
</Video>

</VideoData>
```

> For your convenience, I have saved a text file version of this XML file. To download it,
> go to http://windowspresentationfoundation.com/Blend3Book/videodata.txt.

Now that we have our assets imported and our XML file created, it is time to parse and serialize the
XML file:

10. In Solution Explorer, click the + symbol next to Page.xaml in the SLVideoPlayer01 project.

11. Double-click Page.xaml.cs to open (see Figure 7-9).

Figure 7-9. Open Page.xaml.cs.

12. Put your cursor right after the line that reads InitializeComponent(); and press the Enter key
to create an empty line.

13. Start typing this.Loaded, and press the Enter key when Visual Studio's IntelliSense tries to finish the line for you.

14. Type +=, and press the Tab key twice so that IntelliSense attaches the RoutedEventHandler and
generates the event handler method stub. Your code should look like the following:

```
namespace SLVideoPlayer01
{
    public partial class Page : UserControl
    {
        public Page ()
        {
            InitializeComponent();
            this.Loaded += new RoutedEventHandler(Page _Loaded);
        }
```

```
void Page _Loaded(object sender, RoutedEventArgs e)
{
    throw new NotImplementedException();
}
}
}
```

15. Erase the throw new... line.

Here is where we would normally start to deal with the XML, but before we do, we are going to need to add a reference to the .NET XML libraries so that our application knows how to deal with XML:

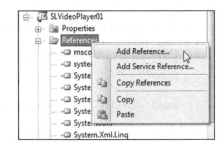

16. In Solution Explorer, right-click the References folder of the SLVideoPlayer01 project.

17. Click Add Reference, as shown in Figure 7-10.

18. When the Add Reference dialog box appears, make sure the .NET tab is selected.

Figure 7-10. Add a Reference to the SLVideoPlayer01 project.

19. Scroll down to System.Xml.Linq and System.Xml. Serialization.

20. Hold down the Ctrl key to select both of these, and click OK as shown in Figure 7-11.

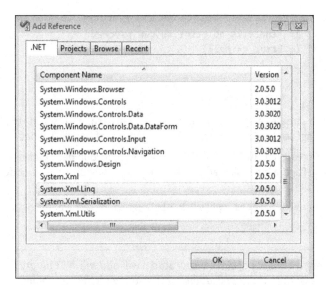

Figure 7-11. Add a reference to System.Xml.Linq and System.Xml.Serialization.

Now that you have done this, you can start dealing with the XML in the Page_Loaded event handler:

21. Add the following code into the Page_Loaded event handler:

```
WebClient xmlClient = new WebClient();
            xmlClient.DownloadStringCompleted += new
 DownloadStringCompletedEventHandler(XMLFileLoaded);
            xmlClient.DownloadStringAsync
(new Uri("videodata.xml", UriKind.RelativeOrAbsolute));
```

This code creates a new WebClient, specifies an event handler that will fire once the download is complete, and then tells the application to start downloading the file videodata.xml. What we need to add now is the event handler that fires once the download is complete:

22. Create a new event handler called XMLFileLoaded as follows:

```
private void XMLFileLoaded(object sender,

DownloadStringCompletedEventArgs e)
        {
            throw new NotImplementedException();
        }
```

23. Erase the throw new. . . code.

24. Now we need to make sure that there was no error in the downloading process:

```
        private void XMLFileLoaded(object sender, DownloadStringCompletedEventArgs
    e)
        {
            // if  there is no error we can proceed.
            if (e.Error == null)
            {
            }
        }
```

25. Next, we can create a string variable called xmlData and set it to the result of our DownloadStringCompletedEventArgs, which is a string of our XML video data.

26. We can then create an HtmlPage alert to make certain our data had been downloaded correctly. An HtmlPage alert is similar to a MessageBox (you can see the code for this after step 27).

27. Note that you will have to right-click HtmlPage and resolve it to use System.Windows. Browser.

> When you resolve a piece of code, Visual Studio will add the .NET library to make that piece of code work to your application in the solution's Reference folder.

```
        private void XMLFileLoaded
(object sender, DownloadStringCompletedEventArgs e)
        {
            // if e.error is null we can proceed.
            if (e.Error == null)
```

```
            {
                string xmlData = e.Result;
                HtmlPage.Window.Alert(xmlData);
            }
        }
```

Now, if you press F5 to compile and run the application, you should see something like what's shown in Figure 7-12.

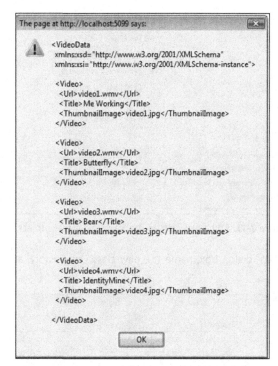

Figure 7-12. The HTML alert shows that our data has been downloaded correctly.

Now that the XML has been properly downloaded, we need to serialize the data into our own data. Before we do that, though, we need to add some classes that the data can serialize into. We are going to start by creating a DataFactory.

> When we serialize XML, it turns the data into data that the application understands.

The DataFactory is a convention that allows developers to place all of their application data into one neat place for easy setting and retrieval. Close the web browser, and let's create the DataFactory now:

1. Right-click the SLVideoPlayer01 project, and click Add ➤ Class, as shown in Figure 7-13.

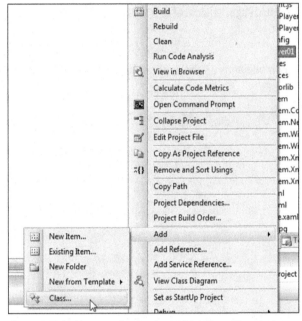

Figure 7-13. Add a new class to the SLVideoPlayer01 project.

2. In the Add New Item dialog box, name the new class DataFactory, and click Add, as shown in Figure 7-14.

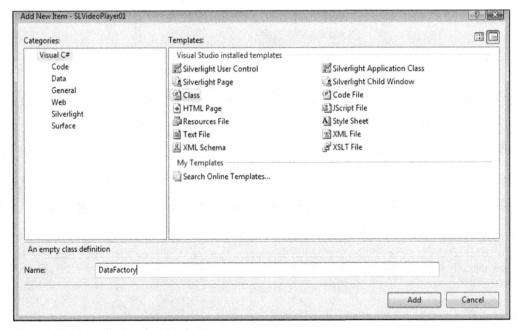

Figure 7-14. Name the new class DataFactory.

3. In the new class, we are going to create a new singleton (a class that can only be created or instantiated once) instance of DataFactory. This will allow us to create a CLR instance memory flow that we can then put our serialized data into for easy retrieval:

```
namespace SLVideoPlayer01
{
    public class DataFactory
    {
        #region Singleton

        protected static DataFactory _Singleton = new DataFactory();
        public static DataFactory CLRInstance
        {
            get
            {
                return _Singleton;
            }
        }
        public DataFactory Instance
        {
            get
            {
                return CLRInstance;
            }
        }

        #endregion Singleton

    }
}
```

> To keep the code clean, I have wrapped it in a region called Singleton. These regions can be collapsed to make reading other parts of the code easier.

Now, we need to add a couple more classes, VideoData and Video:

1. Right-click SLVideoPlayer01, and create a new class called VideoData.

2. Right-click SLVideoPlayer01, and create a new class called Video.

3. Open VideoData.

4. The first thing we need to do in VideoData is to specify the root (highest level node) of our XML file (note that you will need to right-click XmlRoot and resolve it to use System.Xml. Serialization). This tells the class where to start looking for data in the XML file. If we don't specify this, Silverlight will not know in which XML node to start looking for data.

```
namespace SLVideoPlayer01
{
    [XmlRoot("VideoData")]
    public class VideoData
    {

    }
}
```

5. The next thing we need to do is to extend VideoData to know that it is going to be a list of Video objects (note you will also need to resolve List to use System.Collections.Generic):

```
namespace SLVideoPlayer01
{
    [XmlRoot("VideoData")]
    public class VideoData : List<Video>
    {
    }
}
```

6. Now, all we need to do is to create a private _Video variable of type Video and then create a public Video variable of type Video:

```
namespace SLVideoPlayer01
{
    [XmlRoot("VideoData")]
    public class VideoData : List<Video>
    {
        private Video _Video = null;
        public Video Video
        {
            get { return _Video; }
            set { _Video = value; }
        }
    }
}
```

We are finished with VideoData. Next, we need to open Video and modify it as follows:

1. We need to create string variables that correspond to our XML nodes (URL, ThumbnailImage, and Title):

```
public class Video
    {
        private string _Url = "";
        public string Url
        {
            get { return _Url; }
            set { _Url = value; }
        }
```

```csharp
        private string _Title = "";
        public string Title
        {
            get { return _Title; }
            set { _Title = value; }
        }

        private string _ThumbnailImage = "";
        public string ThumbnailImage
        {
            get { return _ThumbnailImage; }
            set { _ThumbnailImage = value; }
        }
    }
}
```

Now, we need to go back to the DataFactory and create the VideoData object, which will give us access to VideoData via our CLR instance of DataFactory:

2. Create the VideoData class:

```csharp
namespace SLVideoPlayer01
{
    public class DataFactory
    {
        #region Singleton

        protected static DataFactory _Singleton = new DataFactory();
        public static DataFactory CLRInstance
        {
            get
            {
                return _Singleton;
            }
        }
        public DataFactory Instance
        {
            get
            {
                return CLRInstance;
            }
        }

        #endregion Singleton


        private VideoData _VideoData = null;
        public VideoData VideoData
        {
            get
            {
```

```
            return _VideoData;
        }
        set { _VideoData = value; }
    }

  }
}
```

Now that we have done this we can go back to Page.xaml.cs and continue to serialize our data:

1. Serialize the data and set it to the DataFactory VideoData object. This will turn the XML data into data that the application can understand:

```
private void XMLFileLoaded(object sender,
DownloadStringCompletedEventArgs e)
        {
            // if there is no error we can proceed.
            if (e.Error == null)
            {
                string xmlData = e.Result;
                HtmlPage.Window.Alert(xmlData);

                // create the XmlSerializer
                XmlSerializer x = new XmlSerializer(typeof(VideoData));
                using (XmlReader reader = XmlReader.Create
(new StringReader(xmlData)))
                {
                    // deserialize the xmlData and set it to our
                    // DataFactory VideoData object
                    DataFactory.CLRInstance.VideoData =
(VideoData)x.Deserialize(reader);
                }
            }
        }
```

2. Now, comment out the HTML alert, as we only need it for testing. Also, you will need to resolve XmlReader and StringReader as follows:

```
        private void XMLFileLoaded(object sender,
    DownloadStringCompletedEventArgs e)
        {
            // if e.error is null we can proceed.
            if (e.Error == null)
            {
                string xmlData = e.Result;
                //HtmlPage.Window.Alert(xmlData);

                // create the XmlSerializer
                XmlSerializer x = new XmlSerializer(typeof(VideoData));
                using (XmlReader reader = XmlReader.Create
(new StringReader(xmlData)))
```

```
                {
                    // deserialize the xmlData and set it to our
                    // DataFactory VideoData object
                    DataFactory.CLRInstance.VideoData =
        (VideoData)x.Deserialize(reader);
                }
            }
        }
```

Now that we have populated the VideoData object with Video objects by way of serialization, we need to make use of it. For each Video object in VideoData, we are going to add an instance of a custom UserControl called UC_VideoDragger ("UC" is short for "UserControl").

1. Right-click SLVideoPlayer01 in Solution Explorer.

2. Click Add ➤ New Item.

3. Click Silverlight User Control.

4. Name it UC_VideoDragger.

5. Click Add (see Figure 7-15).

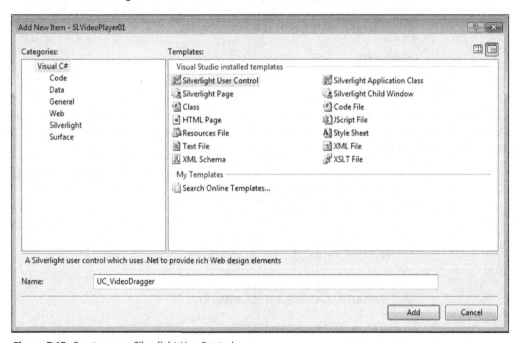

Figure 7-15. Create a new Silverlight UserControl.

6. In UC_VideoDragger's XAML file, change the Height and Width to 100.

7. Change the LayoutRoot Grid to have a Transparent background.

8. Add a StackPanel with an Orientation of Vertical (so the pieces of content stack on top of each other).

9. Add an Image named PreviewImage with a Height of 80.

10. Add a TextBlock named PreviewTextBlock with a TextAlignment of Center and a Foreground of Black:

```xml
<UserControl x:Class="SLVideoPlayer01.UC_VideoDragger"
    xmlns="http://schemas.microsoft.com/winfx/2006/xaml/presentation"
    xmlns:x="http://schemas.microsoft.com/winfx/2006/xaml"
    Width="100" Height="100">
    <Grid
        x:Name="LayoutRoot"
        Background="Transparent">

        <StackPanel
            Orientation="Vertical">

            <Image
                x:Name="PreviewImage"
                Height="80" />

            <TextBlock
                x:Name="PreviewTextBlock"
                TextAlignment="Center"
                Foreground="Black" />

        </StackPanel>
    </Grid>
</UserControl>
```

Now that we have created the UserControl, we can go back to Page.xaml.cs and loop through our list of Video objects. For each one, we are going to create an instance of UC_VideoDragger and set its PreviewImage and PreviewTextBlock:

1. The first thing we need to do is to create a method called CreateVideoDraggerUserControls:

```csharp
    private void XMLFileLoaded(object sender,
DownloadStringCompletedEventArgs e)
    {
        // if e.error is null we can proceed.
        if (e.Error == null)
        {
            string xmlData = e.Result;
            //HtmlPage.Window.Alert(xmlData);

            // create the XmlSerializer
            XmlSerializer x = new XmlSerializer(typeof(VideoData));
            using (XmlReader reader = XmlReader.Create
(new StringReader(xmlData)))
                {
                    // deserialize the xmlData and set it to our

                    // DataFactory VideoData object
                    DataFactory.CLRInstance.VideoData =
```

```
(VideoData)x.Deserialize(reader);
                }
            }
    }
    private void CreateVideoDraggerUserControls()
    {

    }
```

2. In this new method, we are going to cycle through the VideoData list:

```
    private void CreateVideoDraggerUserControls()
    {
        foreach (Video v in DataFactory.CLRInstance.VideoData)
        {

        }
    }
```

Here is where we are going to create a new instance of UC_VideoDragger. We can then set the PreviewImage and PreviewTextBlock. But we also need to be able to tell the UC_VideoDragger what the URL is for its video. There is no built-in property for this in UC_VideoDragger, so we are going to need to create a custom DependencyProperty to store this information:

3. Open UC_VideoDragger.xaml.cs (note that this is the CS file, not the XAML file we were editing earlier), and create the DependencyProperty called VideoURL:

```
namespace SLVideoPlayer01
{
    public partial class UC_VideoDragger : UserControl
    {
        #region VideoURL (DependencyProperty)


        public string VideoURL
        {
            get { return (string)GetValue(VideoURLProperty); }
            set { SetValue(VideoURLProperty, value); }
        }
        public static readonly DependencyProperty VideoURLProperty =
            DependencyProperty.Register("VideoURL", typeof(string),
    typeof(UC_VideoDragger),
                new PropertyMetadata(string.Empty));

        #endregion

        public UC_VideoDragger()
        {
            InitializeComponent();
        }
    }
}
```

We are going to amend the application so you can drag a `UC_VideoDragger` onto a `MediaElement` to play the corresponding video. We also want the `UC_VideoDragger` to snap back to its original position when dropped. To do that, we need to store its x and y positions when it is created. To do this, we can create two more DependencyProperties called Xprop and Yprop. Do that now:

```
namespace SLVideo
{
    public partial class UC_VideoDragger : UserControl
    {
        #region VideoURL (DependencyProperty)

        public string VideoURL
        {
            get { return (string)GetValue(VideoURLProperty); }
            set { SetValue(VideoURLProperty, value); }
        }
        public static readonly DependencyProperty VideoURLProperty =
            DependencyProperty.Register("VideoURL", typeof(string),
 typeof(UC_VideoDragger),
                new PropertyMetadata(string.Empty));

        #endregion VideoURL (DependencyProperty)

        #region Xprop (DependencyProperty)

        public double Xprop
        {
            get { return (double)GetValue(XpropProperty); }
            set { SetValue(XpropProperty, value); }
        }
        public static readonly DependencyProperty XpropProperty =
            DependencyProperty.Register("Xprop", typeof(double),
 typeof(UC_VideoDragger),
                new PropertyMetadata(0.0));

        #endregion Xprop (DependencyProperty)

        #region YProp (DependencyProperty)

        public double YProp
        {
            get { return (double)GetValue(YPropProperty); }
            set { SetValue(YPropProperty, value); }
        }
        public static readonly DependencyProperty YPropProperty =
            DependencyProperty.Register("YProp", typeof(double),
 typeof(UC_VideoDragger),
                new PropertyMetadata(0.0));
```

```
#endregion YProp (DependencyProperty)

    public UC_VideoDragger()
    {
        InitializeComponent();
    }
  }
}
```

Now that we have stored the x and y positions, we can go back to Page.xaml.cs and finish adding our UC_VideoDraggers:

1. We can make two private variables in Page.xaml.cs called Xprop and Yprop. You will see why in a bit:

```
public partial class Page : UserControl
    {
        private double Xprop = 10;
        private double Yprop = 10;
```

In Page.xaml, we need to add a Canvas that will hold our soon-to-be instances of UC_VideoDragger.

2. In Page.xaml, add a Canvas to the main grid, and call it DragCanvas:

```
<UserControl x:Class="SLVideoPlayer01.Page"
    xmlns="http://schemas.microsoft.com/winfx/2006/xaml/presentation"
    xmlns:x="http://schemas.microsoft.com/winfx/2006/xaml"
    Width="400" Height="300">
    <Grid x:Name="LayoutRoot" Background="White">

        <Canvas
            x:Name="DragCanvas" />


    </Grid>
</UserControl>
```

Now, we can go back to our foreach loop in Page.cs. You can see what we are doing by reading the commented code:

```
        private void CreateVideoDraggerUserControls()
        {
            foreach (Video v in DataFactory.CLRInstance.VideoData)
            {
                // instantiate a new instance of UC_VideoDragger called
videoDragger
                UC_VideoDragger videoDragger = new UC_VideoDragger();
                // set the PreviewImage source
                videoDragger.PreviewImage.Source = new BitmapImage(new
```

```
Uri(v.ThumbnailImage, UriKind.RelativeOrAbsolute));
                    // set the PreviewTextBlock Text
                    videoDragger.PreviewTextBlock.Text = v.Title;
                    // set the VideoURL DependencyProperty
                    videoDragger.VideoURL = v.Url;
                    // set the Xprop and Yprop to our local variables
(Xprop and Yprop)
                    videoDragger.Xprop = Xprop;
                    videoDragger.YProp = Yprop;
                    // set the values for where the videoDragger appears
                    videoDragger.SetValue(Canvas.LeftProperty, Xprop);
                    videoDragger.SetValue(Canvas.TopProperty, Yprop);
                    // set videoDragger so it has a hand cursor
                    videoDragger.Cursor = Cursors.Hand;
                    // add videoDragger to the workspace
                    DragCanvas.Children.Add(videoDragger);
                    // add 150 units to local Xprop
                    Xprop += 150;


            }
```

> You will need to resolve BitmapImage in the preceding code.

As you can see in the preceding listing, we are accomplishing the following:

- Instantiating a new UC_VideoDragger called videoDragger
- Setting the Source and Text of the Image and TextBlock
- Setting the DependencyProperties for VideoURL, Xprop, and Yprop
- Setting where videoDragger will appear in the DragCanvas
- Setting the cursor of videoDragger to be a hand cursor
- Adding videoDragger to DragCanvas
- Increasing the local Xprop by 150

At this point, if we run the application, we will not see anything. Why? Because we never called the CreateVideoDraggerUserControls method. Right after we serialize the XML, we need to call this method:

```
        private void XMLFileLoaded(object sender,
    DownloadStringCompletedEventArgs e)
        {
            // if e.error is null we can proceed.
            if (e.Error == null)
            {
                string xmlData = e.Result;
                //HtmlPage.Window.Alert(xmlData);
```

```
                    // create the XmlSerializer
                    XmlSerializer x = new XmlSerializer(typeof(VideoData));
                    using (XmlReader reader = XmlReader.Create(new

StringReader(xmlData)))
                    {
                        // deserialize the xmlData and set it to our
                        //DataFactory VideoData object
                        DataFactory.CLRInstance.VideoData =

(VideoData)x.Deserialize(reader);
                        CreateVideoDraggerUserControls();
                    }
                }
            }
```

Now, if you press F5 to compile and run the application, you should see something like I have in Figure 7-16.

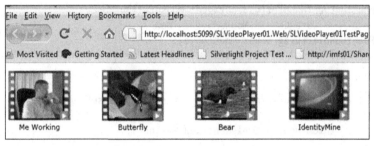

Figure 7-16. The running application

Our application is coming along nicely, but we now need to add the ability to drag each UC_VideoDragger.

1. Right after we add videoDragger to DragCanvas, we need to raise MouseLeftButtonDown and MouseLeftButtonUp events and create the event handlers for them.

2. We also need to raise an event for MouseMove on the DragCanvas:

```
        private void CreateVideoDraggerUserControls()
        {
            foreach (Video v in DataFactory.CLRInstance.VideoData)
            {
                // instantiate a new instance of UC_VideoDragger called
    videoDragger
                UC_VideoDragger videoDragger = new UC_VideoDragger();
                // set the PreviewImage source
                videoDragger.PreviewImage.Source = new BitmapImage(new
Uri(v.ThumbnailImage, UriKind.RelativeOrAbsolute));
                // set the PreviewTextBlock Text
                videoDragger.PreviewTextBlock.Text = v.Title;
```

```
                    // set the VideoURL DependencyProperty
                    videoDragger.VideoURL = v.Url;
                    // set the Xprop and Yprop to our local variables
        (Xprop and Yprop)
                    videoDragger.Xprop = Xprop;
                    videoDragger.YProp = Yprop;
                    // set the values for where the videoDragger appears
                    videoDragger.SetValue(Canvas.LeftProperty, Xprop);
                    videoDragger.SetValue(Canvas.TopProperty, Yprop);
                    // set videoDragger so it has a hand cursor
                    videoDragger.Cursor = Cursors.Hand;
                    // add videoDragger to the workspace
                    DragCanvas.Children.Add(videoDragger);
                    // add 150 units to local Xprop
                    Xprop += 150;

                    videoDragger.MouseLeftButtonDown += new
        MouseButtonEventHandler(videoDragger_MouseLeftButtonDown);
                    videoDragger.MouseLeftButtonUp += new
        MouseButtonEventHandler(videoDragger_MouseLeftButtonUp);
                    DragCanvas.MouseMove += new
        MouseEventHandler(DragCanvas_MouseMove);
                }
            }

        void DragCanvas_MouseMove(object sender, MouseEventArgs e)
        {
            throw new NotImplementedException();
        }

        void videoDragger_MouseLeftButtonUp(object sender,
        MouseButtonEventArgs e)
        {
            throw new NotImplementedException();
        }

        void videoDragger_MouseLeftButtonDown(object sender,
        MouseButtonEventArgs e)
        {
            throw new NotImplementedException();
        }
    }
}
```

What we want to do is to create a variable called _draggedElement and then set that variable to the UC_VideoDragger when the mouse is clicked and release it when the mouse is released. Later, in the MouseMove event handler, if draggable is not null, we run the drag code. If it is null, we will not do anything, because the user had not clicked anything to drag. If this does not make sense now, trust me; it will! With that, we first need to create the variable of type UIElement:

```
public partial class Page : UserControl
{
    private double Xprop = 10;
    private double Yprop = 10;
    private UIElement draggedElement;
```

1. Now, on MouseDown, set this variable, and release it on MouseUp.

2. Also, make sure to set _lastMousePosition in the MouseLeftButtonDown handler:

```
void videoDragger_MouseLeftButtonUp(object sender,
MouseButtonEventArgs e)
{
    _draggedElement = null;
}

void videoDragger_MouseLeftButtonDown(object sender,
MouseButtonEventArgs e)
{
    _draggedElement = sender as UIElement;
    _lastMousePosition = e.GetPosition(DragCanvas);
}
```

Now, in the MouseMove handler, we can add the code that allows users to drag the objects. Before we do that, we need to add two local variables called _newPosition and _lastPosition. We will use these to make the UC_VideoDragger draggable. If you don't understand what's happening right away, fear not; you will understand after the next few steps:

```
public partial class Page : UserControl
{
    private double Xprop = 10;
    private double Yprop = 10;

    private UIElement _draggedElement;

    private Point _newposition = new Point(0, 0);
    private Point _lastMousePosition;
```

3. Now, we can add the code that makes each UC_VideoDragger draggable:

```
void DragCanvas_MouseMove(object sender, MouseEventArgs e)
{
    if (_draggedElement != null)
    {
        _newposition = e.GetPosition(DragCanvas);
        double OffsetX = _newposition.X - _lastMousePosition.X;
        double OffsetY = _newposition.Y - _lastMousePosition.Y;
        Canvas.SetTop(_draggedElement,
Canvas.GetTop(_draggedElement) + OffsetY);
        Canvas.SetLeft(_draggedElement,
```

```
Canvas.GetLeft(_draggedElement) + OffsetX);
            _lastMousePosition = _newposition;
        }
    }
}
```

If you press F5 and run the application, you can drag around each UC_VideoDragger (see Figure 7-17).

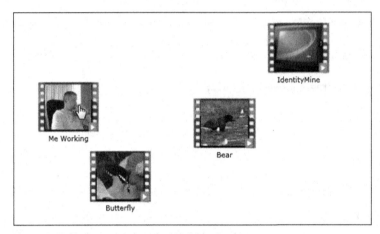

Figure 7-17. You can now drag the UC_VideoDraggers.

Great! Next, when we drop the videos, we want the video associated with the dragger to start to play, and we want the dragger to snap back to its original position:

4. The first thing we need to do is to add a MediaElement to Page.xaml:

```xml
<UserControl x:Class="SLVideoPlayer01.Page"
    xmlns="http://schemas.microsoft.com/winfx/2006/xaml/presentation"
    xmlns:x="http://schemas.microsoft.com/winfx/2006/xaml"
    Width="800" Height="600">
    <Grid x:Name="LayoutRoot" Background="White">

        <MediaElement
            x:Name="ME"
            Source="video1.wmv"
            Margin="140,160,360,260"
            AutoPlay="True"
            Position="00:00:03"
            Stretch="Uniform" />

        <Canvas
            x:Name="DragCanvas" />
    </Grid>
</UserControl>
```

> *Your margins may be different from mine. If you run the application and don't see any
> video, set your MediaElement to have a margin of 0, run the application again, and
> adjust it accordingly.*

Notice that I set the Source of the MediaElement to be video1.wmv. In the MouseUp handler, we need
to get a list of all visual elements in the visual tree. We then need to cycle through that list, and if
that list contains a MediaElement, we need to set the Source of the MediaElement to the VideoURL
property of the UC_VideoDragger:

```
        void videoDragger_MouseLeftButtonUp(object sender,
    MouseButtonEventArgs e)
        {
draggedElement = null;
            // get a list of all visual elements in the VisualTree
            IEnumerable<UIElement> mylist =

VisualTreeHelper.FindElementsInHostCoordinates(e.GetPosition(this),
  this);
            //cycle through each element
            foreach (UIElement uie in mylist)
            {
                // if this element is a MediaElement
                if (uie is MediaElement)
                {
                    // create a UC_VideoDragger element
                    UC_VideoDragger videoDragger = sender as
UC_VideoDragger;
                    // make sure it is not null
                    if (videoDragger != null)
                    {
                        // pause the MediaElement (named ME)
                        ME.Pause();
                        // create the URI based upon the videoDraggers
VideoURL DependencyProperty
                        Uri srcUri = new Uri(videoDragger.VideoURL,
UriKind.RelativeOrAbsolute);
                        // set the Source of ME
                        ME.Source = srcUri;
                        // Send videoDragger back to its original
                                        //position using the Xprop and Yprop
DependencyProperties.
                        videoDragger.SetValue(Canvas.LeftProperty,
  videoDragger.Xprop);
                        videoDragger.SetValue(Canvas.TopProperty,
```

```
        videoDragger.YProp);
                            // tell ME to play
                            ME.Play();
                    }
                }
            }
```

If you press F5 to compile and run the application now, you will see that you can drag a UC_VideoDragger onto the MediaElement. The MediaElement will play the associated video and the UC_VideoDragger will return to its original x and y position. Cool, huh?

That's it! You have a cool Silverlight video player with drag capabilities. My challenge to you is to make the video for the UC_VideoDragger play when you click it.

Summary

In this chapter, you learned about the Silverlight MediaElement and some situations where you would want to use Silverlight for video rather than Flash. You then created a Silverlight video player complete with XML data, a DataFactory, and drag-and-drop capabilities.

In the next chapter, we are going to learn all about the WPF Toolkit and the Visual State Manager (VSM). Exciting!

Chapter 8

THE WPF TOOLKIT

What this chapter covers:

- What the WPF Toolkit is
- The Visual State Manager and the WPF Toolkit
- Other controls featured in the WPF Toolkit
- Where to get the WPF Toolkit
- Installing the WPF Toolkit
- Setting up a WPF application to use the WPF Toolkit
- Creating a simple VSM WPF application and adding button states
- How to get the States panel working in Blend

My guess is that right now you are scratching your head and saying something like, "Hey, this is a Silverlight book, so why are we talking about WPF?" For that matter, you may even be asking yourself what WPF is. If you are asking such questions, let me take a minute to answer them. First, yes, this is a book on Silverlight development, but the new release of Silverlight includes something very cool called the Visual State Manager (VSM) (you should be familiar with this already, as we used it extensively in Chapter 6 to build an interactive video player). The problem is that the VSM was not included in the most recent version of WPF (3.5 SP1). So that brings me to the second question: what is WPF? Windows Presentation Foundation (WPF) is a set of libraries that are used to develop, run, compile, and manage Windows Vista applications. It, like Silverlight, makes use of the .NET libraries. In fact, Silverlight could be thought of as WPF's little brother, because Silverlight is basically a subset of the libraries that are part of WPF. So, in a nutshell, if you want to develop Windows desktop applications, you should use WPF, and if you want to create cross-platform web applications, you should use Silverlight.

I realize that I still haven't explained why I am bringing WPF up in this chapter. The reason is that, if you want to learn how to develop in Silverlight, then you probably will want to develop in WPF as well, because the two are so similar. I can guarantee that any professional Silverlight developer right now could create at least a basic WPF application. Further, if you have invested this much time in learning Silverlight, I am certain you have at least heard of WPF already, and you may have even played around with it as well. That being the case, I thought it would be an extra bonus for me to show you how to use Silverlight's VSM in a WPF application with the WPF Toolkit.

What is the WPF Toolkit?

The WPF Toolkit is an open source set of components and features created by Microsoft that do not ship with the current version of the .NET libraries. This toolkit can be easily installed and then added to a WPF project so that the developer has easy access to these new components. Following are some of the WPF Toolkit components and features:

- The DataGrid
- The MS Office Ribbon control
- The DatePicker and the Calendar control
- The ability to enable Blend's States panel for WPF applications
- VSM support for WPF

Because this is a Silverlight book, I am only going to cover how you can use the VSM in a WPF application. But I encourage you to go back and play with the other components, because they can be handy and fun to play with. Let's go ahead and download the WPF Toolkit.

Downloading and installing the WPF Toolkit

Perform the following steps to download the WPF Toolkit:

1. Open a browser and navigate to www.codeplex.com/wpf/Release/ProjectReleases.aspx. Click WPFToolkit Binaries, as shown in Figure 8-1.

2. Save the file to your local hard drive.

3. When it has finished downloading, double-click it.

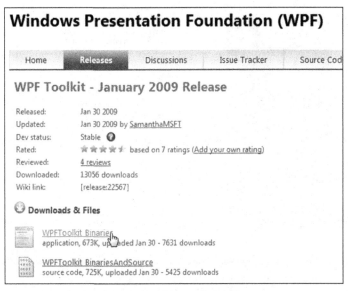

Figure 8-1. Download the WPF Toolkit installation file.

4. When the Open File – Security Warning **dialog appears, click** Run, **as shown in Figure 8-2.**

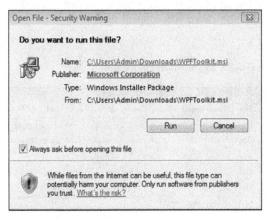

Figure 8-2. Click Run.

5. In the WPF Toolkit Setup **dialog box that appears, check the** I accept the terms in the License Agreement **box, and click** Install, **as shown in Figure 8-3.**

6. Once the WPF Toolkit installs, click Finish.

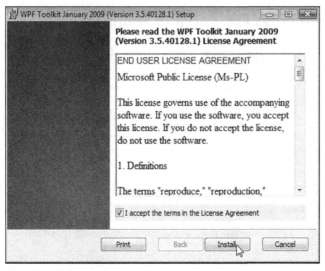

Figure 8-3. Click Install.

Creating a new WPF application

Now that we have the WPF Toolkit installed, we are going to need to use it. So, let's open Visual Studio and create a new WPF application called WPFToolkitProject.

1. Open Visual Studio.
2. Click File ➤ New ➤ Project, as shown in Figure 8-4.

Figure 8-4. Create a new project in Visual Studio.

3. When the New Project dialog box appears, choose Windows for the project type.

4. Choose WPF application for the template.

5. Name the project WPFToolkitProject.

6. Make a mental note of where the project is being saved so you can find it again later, and click OK, as shown in Figure 8-5.

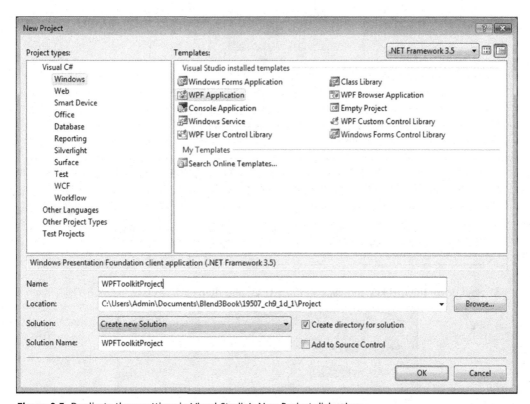

Figure 8-5. Duplicate these settings in Visual Studio's New Project dialog box.

Setting up the application for the WPF Toolkit

Now that we have downloaded and installed the WPF Toolkit and created the WPFToolkitProject, it is time we got the application ready to use the WPF Toolkit. The first thing we are going to need to do is add a reference to the dynamic link libraries (DLLs) for the WPF Toolkit. Follow these instructions to do this:

1. In Visual Studio's Solution Explorer, right-click the References folder of the application, and then click Add Reference, as shown in Figure 8-6.

Figure 8-6. Start to add a reference in the new application.

2. When the Add Reference dialog box appears, click the Browse tab and then navigate to the most recent folder within c:\ProgramFiles\WPFToolkit.

> By the time you add these references, the version may have changed from v3.5.40128.1, and thus the path you enter will change accordingly.

3. Hold down the Ctrl key and click all three DLLs, and then click OK (see Figure 8-7).

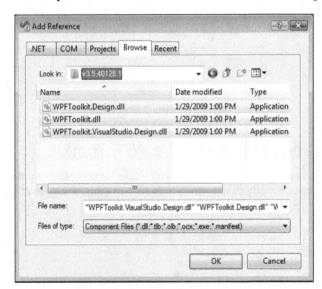

Figure 8-7. Add references to the three WPF Toolkit DLLs.

Now that our application has a reference to the WPF Toolkit DLLs, we are ready to use it, right? Wrong. In order to use the WPF Toolkit, we need to tell both our code-behind file and our XAML files to make use of these DLLs. Let's do that now:

4. Open Window1.xaml and add the following namespace:

```
<Window
    x:Class="WPFToolkitProject.Window1"
    xmlns="http://schemas.microsoft.com/winfx/2006/xaml/presentation"
    xmlns:x="http://schemas.microsoft.com/winfx/2006/xaml"
    xmlns:toolkit="http://schemas.microsoft.com/wpf/2008/toolkit"
    Title="Window1"
    Height="300"
    Width="300">
    <Grid>

    </Grid>
</Window>
```

5. Now open the Window1.xaml.cs code-behind file and add the following using statement:

```
using System;
using System.Collections.Generic;
using System.Linq;
using System.Text;
using System.Windows;
using System.Windows.Controls;
using System.Windows.Data;
using System.Windows.Documents;
using System.Windows.Input;
using System.Windows.Media;
using System.Windows.Media.Imaging;
using System.Windows.Navigation;
using System.Windows.Shapes;
using Microsoft.Windows.Controls;


namespace WPFToolkitProject
{
    /// <summary>
    /// Interaction logic for Window1.xaml
    /// </summary>
    public partial class Window1 : Window
    {
        public Window1()
        {
            InitializeComponent();
        }
    }
}
```

Now your application is all ready to use WPF Toolkit. So let's use it!

Using the WPF Toolkit

Because I am such a big fan of the VSM, I will start off with an exercise to show you how to use it. We'll make a button UserControl that has a glassy look to it (and so it will be called the Glass button). The new Glass button control will use the VSM to control its states (MouseEnter and MouseLeave).

1. Fire up Blend 3.

2. Click File ➤ Open Project/Solution.

3. Navigate to where you saved your WPFToolkitProject project and double-click it to open it.

4. Click the Rectangle tool on the toolbar and draw a Rectangle, as shown in Figure 8-8.

Figure 8-8. Draw a Rectangle in the workspace.

5. Next, give the new Rectangle a gradient fill. Make the first color blue and the second a lighter blue, as shown in Figure 8-9.

6. Next, remove the Rectangle's stroke in the Properties panel by clicking the No brush button, as shown in Figure 8-10.

Figure 8-9. Give the Rectangle a gradient fill.

Figure 8-10. Remove the Rectangle's stroke.

7. Next, use the radius handles to give the Rectangle rounded edges, as shown in Figure 8-11.

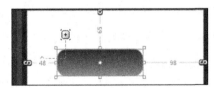

Figure 8-11. Give the Rectangle rounded edges.

8. Now select the Rectangle and press Ctrl+C to copy it and Ctrl+V to paste in a new one.

9. Give the new Rectangle a gradient fill that goes from white to white (you will see why in a moment).

10. Next, make the new Rectangle a little smaller, as shown in Figure 8-12.

Figure 8-12. The new Rectangle

11. Now make the bottom color stop have an alpha value of 0 in the Properties panel, as shown in Figure 8-13.

Figure 8-13. Give the new Rectangle's lower gradient color stop an alpha of 0.

You should now have something like what is shown in Figure 8-14.

This looks pretty cool, so we can now go ahead and turn this into a UserControl.

Figure 8-14. Your two Rectangles should now look like this.

12. Select both Rectangles, and in the Objects and Timeline panel, group them into a Canvas.

13. Right-click the newly created Canvas, and then click Make Into UserControl, as shown in Figure 8-15.

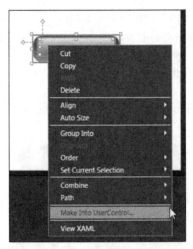

Figure 8-15. Turn the two Rectangles into a UserControl.

14. When the Make Into UserControl dialog box appears, name the new UserControl BlueButtonUC, as shown in Figure 8-16. Click OK.

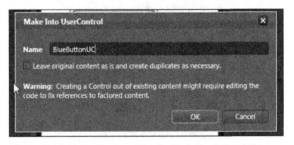

Figure 8-16. Name the new UserControl BlueButtonUC.

Once you have done this, Blend 3 will open BlueButtonUC, and the States panel should appear. Now we can start adding our states.

15. In the States panel, click the Add state group, as shown in Figure 8-17.

Figure 8-17. Add a new state group.

16. Name the new state group BlueButtonStateGroup, as shown in Figure 8-18.

Figure 8-18. Name the new state group BlueButtonStateGroup.

17. Next, set Default transition to 0.5s, as shown in Figure 8-19.

Figure 8-19. Set the default transition to .5 seconds.

18. Next, click the Add state button, as shown in Figure 8-20.

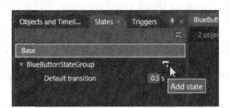

Figure 8-20. Click the Add state button.

19. Name the new state MouseIsOver, as shown in Figure 8-21.

Figure 8-21. Name the new state MouseIsOver.

A red line will appear around the workspace, indicating that anything we do now is being recorded into the visual state. So, let's make some changes to the UserControl.

20. In the Brushes bucket of the Properties panel, change the bottom Rectangle's top color to red, as shown in Figure 8-22.

Figure 8-22. Change the bottom Rectangle's top gradient color to red.

21. Now you can stop recording by clicking Base in the Properties panel to change back to the Base state, as shown in Figure 8-23.

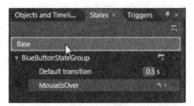

Figure 8-23. Click Base to stop recording.

If we were to wire up this state now in code-behind, we would put our mouse over the button and it would change colors, but it would never change back. To make it change back, we need another state, which we'll call MouseIsOff. Let's create that state now.

22. Click the Add state button again and name the new state MouseIsOff.

As you learned in Chapter 6 when you made your first Silverlight VSM project, you don't need to do anything in this state, as this is exactly how you want the button to look when the mouse is not over it. So, let's now be fancy and add a new state for when the button is pressed. I think it would look cool if the button when pressed glows yellow, and then returns back to normal when the mouse is up. Let's implement that now.

23. The first thing you need to do is click Base to stop recording, and then add a new Rectangle that is behind the two existing Rectangles. You can send it to the back by dragging it in the Objects and Timeline panel so that it is above the two existing Rectangles.

24. Make it slightly bigger and make it a solid fill of yellow, as shown in Figure 8-24 (make sure you are in the Base state so that nothing is being recorded at this time).

Figure 8-24. Add a new, slightly bigger Rectangle behind the two existing ones, and give it a yellow fill.

25. Next, in the Properties panel's Appearance bucket, set the new Rectangle's opacity to 0%, as shown in Figure 8-25.

Figure 8-25. Set the new Rectangle to have an opacity of 0%.

26. In the States panel, click the Add state button, and name the new state MouseIsDown.

27. Give the new Rectangle an opacity of 100%.

Now we need to add a MouseIsUp state so that the yellow Rectangle disappears when the mouse is up.

28. Click the Add state button in the States panel and name it MouseIsUp. Your States panel should look like Figure 8-26.

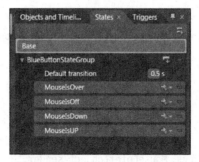

Figure 8-26. Add a new state named MouseIsUp.

Again, because this is the default state, we don't need to do anything. We just need to go into code-behind and wire up the states. Even though Blend 3 now has IntelliSense, it's generally still better to do your C# coding in Visual Studio. So, in Blend, press Ctrl+Shift+B to compile the application, and then fire up Visual Studio and open the WPFToolkitProject project.

29. Open BlueButtonUC.xml.cs. Underneath the InitializeComponent() line of code, add a Loaded handler. Type this.loaded+=, and when IntelliSense prompts you, press the Tab key twice to complete the Raise event call as well as the event handler. Your code should look like the following:

```
namespace WPFToolkitProject
{
 /// <summary>
 /// Interaction logic for BlueButtonUC.xaml
 /// </summary>
 public partial class BlueButtonUC
 {
 public BlueButtonUC()
 {
 this.InitializeComponent();
          this.Loaded += new RoutedEventHandler(BlueButtonUC_Loaded);
 }

         void BlueButtonUC_Loaded(object sender, RoutedEventArgs e)
         {
             throw new NotImplementedException();
         }
 }
 }
```

30. Now erase the default throw new... code, raise the MouseEnter event, and create the event handler as well, as shown in the following code:

```
        void BlueButtonUC_Loaded(object sender, RoutedEventArgs e)
        {
            this.MouseEnter += new
MouseEventHandler(BlueButtonUC_MouseEnter);
        }

        void BlueButtonUC_MouseEnter(object sender, MouseEventArgs e)
        {
            throw new NotImplementedException();
        }
    }
```

31. In the MouseEnter event handler, erase the default throw new... code and create the VSM code, as shown here:

```
        void BlueButtonUC_MouseEnter(object sender, MouseEventArgs e)
        {
            VisualStateManager.GoToState(this, "MouseIsOver", true);
        }
```

Press F5 to compile and run the application. Place your mouse over the button and it should apply the MouseIsOver state (see Figure 8-27).

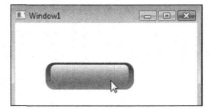

Figure 8-27. If you place your mouse over the button now, it applies the MouseIsOver state.

Great, it works just as we'd hoped. But notice that if you move your mouse off of the button, it stays in the MouseIsOver state. Let's change that now by wiring up the other states.

32. In the Loaded event handler, raise the MouseLeave, MouseDown, and MouseUp events, and create the event handlers, as shown in the following code:

```
void BlueButtonUC_Loaded(object sender, RoutedEventArgs e)
{
    this.MouseEnter += new
MouseEventHandler(BlueButtonUC_MouseEnter);
    this.MouseLeave += new
MouseEventHandler(BlueButtonUC_MouseLeave);
    this.MouseDown += new
MouseButtonEventHandler(BlueButtonUC_MouseDown);
    this.MouseUp += new
MouseButtonEventHandler(BlueButtonUC_MouseUp);
}

void BlueButtonUC_MouseUp
(object sender, MouseButtonEventArgs e)
{
    throw new NotImplementedException();
}

void BlueButtonUC_MouseDown
(object sender, MouseButtonEventArgs e)
{
    throw new NotImplementedException();
}

void BlueButtonUC_MouseLeave(object sender, MouseEventArgs e)
{
    throw new NotImplementedException();
}
```

195

```
void BlueButtonUC_MouseEnter(object sender, MouseEventArgs e)
{
    VisualStateManager.GoToState(this, "MouseIsOver", true);
}
```

33. Now wire up the corresponding states in each of the new event handlers:

```
public partial class BlueButtonUC
{
public BlueButtonUC()
{
this.InitializeComponent();
        this.Loaded += new RoutedEventHandler(BlueButtonUC_Loaded);
}

    void BlueButtonUC_Loaded(object sender, RoutedEventArgs e)
    {
        this.MouseEnter += new
MouseEventHandler(BlueButtonUC_MouseEnter);
        this.MouseLeave += new
MouseEventHandler(BlueButtonUC_MouseLeave);
        this.MouseDown += new
MouseButtonEventHandler(BlueButtonUC_MouseDown);
        this.MouseUp += new
MouseButtonEventHandler(BlueButtonUC_MouseUp);
    }

    void BlueButtonUC_MouseUp
(object sender, MouseButtonEventArgs e)
    {
        VisualStateManager.GoToState(this, "MouseIsUp", true);
    }

    void BlueButtonUC_MouseDown
(object sender, MouseButtonEventArgs e)
    {
        VisualStateManager.GoToState(this, "MouseIsDown", true);
    }

    void BlueButtonUC_MouseLeave(object sender, MouseEventArgs e)
    {
        VisualStateManager.GoToState(this, "MouseIsOff", true);
    }

    void BlueButtonUC_MouseEnter(object sender, MouseEventArgs e)
    {
        VisualStateManager.GoToState(this, "MouseIsOver", true);
    }
  }
}
```

Now if you press F5 to compile and run the application, you will see that it reacts to our mouse events just as we'd hoped. That is, the button's top gradient changes to red when the mouse is over and changes back to the default color when the mouse is off. The button also has a yellow glow when it is clicked.

You can download this project here: http://windowspresentationfoundation.com/Blend3Book/ WPFToolkitProject.zip.

Summary

In this chapter, you learned about a set of components and features that do not ship with the .NET libraries, called the WPF Toolkit. You also learned how to download it, install it, and make a WPF application ready to use it. You learned how to use the VSM (a powerful Silverlight feature that allows the developer and/or designer to easily create states in their Silverlight applications) with WPF, and then created a new WPF application with a custom UserControl. You then used the VSM to give your new control MouseEnter, MouseLeave, MouseDown, and MouseUp states.

As mentioned at the beginning of the chapter, there are a few other very cool controls that are part of the WPF Toolkit, including the Calendar control and the DataGrid. I encourage you to play around with them. You can find tutorials, forums, and other good information on the WPF Toolkit at http:// wpf.codeplex.com/Release/ProjectReleases.aspx?ReleaseId=22567.

In the next chapter, we are going to discuss events, event handling, and a popular software design pattern called Model-View-ViewModel (MVVM).

Chapter 9

EVENTS AND EVENTHANDLERS

What this chapter covers:

- What are events and EventHandlers
- Creating a project and exploring and creating some different events
- Learn about a popular design pattern called Model-View-ViewModel (MVVM)

Most Silverlight objects have a set of events that fire when users interact with them. You have already seen some events in earlier chapters. You also know that any method or function that is called when an event is fired is called an EventHandler. In this chapter, I am going to discuss the many different events that objects have, from the Click event to the MouseWheel event. You are going to create EventHandlers for all of these different events as well, so let's get started and create a new Silverlight project.

Creating the EventAndEventHandlers project

As I have stated so many times before, this is a very hands-on book, so now would be a great time to create a new Silverlight Application project and start exploring events and EventHandlers with practical examples (as you might have guessed, I am of the opinion that people learn best by doing rather than just reading). So let's get started:

1. Open Visual Studio 2008.

2. Select File ➤ New ➤ Project, and choose Silverlight Application.

3. Give the project the name EventsAndEventHandlers. Choose a location to save the project, and click OK (see Figure 9-1). Click OK again when the New Silverlight Application dialog box appears.

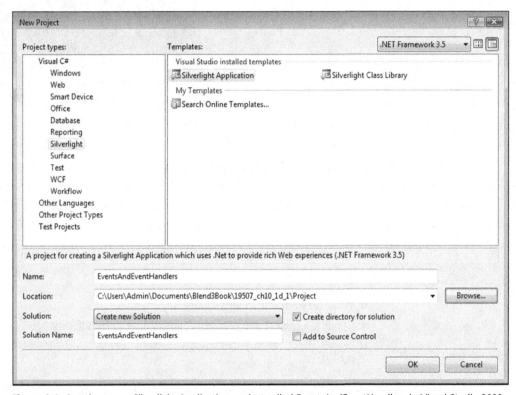

Figure 9-1. Creating a new Silverlight Application project called EventsAndEventHandlers in Visual Studio 2008

4. Note where the project was created, as we are about to open it in Blend 3.

5. Now, open Blend 3, navigate to where you saved the project, and open it.

6. With your project created in Blend 3, double-click MainPage.xaml from the Projects panel, select the Button tool from the toolbar, and draw a Button control in the workspace like the one shown in Figure 9-2.

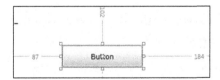

Figure 9-2. Drawing a Button control in the workspace in Blend

7. Now, build the project by pressing Ctrl+Shift+B, and switch back to Visual Studio 2008. When you're prompted to reload the project, select Yes.

8. Now that you have a Button in the XAML, you need to give it a unique name so that you can control it programmatically in the C# of MainPage.xaml.cs. So in MainPage.xaml, locate the XAML for your Button, and give it the name of MyButton, as shown in the following code:

```
<UserControl x:Class="EventsAndEventHandlers.Page"
    xmlns="http://schemas.microsoft.com/winfx/2006/xaml/presentation"
    xmlns:x="http://schemas.microsoft.com/winfx/2006/xaml"
    Width="400" Height="300">
    <Grid x:Name="LayoutRoot" Background="White">
        <Button
            x:Name="MyButton"
            Height="33"
            Width="100"
            Margin="87,102,184,0"
            VerticalAlignment="Top"
            Content="Button" />

    </Grid>
</UserControl>
```

> For easier-to-read XAML, you can restructure your code so that each property is on its own line.

9. Press F6 to recompile the project without running it.

10. Now that you have named your Button and recompiled the application, open MainPage. xaml.cs, and in the constructor below the code that reads InitializeComponent();, type the Button name and type a . (period). You will see an IntelliSense drop-down menu of the events that your Button has. Events have an icon of a lightning bolt next to them.

Let's go over the events that you would commonly use for a Button.

Click

Click, obviously, is the event that occurs when the Button is clicked.

1. Directly under the InitializeComponent(); line of code type Click. After you type "click", type +=, and press the Tab key twice. Visual Studio 2008 attaches the Click event to the EventHandler method stub for you. My code follows:

```
namespace EventsAndEventHandlers
{
    public partial class Page : UserControl
    {
        public Page()
        {
            InitializeComponent();
```

```
        MyButton.Click += new RoutedEventHandler(MyButton_Click);
    }

    void MyButton_Click(object sender, RoutedEventArgs e)
    {
        throw new NotImplementedException();
    }
  }
}
```

2. In the new method stub, remove the default text of throw new NotImplementedException();. Replace it with a MessageBox, as shown here:

```
namespace EventsAndEventHandlers
{
    public partial class Page : UserControl
    {
        public Page()
        {
            InitializeComponent();
            MyButton.Click += new RoutedEventHandler(MyButton_Click);
        }

        void MyButton_Click(object sender, RoutedEventArgs e)
        {
            MessageBox.Show("I was clicked");
        }
    }
}
```

3. Press F5 to compile and run the application.

Now, you can click the Button and see a MessageBox with the message "I was clicked."

That was simple enough, so let's move on to mouse events.

Mouse events

In C#, there are many ways to handle events that involve users interacting with objects using the mouse. I am now going to discuss some of these events. It is also important to note that you are going to create examples of these events using a Button control, but most of these events can just as easily be applied to other objects such as a simple Rectangle, a MediaElement, or even the main application itself.

Before I start talking about these events, you'll need to do some maintenance to your application to give you some breathing room:

1. Make sure your application is saved, and switch back to Blend 3.

2. Change the width and height of your application to 800×600. I find the easiest way to do this is to alter the XAML in the Split view and just change the Height and Width properties in the Page node to 800 and 600 (by default, Visual Studio made my Page 400×300).

I find developing visually in Blend 3 easier with the Design view rather than the Split view, as I do most of my XAML coding in Visual Studio 2008—primarily because it formats my code and Blend 3 does not. With its new size, the application in Blend should look similar to the one shown in Figure 9-3.

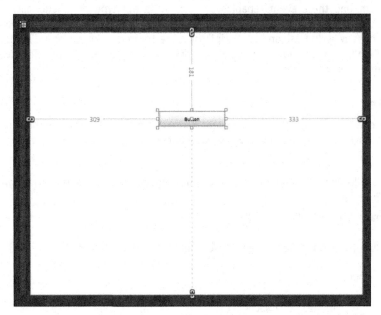

Figure 9-3. After changing the size of the application, your application should resemble this.

3. With the Button selected, go to the Common Properties bucket of the Properties panel, and change the Content property to read Press Me!.

4. In XAML view, your code should look similar to this:

```
<UserControl x:Class="EventsAndEventHandlers.Page"
    xmlns="http://schemas.microsoft.com/winfx/2006/xaml/presentation"
    xmlns:x="http://schemas.microsoft.com/winfx/2006/xaml"
    Width="800" Height="600">
    <Grid x:Name="LayoutRoot" Background="White">
        <Button
            x:Name="MyButton"
            Height="33"
            Margin="309,181,333,0"
            VerticalAlignment="Top"
            Content="Press Me!" />

    </Grid>
</UserControl>
```

5. Press Ctrl+Shift+B to compile the application, and switch back to Visual Studio so you can explore more events.

MouseEnter and MouseLeave

MouseEnter and MouseLeave are two very important events. Most rich media applications have buttons that do *something* when your mouse is over them and then do *something else* when your mouse is not over them, and these events enable you to provide this type of functionality. For example, navigation buttons commonly glow when your mouse is over them, and the glow will disappear when your mouse moves away. In Flash and JavaScript, these are commonly known as RollOver and RollOut states, but in Blend, they are known as MouseEnter and MouseLeave, respectively. Try these events out yourself in the following sections.

MouseEnter

As you can probably guess, a MouseEnter event is fired when the user moves their mouse over an object. To see how this works, you'll add the MouseEnter event and EventHandler to the MyButton control.

1. Use the following code as a guide to wire your MyButton control up to listen for and handle the MouseEnter event:

```
namespace EventsAndEventHandlers
{
    public partial class Page : UserControl
    {
        public Page()
        {
            InitializeComponent();
            MyButton.MouseEnter += new MouseEventHandler
(MyButton_MouseEnter);
        }

        void MyButton_MouseEnter(object sender, MouseEventArgs e)
        {
            MessageBox.Show("MouseEnter");

        }
    }
}
```

2. Press F5 to compile and run the application. You will see a MessageBox appear when you place your mouse over the button (see Figure 9-4).

Erase the event and EventHandler you just coded, and let's move on to looking at the MouseLeave event.

MouseLeave

The following code will fire when you move your mouse over the button and then off of it:

```
namespace EventsAndEventHandlers
{
    public partial class Page : UserControl
```

Figure 9-4.
The MouseEnter event was fired.

```
    {
        public Page()
        {
            InitializeComponent();
            MyButton.MouseLeave += new MouseEventHandler
(MyButton_MouseLeave);
        }

        void MyButton_MouseLeave(object sender, MouseEventArgs e)
        {
            MessageBox.Show("MouseLeave event fired");
        }

    }
}
```

MouseLeftButtonDown

The MouseLeftButtonDown event is fired when you click your left mouse button on an object. This seems pretty straightforward, but there is a catch: if you were to listen for the MouseLeftButtonDown event on your Button, you would not get any results, because a Button control has a Click event. So, you may be asking, why would you want to use a MouseLeftButtonDown event on a Button? Good question; the simple answer is you wouldn't because the MouseLeftButtonDown event is primarily used for controls that do not have a Click event such a Grid. That being said, let's code for a MouseLeftButtonDown event on the application's main Grid named LayoutRoot:

1. In MainPage.xaml.cs, add a MouseLeftButtonDown event for your LayoutRoot control that shows a MessageBox. The code is as follows:

```
namespace EventsAndEventHandlers
{
    public partial class Page : UserControl
    {
        public Page()
        {
            InitializeComponent();
            LayoutRoot.MouseLeftButtonDown +=
new MouseButtonEventHandler(LayoutRoot_MouseLeftButtonDown);
        }

        void LayoutRoot_MouseLeftButtonDown
(object sender, MouseButtonEventArgs e)
        {
            MessageBox.Show("MouseLeftButtonDown event fired");
        }

    }
}
```

2. Run the application, and try it out. As you can see in Figure 9-5, you get the results that you would expect.

Figure 9-5. Your MessageBox appears when you MouseLeftButtonDown on LayoutRoot Grid.

MouseLeftButtonUp

The MouseLeftButtonUp event is much like the MouseLeftButtonDown event, except it fires when, of course, the left mouse button is released over an object. Go ahead and make a new MessageBox appear when you MouseLeftButtonUp over the LayoutRoot Grid:

```
namespace EventsAndEventHandlers
{
    public partial class Page : UserControl
    {
        public Page()
        {
            InitializeComponent();
            LayoutRoot.MouseLeftButtonUp +=
new MouseButtonEventHandler(LayoutRoot_MouseLeftButtonUp);

        }

        void LayoutRoot_MouseLeftButtonUp
(object sender, MouseButtonEventArgs e)
        {
            MessageBox.Show("MouseLeftButtonUp event fired");
        }

    }
}
```

The Model-View-ViewModel Pattern and Commands

Design patterns are software patterns that offer architectural solutions to problems that frequently occur in software development. They describe structural organization, responsibilities, and object interaction. A very popular model for building WPF and, recently, Silverlight applications, is called the Model-View-ViewModel pattern (MVVM). This pattern for building applications is the next logical step in design patterns and usually has three distinct parts:

- *Model (sometimes called the data model)*: This is responsible for exposing application data.

- *View*: This is the user interface of the application. The objects here can bind to the ViewModel's behaviors. Ideally, a View has no code-behind whatsoever, but in the case of Silverlight, this is not yet possible. The View should be as dumb as possible (it should contain as little logic as possible).

- ViewModel: This is a Model for an application View. It exposes data from the Model that is relevant for the View. It also exposes behaviors for the views. These behaviors usually come in the form of commands.

> If you're familiar with design patters, MVVM is an adaptation of the MVC design pattern.

In this section, I am going to create a Silverlight application that makes use of a command manager and a ViewModel to expose behaviors in the way of commands. "Why do we need a CommandManager utility class?" you ask. Here is why:

In the MVVM design pattern, the ViewModel contains the data the View needs for presentation. The ViewModel exposes this data to the View as bindable properties. The View (Controls, UserControls, and the like) binds to those properties. When the data changes in a way that should cause an update in the view, like if a button needs to change from enabled to disabled, the properties in the ViewModel change and cause the bindings in the View to update. This elegantly encapsulates updates from the ViewModel to the View.

The problem lies in updates in the other direction, when the View receives user input, like a button click, and needs to forward that input to the ViewModel. One way to handle user input is to create event handlers in the code-behind of your UserControls, like a button click handler, for example. In this pattern, the application will receive input from the user and route the call to the ViewModel. The ViewModel then makes some changes to its data that are reflected in the View through its bindings. The disadvantage of this pattern is that it closely couples the View and the ViewModel. The View must know enough about the ViewModel to be able to translate a Click event into a method call on its ViewModel—not an ideal scenario. Alternatively, we could create event handlers directly in the ViewModel and bind the Button's Click event to that handler. However, this pattern is no better because, again, the View and ViewModel are tightly coupled.

In WPF, commands are used to avoid tight coupling of View and ViewModel. Several controls in WPF support a Command property of type ICommand. Developers can define an ICommand object in the ViewModel. The View can bind the Click event to that ICommand object. When the Click event is raised, WPF will route the event to the command with the help of a utility class called CommandManager, effectively allowing the ViewModel to handle the event without any code-behind or coupling the View to the ViewModel. Unfortunately, no Silverlight controls expose a Command property, and there is no CommandManager utility class. However, we can write our own CommandManager to mimic the sophisticated command routing in WPF, allowing us to create a nicely decoupled MVVM architecture. (Thank my technical editor Jason Cook for this in-depth reason for our need for a CommandManager utility class.)

So, commands allow the view to execute code-behind directly on the ViewModel without caring what happens when that code is executed, thus decoupling the View and ViewModel. The following tutorial is based on a wonderful tutorial by Chris Klug (screename ZeroKoll), who keeps a great blog at http://chris.59north.com. Close the project you currently have open, and let's get to it!

1. In Visual Studio, create a new Silverlight Class Library called CommandManager, as shown in Figure 9-6.

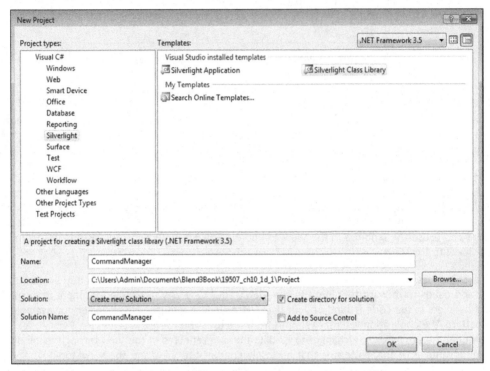

Figure 9-6. Create a new Silverlight Class Library in Visual Studio called CommandManager.

2. In the Solution Explorer, add a new Class, as shown in Figure 9-7.

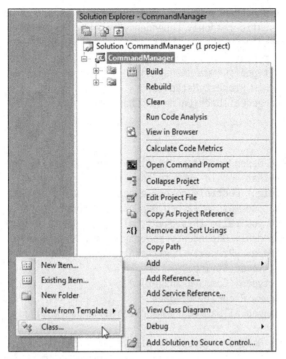

Figure 9-7. Add a new class.

3. In the Add New Item dialog box, name the new class CommandManager, and click Add.

4. The following code should be in your new class. You can download a text version of this code at http://windowspresentationfoundation.com/Blend3Book/commandmanager.txt. The code has also been commented in detail if you want to know exactly what it is doing.

```
using System;
using System.Net;
using System.Windows;
using System.Windows.Controls;
using System.Windows.Documents;
using System.Windows.Ink;
using System.Windows.Input;
using System.Windows.Media;
using System.Windows.Media.Animation;
using System.Windows.Shapes;
using System.Collections.Generic;
using System.Reflection;

namespace CommandManager
{
    public static class CommandManager
    {
        #region DependencyProperty declarations
```

```
                        // This DependencyProperty defines what ICommand object to use
                        public static readonly DependencyProperty CommandProperty =
                            DependencyProperty.RegisterAttached("Command",
                                typeof(ICommand),
                                typeof(CommandManager),
                                new PropertyMetadata
(new PropertyChangedCallback(OnCommandChanged)));



        // This Attached DependencyProperty allows you to specify the name
        // of the event that should execute the Command.
        // Since Silverlight Controls do not expose a Command property,
        //we can instead use this Attached DependencyProperty to tell the
        // control "when you raise this event, also execute this ICommand"
        public static readonly DependencyProperty CommandEventNameProperty =
                    DependencyProperty.RegisterAttached("CommandEventName",
                        typeof(String),
                        typeof(CommandManager),
                        new PropertyMetadata
(new PropertyChangedCallback(OnCommandEventNameChanged)));

        // This Attached DependencyProperty allows the control to optionally
        //pass a single object to the Command as a parameter, much like the
        // WPF CommandParameter.
                public static readonly DependencyProperty
CommandParameterProperty =
                    DependencyProperty.RegisterAttached("CommandParameter",
                        typeof(object),
                        typeof(CommandManager),
                        new PropertyMetadata
(new PropertyChangedCallback(OnCommandParameterChanged)));
                #endregion

        // These are simple Getters and Setters for the Command,
        //CommandEventName and CommandParameter DependencyProperties.
                #region DependencyProperty Get and Set methods
                public static ICommand GetCommand(DependencyObject obj)
                {
                    return (ICommand)obj.GetValue(CommandProperty);
                }
                public static void SetCommand
(DependencyObject obj, ICommand command)
                {
                    obj.SetValue(CommandProperty, command);
                }

                public static string GetCommandEventName(DependencyObject obj)
                {
```

```
                return (string)obj.GetValue(CommandEventNameProperty);
        }
        public static void SetCommandEventName
(DependencyObject obj, string commandEventName)
        {
                obj.SetValue(CommandEventNameProperty, commandEventName);
        }


        public static string GetCommandParameter(DependencyObject obj)
        {
                return (string)obj.GetValue(CommandParameterProperty);
        }
        public static void SetCommandParameter
(DependencyObject obj, string commandParameter)
        {
                obj.SetValue(CommandParameterProperty, commandParameter);
        }
        #endregion

        static CommandManager()
        {
                // This initializes the CommandDeclaration Dictionary,
                // shown below
                _commandDeclarations = new
Dictionary<DependencyObject, CommandDeclaration>();
        }

// These are callback methods invoked when the value of the Command,
// CommandEventName or CommandParameter properties change.
//They all use a utility method GetCommandDeclaration, shown below.
        #region DependencyProperty Changed Callbacks
        static void OnCommandChanged
(DependencyObject obj, DependencyPropertyChangedEventArgs e)
        {
                GetCommandDeclaration(obj).Command = (ICommand)e.NewValue;
        }
        static void OnCommandEventNameChanged
(DependencyObject obj, DependencyPropertyChangedEventArgs e)
        {
                GetCommandDeclaration(obj).EventName = (string)e.NewValue;
        }
        static void OnCommandParameterChanged
(DependencyObject obj, DependencyPropertyChangedEventArgs e)
        {
                GetCommandDeclaration(obj).CommandParameter = e.NewValue;
        }
        #endregion

        #region CommandDeclaration dictionary
```

```
//This is a Dictionary where the Key is the DependencyObject with the
//Event we want to connect to an ICommand and the Value is a
//CommandDeclaration object, described below.
static Dictionary<DependencyObject,
CommandDeclaration> _commandDeclarations;

//This method returns the CommandDeclaration associated with the
//DependencyObject obj. If this object is not yet in the
//commandDeclarations Dictionary, this method adds it and creates a
//new CommandDeclaration.
private static CommandDeclaration GetCommandDeclaration
(DependencyObject obj)
        {
            if (!_commandDeclarations.ContainsKey(obj))
            {
                CommandDeclaration decl = new CommandDeclaration(obj);
                _commandDeclarations.Add(obj, decl);
            }
            return _commandDeclarations[obj];
        }
        #endregion

// This class handles associating an ICommand with an Event.
        private class CommandDeclaration
        {
// The DependencyObject where the Event should exist
            DependencyObject _object;
// The ICommand to execute when the Event is raised
ICommand _cmd = null;
// The name of the Event to associate with the ICommand
            string _eventName = String.Empty;

            public CommandDeclaration(DependencyObject obj)
            {
                _object = obj;
            }

// This method connects the ICommand to the Event.
            internal void ConnectHandler()
            {
                if (Command != null &&
!String.IsNullOrEmpty(EventName))
                {
                    EventInfo ev = GetEventInfo(_eventName);
// This will throw an exception if the Event with the name _
// eventName was not found on the DependencyObject _object.
                    if (ev == null)
                        throw new Exception
("Cannot find event: " + _eventName);
```

```csharp
            // The event was found. Now add an EventHandler to it to
            //execute the command when the Event is raised.
                    ev.AddEventHandler(_object, GetDelegate());
                }
            }

            internal void DisconnectHandler()
            {
                if (!String.IsNullOrEmpty(EventName))
                {
                    EventInfo ev = GetEventInfo(EventName);
                    if (EventName != null)
                    {
                        ev.RemoveEventHandler(_object, GetDelegate());
                    }
                }
            }

    // When the _object raises the event _eventName, the Delegate
    //created by GetDelegate will call this method which checks to
    //see if the Command can be executed, then Executes the Command.
            public void Handler(object sender, EventArgs e)
            {
                if (Command != null &&
    Command.CanExecute(CommandParameter))
                    Command.Execute(CommandParameter);
            }

            private EventInfo GetEventInfo(string eventName)
            {
                Type t = _object.GetType();
                EventInfo ev = t.GetEvent(eventName);
                return ev;
            }
    // This method returns a Delegate that represents a suitable
    //event handler for the event EventName.
            private Delegate GetDelegate()
            {
                EventInfo ev = GetEventInfo(EventName);
    // Type type: The Type of the delegate to create.
    //This Type will depend on the Type of the Event.
                return Delegate.CreateDelegate
    (ev.EventHandlerType, this, this.GetType().GetMethod("Handler"), true);
    // Arguments passed to the Delegate:
    // Object firstArgument:
    //This object will be the "sender"
    //argument in the delegate method.
```

```csharp
    // MethodInfo method: A MethodInfo object describing
    //the method the delegate represents. This will tell
    //the delegate to invoke the method called "Handler".

    // Bool throwOnBindFailure: A Boolean determining whether
    //or not to throw an exception if the method cannot be found.
                }

        public DependencyObject Object
        {
            get
            {
                return _object;
            }
        }
        public object CommandParameter
        {
            get;
            set;
        }
        public ICommand Command
        {
            get
            {
                return _cmd;
            }
            set
            {
                if (_cmd == value)
                    return;

                if (_cmd != null)
                    DisconnectHandler();

                _cmd = value;

                if (_cmd != null)
                    ConnectHandler();
            }
        }
        public string EventName
        {
            get
            {
                return _eventName;
            }
            set
            {
                if (_eventName == value)
                    return;
```

```
            if (!string.IsNullOrEmpty(_eventName))
                DisconnectHandler();

            _eventName = value;

            if (string.IsNullOrEmpty(_eventName))
                return;

            if (!String.IsNullOrEmpty(_eventName))
                ConnectHandler();
        }
    }
  }
 }
}
```

For a detailed explanation of what this class is doing, you can read ZeroKoll's brilliant tutorial here: http://chris.59north.com/post/Creating-a-command-manager-in-Silverlight-2.aspx.

5. Next add a new Silverlight project to the Solution Explorer, as shown in Figure 9-8.

Figure 9-8. Add a new Project to the Solution.

6. In the Add New Project dialog box, select Silverlight Application; name it SLViewModelExample, and Click OK, as shown in Figure 9-9.

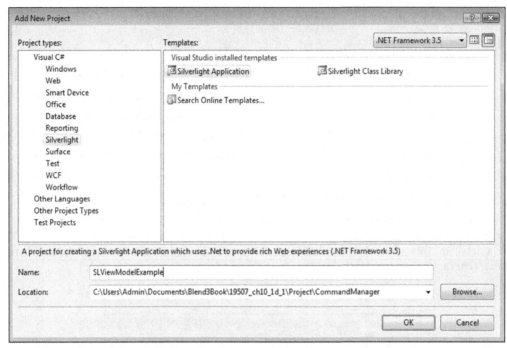

Figure 9-9. Name the new Silverlight Application SLViewModelExample.

7. In the New Silverlight Application dialog box, leave the default settings, and click OK.

8. Next, add a new class to the SLViewModelExample, and call it ApplicationCommands (see Figure 9-10).

9. Have this class extend the ICommand object by typing " : ICommand" after the class declaration as shown in the following code. This addition makes the ApplicationCommands class a child of ICommand and will allow us to implement ICommand:

```
namespace SLViewModelExample
{
    public class ApplicationCommands : ➡
ICommand
    {

    }
}
```

10. Next, place your cursor on ICommand, press Ctrl+. (period), and click Implement interface "ICommand" as shown in Figure 9-11.

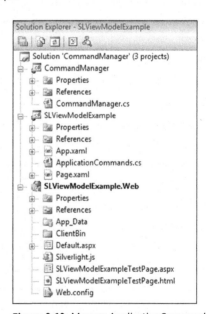

Figure 9-10. My new ApplicationCommands in the Solution Explorer

> *You can also right-click* ICommand, *and click* Implement interface "ICommand", *but I find it much easier to use the keyboard shortcut.*

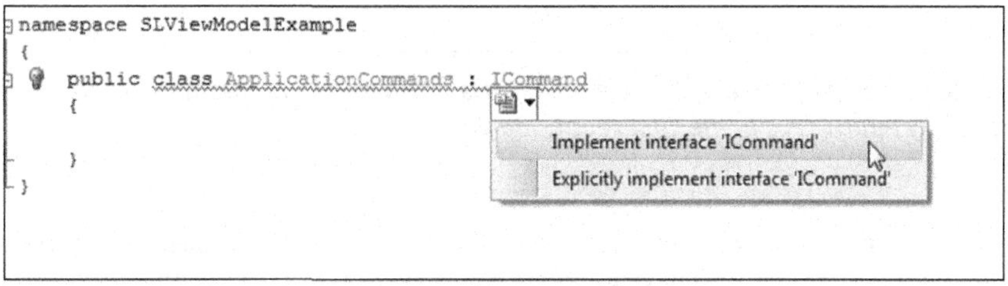

```
namespace SLViewModelExample
{
    public class ApplicationCommands : ICommand
    {

    }
}
```
                                              Implement interface 'ICommand'
                                              Explicitly implement interface 'ICommand'

Figure 9-11. Implement the ICommand Interface.

Your code should now look like this:

```
namespace SLViewModelExample
{
    public class ApplicationCommands : ICommand
    {

        #region ICommand Members

        public bool CanExecute(object parameter)
        {
            throw new NotImplementedException();
        }

        public event EventHandler CanExecuteChanged;

        public void Execute(object parameter)
        {
            throw new NotImplementedException();
        }

        #endregion
    }
}
```

The first member is a Boolean variable that simply asks to see if it is OK to execute the command, and the second member is an event called CanExecuteChanged. This listens and can react whenever the CanExecute Boolean has changed. Finally, there is an Execute method that actually executes the command, as you may have guessed from its name.

11. Set the CanExecute to always return true as follows:

```
public bool CanExecute(object parameter)
{
    return true;
}
```

> For the purposes of this exercise, we are always going to let the command execute, so we simply return true in the CanExecute Boolean.

12. Next, you are going to have the ApplicationCommands raise an event called Executing whenever it is executed. To do this, you have to create a new EventArgs class called ParameterEventArgs (see the following for both the event and the EventArgs class):

```
namespace SLViewModelExample
{
    public class ApplicationCommands : ICommand
    {

        #region ICommand Members

        public bool CanExecute(object parameter)
        {
            return true;
        }

        public event EventHandler CanExecuteChanged;

        public void Execute(object parameter)
        {
            throw new NotImplementedException();
        }

        #endregion

        public event EventHandler<ParameterEventArgs> Executing;
    }

    public class ParameterEventArgs : EventArgs
    {
        public object Parameter;
    }
}
```

13. Next, we will raise the Executing event in the Execute method. This will then raise the Execute command, which fires the ShowMsgBox_Executing method (we will create this method soon). The Button is bound to this Execute command in the XAML:

```
namespace SLViewModelExample
{
    public class ApplicationCommands : ICommand
    {

        #region ICommand Members

        public bool CanExecute(object parameter)
        {
            return true;
        }

        public event EventHandler CanExecuteChanged;

        public void Execute(object parameter)
        {
            if (Executing != null)
                Executing(this, new ParameterEventArgs()
{ Parameter = parameter });
        }

        #endregion

        public event EventHandler<ParameterEventArgs> Executing;
    }

    public class ParameterEventArgs : EventArgs
    {
        public object Parameter;
    }
}
```

Remember the explanation of MVVM earlier? I told you a model never has any logic about what its objects do. It should only tell (via a CommandBinding) its ViewModel that it has been interacted with (via a Click event, for instance). MainPage.xaml will act as our Model, so now we need to create a ViewModel. This is where we are going to create a new ApplicationsCommand and hook it up to the method called ShowMsgBox_Executing. We are then going to create a new ICommand called ShowMsgBox and wire it up to our ApplicationsCommand. Whew, that was a lot of explanation, so let's take it step by step.

14. The first thing we need to do is to create a new class in the SLViewModelExample project called ViewModel. The Solution Explorer should look like the one shown in Figure 9-12.

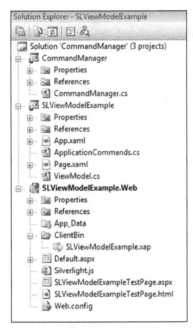

Figure 9-12. The Solution Explorer should look like this now.

15. After the class declaration type " : INotifyPropertyChanged" as follows:

```
namespace SLViewModelExample
{
    public class ViewModel : ➡
INotifyPropertyChanged
    {

    }
}
```

16. Now, press Ctrl+. (period), and click using System.ComponentModel, as shown in Figure 9-13.

> *You can also do this by right-clicking* INotifyPropertyChange *and clicking* using Sytem.ComponentModel;.

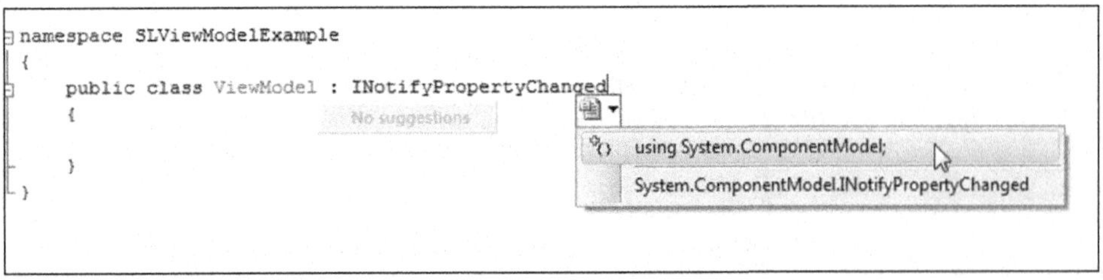

```
namespace SLViewModelExample
{
    public class ViewModel : INotifyPropertyChanged
    {                          No suggestions
                                                  using System.ComponentModel;
    }
                                                  System.ComponentModel.INotifyPropertyChanged
}
```

Figure 9-13. Resolve INotifyPropertyChanged.

17. Now, press Ctrl+. (period) again, and implement the interface as shown in Figure 9-14.

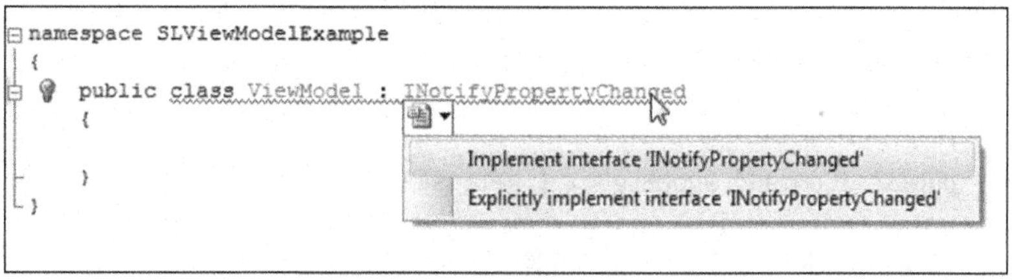

```
namespace SLViewModelExample
{
    public class ViewModel : INotifyPropertyChanged
    {
        [icon ▼]
                    Implement interface 'INotifyPropertyChanged'
                    Explicitly implement interface 'INotifyPropertyChanged'
    }
}
```

Figure 9-14. Implement the INotifyPropertyChanged interface.

Your code should now look like this:

```
namespace SLViewModelExample
{
    public class ViewModel : INotifyPropertyChanged
    {

        #region INotifyPropertyChanged Members

        public event PropertyChangedEventHandler PropertyChanged;

        #endregion
    }
}
```

18. At this point, we can go ahead and make our commands. Make a command in ViewModel.cs called ShowMsgBox as follows:

```
namespace SLViewModelExample
{
    public class ViewModel : INotifyPropertyChanged
    {

        public ICommand ShowMsgBox { get; set; }

        #region INotifyPropertyChanged Members

        public event PropertyChangedEventHandler PropertyChanged;

        #endregion
    }
}
```

19. Now, create a constructor method for ViewModel.cs like so:

```
namespace SLViewModelExample
{
    public class ViewModel : INotifyPropertyChanged
    {
```

```
    public ViewModel()
    {


    }

    public ICommand ShowMsgBox { get; set; }

    #region INotifyPropertyChanged Members

    public event PropertyChangedEventHandler PropertyChanged;

    #endregion
    }
}
```

20. Next, in the constructor, create a new ApplicationCommand:

```
namespace SLViewModelExample
{
    public class ViewModel : INotifyPropertyChanged
    {

        public ViewModel()
        {
            ApplicationCommands cmd = new ApplicationCommands();
        }

        public ICommand ShowMsgBox { get; set; }

        #region INotifyPropertyChanged Members

        public event PropertyChangedEventHandler PropertyChanged;

        #endregion
    }
}
```

21. Now, we need to create the Executing event handler (type cmd.Executing+=, and press the Tab key twice to raise the event and create the event handler):

```
namespace SLViewModelExample
{
    public class ViewModel : INotifyPropertyChanged
    {

        public ViewModel()
        {
            ApplicationCommands cmd = new ApplicationCommands();
```

```
        cmd.Executing += new EventHandler<ParameterEventArgs>
(cmd_Executing);
    }

    void cmd_Executing(object sender, ParameterEventArgs e)
    {
        throw new NotImplementedException();
    }

    public ICommand ShowMsgBox { get; set; }

    #region INotifyPropertyChanged Members

    public event PropertyChangedEventHandler PropertyChanged;

    #endregion
    }
}
```

22. Change the name of the method from cmd_Executing to ShowMsgBox_Executing. Then, erase the default throw new... code, and create the MessageBox code:

```
namespace SLViewModelExample
{
    public class ViewModel : INotifyPropertyChanged
    {

        public ViewModel()
        {
            ApplicationCommands cmd = new ApplicationCommands();
            cmd.Executing += new EventHandler<ParameterEventArgs>
(ShowMsgBox_Executing);
        }

        void ShowMsgBox_Executing(object sender, ParameterEventArgs e)
        {
            MessageBox.Show("ShowMsgBox Command Fired");
        }

        public ICommand ShowMsgBox { get; set; }

        #region INotifyPropertyChanged Members

        public event PropertyChangedEventHandler PropertyChanged;

        #endregion
    }
}
```

23. Now, go in and associate the ShowMsgBox command with cmd as follows:

```
public ViewModel()
{
    ApplicationCommands cmd = new ApplicationCommands();
    cmd.Executing += new EventHandler<ParameterEventArgs>
(ShowMsgBox_Executing);
    ShowMsgBox = cmd;
}
```

24. The next thing you need to do is right-click the SLViewModelExample.Web project in the Solution Explorer and make sure it is set to be the StartUp Project (see Figure 9-15).

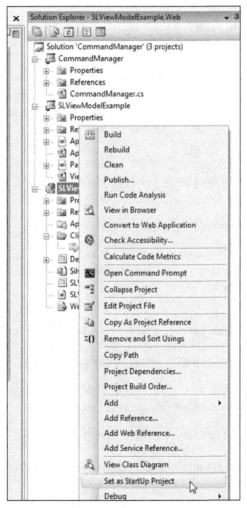

Figure 9-15. Make sure that SLViewModelExample.Web is set as the StartUp Project.

25. Next, right-click the SLViewModelExample project's References folder, and click Add Reference, as shown in Figure 9-16.

Figure 9-16. Start to add a reference to SLViewModelExample.

26. In the Add Reference dialog box, select the Projects tab, click CommandManager, and click OK (see Figure 9-17).

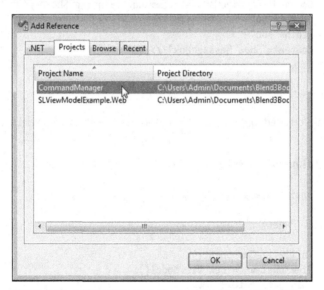

Figure 9-17. Add a reference to the CommandManager project.

27. Now, in MainPage.xaml, we need to add a namespace that we will call Commands that references the CommandManager project:

```
<UserControl
    x:Class="SLViewModelExample.Page"
    xmlns="http://schemas.microsoft.com/winfx/2006/xaml/presentation"
    xmlns:x="http://schemas.microsoft.com/winfx/2006/xaml"
```

```
    xmlns:Commands="clr-namespace:CommandManager;assembly=
CommandManager"
        Width="400"
        Height="300">
```

28. After that, we can create a Button control that uses the CommandManager to fire the ShowMsgBox command:

```
<UserControl
    x:Class="SLViewModelExample.Page"
    xmlns="http://schemas.microsoft.com/winfx/2006/xaml/presentation"
    xmlns:x="http://schemas.microsoft.com/winfx/2006/xaml"
    xmlns:Commands="clr-namespace:CommandManager;assembly=
CommandManager"
        Width="400"
        Height="300">
        <Grid
            x:Name="LayoutRoot"
            Background="White">

            <Button
                Commands:CommandManager.CommandEventName="Click"
                Commands:CommandManager.Command="{Binding ShowMsgBox}"
                Height="50"
                Width="100"
                Content="Show MessageBox" />

        </Grid>
</UserControl>
```

29. The final thing you need to do is to set the DataContext in MainPage.xaml.cs to a new instance of ViewModel:

```
namespace SLViewModelExample
{
    public partial class Page : UserControl
    {
        public Page()
        {
            InitializeComponent();
            ViewModel vm = new ViewModel();
            this.DataContext = vm;
        }
    }
}
```

If you press F5 to compile and run the application, you can click the Button and see the MessageBox that shows us that our command is firing correctly (see Figure 9-18).

Figure 9-18. This MessageBox shows us that our ShowMsgBox Command is firing correctly.

And there you have it, a very good implementation of the MVVM: Our View is, in fact, very dumb in that it is not firing any of its own code-behind when the Button is clicked. Rather, it merely specifies in XAML what command, contained in the ViewModel, it would like to run. The MVVM then runs code that provides the functionality.

"Why go through all of the trouble we have gone through here to learn the MVVM UI design pattern?" you ask. Good question. MVVM has advantages when creating applications. First, it greatly improves the already improved designer-developer workflow. The developers now do not have to even touch the View; they work strictly in the ViewModel. Conversely, the use of MVVM means the designers work strictly in the View. Further, the most cost in an application's lifetime is due to maintenance. Unfortunately, maintenance can and often does cause bugs that break the application. Using MVVM allows for unit testing, that is, software validation that a unit of code works. Because there is such a strict disconnect between the Model, View, and ViewModel, unit testing is very simple and effective. This means your MVVM application will have less bugs and thus be more cost effective during its lifetime. Finally, MVVM allows for two-way data binding between a View and a ViewModel. For example, say you have a variable x located in a ViewModel that is equal to 0. You can use a DataTrigger to bind what View represents this ViewModel based on the value of x. So, if x is 0, the View named ZeroView is used. If x is 1, OneView is used. And you can be sure this variable will not break anything, because the views have no logic and can be swapped out quite easily. Being able to interchange views also allows for greater templating, and as you already know, templates save time and money.

You can download my project at http://windowspresentationfoundation.com/Blend3Book/CommandManager.zip.

Summary

In this chapter, you learned about some of the most-often-used EventHandlers. You also learned how to use MouseEnter and MouseLeave to create rollover effects for buttons. Finally, you learned about a very popular application pattern called Model-View-ViewModel (MVVM). You then created a reusable Silverlight class library and a ViewModel class that contained a command called ShowMsgBox. After that, you wired up a button in the View that specified what command in the ViewModel it wanted to fire. In the next chapter, you are going to learn all about classes, interfaces, and how to create polymorphic classes.

Chapter 10

CLASSES AND INTERFACES

What this chapter covers:

- Different types of classes
- Using interfaces to crate polymorphic classes

As we briefly discussed back in Chapter 3, classes are a very important construct of object-oriented programming and could be considered a blueprint for creating objects. Classes encapsulate state and behavior. Behavior is further encapsulated into methods (sometimes referred to as functions), and state is encapsulated in data placeholders called member variables (also known as properties). There are different types of classes, and we will go over many of them in this chapter. Interfaces are an object-oriented programming construct similar to classes. I will show you how you can use interfaces to create polymorphic classes. Finally, I am going to show you a typical scenario in which you would want to refactor behaviors into a separate class object.

Static classes vs. concrete classes

You already know a little bit about creating classes, as we created a Storyboard helper class back in Chapter 5. This was what is known as a **static class**, which is a class that has methods that can be run without actually instantiating an instance of the class. A **concrete class**, on the other hand, is a class that can have either static or concrete members, methods, or properties. If the member says a method is concrete, the class would need to be instantiated before it is used. For example, say I create a concrete class named Peter. In the Peter class, I have a concrete property named Occupation. I also have a concrete method that encapsulates a behavior; let's call that method GotoTheGym. In order for me to be able to read or set the Occupation property or for me to make use of the GotoTheGym method, I would have to create an instance of the Peter class like so:

```
Peter myPeterInstance = new Peter();
```

Now, I can set the Occupation property as follows:

```
myPeterInstance.Occupation = "IT Engineer";
```

I can also use the methods of the Peter class like this:

```
myPeterInstance.GotoTheGym();
```

I find that static classes are very good for helper classes that encapsulate functionality used throughout an application. A great example of this is the fader Storyboard helper class we created back in Chapter 5.

Abstract classes

An **abstract class** is a class that cannot be instantiated. These classes are designed to be parent classes that child classes can inherit from (we discussed class inheritance back in Chapter 3). Abstract classes contain undefined and unimplemented abstract method bodies that the children are required to implement and define. It is this construct that allows for polymorphic classes, as the parent abstract class only requires that the concrete child classes define and implement its methods. It does not care how those child classes actually implement them, so two different child classes can implement the parent's abstract methods differently. I will show you an example of this later in the chapter.

Sealed classes

The sealed modifier is used to make certain that the class cannot be used as a base class for another class. This also means that a sealed class cannot be an abstract class. Declaring a class as sealed also enables some runtime optimizations. The most notable optimization occurs because it is possible to transform virtual function member invocations on sealed class instances into nonvirtual invocations.

Partial classes

Partial classes are classes that can be split over multiple definitions. This is usually done to deal with large amounts of code. In Silverlight, however, classes are commonly split in UserControls because the XAML portion and code-behind are both partial classes that are merged by the complier at runtime. As a matter of fact, when you create a new Silverlight project, you will see that a default Page. xaml with a code-behind page of Page.xam.cs is created for you. These two files are in fact partial classes, as shown in the following example:

```
namespace SilverlightApplication1
{
    public partial class Page : UserControl
    {
        public Page()
        {
            InitializeComponent();
        }
    }
}
```

InitializeComponent(); is the method that actually merges the two partial class classes definitions into one class.

Access modifiers: public vs. private classes

Both classes and class members (properties and methods) can be declared as public or private (among other things). The following C# examples show both private and public classes:

```
public class PublicClass
{

}

private class PrivateClass
{

}
```

If a class property is set to private, it can only be set within the class itself. Further, even if the class is instantiated, the private members cannot be accessed from outside the class. For example, if in the Occupation property in the Peter class that we created earlier, we instantiated an instance of Peter, we would not be able to read or write the value of that property. If you were to declare a public class, and in that same file declare a private class within this new public class, only the public class (in the same file) would have access to the private class. More commonly, though, classes are declared as public, and certain members are subsequently declared as private or public.

Internal classes

Internal classes are classes that are only accessible from other classes located in the same project or assembly. If you were to create a new Silverlight project called MySLProject and create an internal class called MyInternalClass, you would be able to access it from anywhere in MySLProject. If you were to add a new project to MySLProject called MyNewSLProject and then try to access MyInternalClass from it, you would not be able to. It is also worth noting that if you do not declare a class modifier, then by default the class will be internal.

Protected classes

Protected classes are like private classes in that they can be nested classes that can be accessed from the public class they are nested in. But unlike private classes, protected classes can be accessed from subclasses of the class that defines the protected member.

Interfaces

Interfaces make up a group of behaviors, mostly methods and properties, that can belong to any class. Any class that inherits an interface is required to implement the methods and/or properties of that interface. This allows for polymorphic classes, because each class can implement the methods and properties of the interface differently. Also, any class that implements a particular interface is guaranteed to contain all the methods and properties that interface defines. To better demonstrate this, let's go ahead and create a new Silverlight project called InterfaceProject in Visual Studio. Use the settings shown in Figure 10-1.

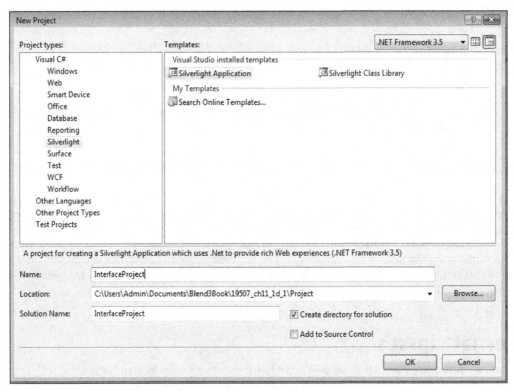

Figure 10-1. Create a new Silverlight project called InterfaceProject.

When the New Silverlight Application dialog box appears, uncheck Host the Silverlight application in a new Web site, and click OK, as shown in Figure 10-2.

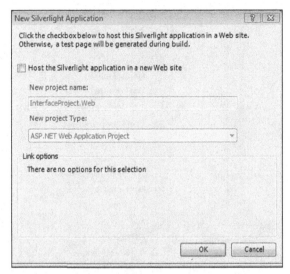

Figure 10-2. Uncheck "Host the Silverlight application in a new Web site", and click OK.

Now, let's create a superclass called Vehicle. This class will be the base class for all of our other types of vehicles, namely Car, Motorcycle, Airplane, Scooter, and Skateboard. Vehicle is going to inherit from two interfaces called IModeOfTransportation (indicates whether the vehicle moves using wheels, wings, etc.) that has a property called ModeOfTransportation and INumberOfSeats (indicates how many seats the vehicle has) that has a method called ShowNumberOfSeats. In Vehicle, we are going to implement ShowModeOfTransportation as an abstract method. This will require classes that derive from it to implement the method. After that, we are going to implement ShowNumberOfSeats as a virtual method, which means that classes that derive from Vehicle can choose to implement it or not. If they do, they can override the default method. If not, they will inherit the parent's implementation. So, let's go ahead and create Vehicle now:

1. Right-click the project in Visual Studio's Solution Explorer.
2. Left-click Add ➤ Class, as shown in Figure 10-3.

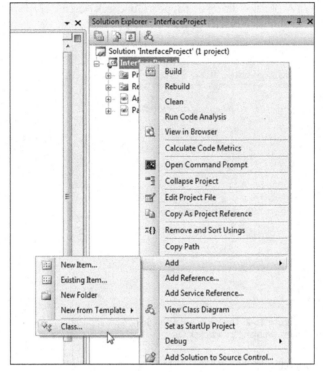

Figure 10-3. Choose to add a new Class in Solution Explorer.

3. Name the new class Vehicle, and click the Add button.

4. Repeat this process, but name the other new class IModeOfTransportation.

5. Change IModeOfTransportation from a public class to an interface (interfaces are public by default, so there's no need to declare it as such). My code follows:

```
namespace InterfaceProject
{
    interface IModeOfTransportation
    {

    }
}
```

6. Add a method in IModeOfTransportation called ShowModeOfTransportation, like I have done in the following lines (notice there is no method body; you will see why shortly):

```
namespace InterfaceProject
{
    interface IModeOfTransportation
    {
        void ShowModeOfTransportation();
    }
}
```

7. Next, create a new class called INumberOfSeats, and change it to an interface as follows:

```
namespace InterfaceProject
{
    interface INumberOfSeats
    {

    }
}
```

8. Add a method called ShowNumberOfSeats:

```
namespace InterfaceProject
{
    interface INumberOfSeats
    {
        void ShowNumberOfSeats();
    }
}
```

9. Now, we need to go into Vehicle and have it inherit IModeOfTransportation by adding : IModeOfTransportation after the class declaration like so:

```
namespace InterfaceProject
{
    public class Vehicle : IModeOfTransportation
    {

    }
}
```

10. When you see the helper icon appear, click it or type Ctrl+. (period), and click Implement interface 'IModeOfTransportation' (see Figure 10-4).

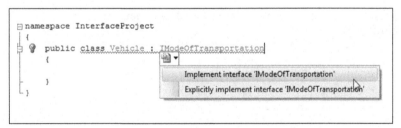

Figure 10-4. Implement IModeOfTransportation.

The resulting code follows:

```
namespace InterfaceProject
{
    public class Vehicle : IModeOfTransportation
    {

        #region IModeOfTransportation Members
```

235

```
        public void ShowModeOfTransportation()
        {
            throw new NotImplementedException();
        }

        #endregion
    }
}
```

11. Now, make the Vehicle class abstract so that it cannot be instantiated:

```
public abstract class Vehicle : IModeOfTransportation
```

12. Still inside the Vehicle class, change IModeOfTransportation to make it abstract and remove the autogenerated method body, as shown in the following code:

```
namespace InterfaceProject
{
    public abstract class Vehicle : IModeOfTransportation
    {

        #region IModeOfTransportation Members

        public abstract void ShowModeOfTransportation();

        #endregion
    }
}
```

13. Now, make Vehicle inherit from INumberOfSeats as well, and press Ctrl+. (period) to implement the interface:

```
namespace InterfaceProject
{
    public abstract class Vehicle : IModeOfTransportation,
INumberOfSeats
    {

        #region IModeOfTransportation Members

        public abstract void ModeOfTransportation();

        #endregion

        #region INumberOfSeats Members

        public void NumberOfSeats()
        {
            throw new NotImplementedException();
        }
```

```
        #endregion
    }
}
```

Because we don't want to force the child classes to implement this method, we are going to make it virtual and provide a default implementation that the children can inherit. We are going to just write a message in Visual Studio's debug window whenever this default implementation is fired. Let's do that now:

14. Change the method to be virtual, and erase the default Throw new. . . line, so your code looks like the following:

```
public virtual void NumberOfSeats()
{

}
```

15. Next, inside the method, type Debug, press Ctrl+. (period), highlight using System.Diagnostics; as show in Figure 10-5. Press Enter.

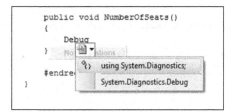

Figure 10-5. Resolve the Debug namespace.

16. Now, write a default debug message like this one:

```
public virtual void NumberOfSeats()
{
    Debug.WriteLine("Vehicle has no seats by default");
}
```

Now that we are done with our superclass and our two interfaces, it is time create some child classes that derive from Vehicle.

17. In Solution Explorer, right-click the project, and click Add ➤ Class.

18. Name the new class Car, and click Add.

19. Have the new Car class extend the Vehicle class like this:

```
namespace InterfaceProject
{
    public class Car : Vehicle
    {

    }
}
```

20. Press Ctrl+. (period), and when IntelliSense gives you the option, click Implement abstract class 'Vehicle', as shown in Figure 10-6.

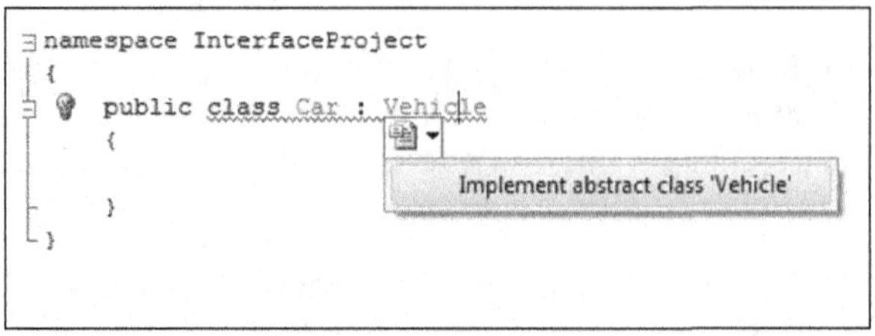

```
namespace InterfaceProject
{
    public class Car : Vehicle
    {
                    [icon] ▼
                         Implement abstract class 'Vehicle'
    }
}
```

Figure 10-6. Implement the Vehicle class.

Your code for the Car class should now look like this:

```
namespace InterfaceProject
{
    public class Car : Vehicle
    {

        public override void ModeOfTransportation()
        {
            throw new NotImplementedException();
        }
    }
}
```

Notice that only the ModeOfTransportation was implemented, because we implemented that method in Vehicle as abstract, meaning that children of Vehicle are required to implement it. Conversely, we implemented NumberOfSeats as virtual so that the children could choose to implement it or not. So, let's go ahead and override the default implementation of NumberOfSeats in the Car class now:

```
namespace InterfaceProject
{
    public class Car : Vehicle
    {

        public override void ModeOfTransportation()
        {
            throw new NotImplementedException();
        }

        public override void NumberOfSeats()
        {
            Debug.WriteLine("A Car has four seats");
        }
    }
}
```

21. Now, erase the default Throw new. . . code from ModeOfTransportation, and put in another Debug statement as I have done in the following example:

```
namespace InterfaceProject
{
    public class Car : Vehicle
    {

        public override void ModeOfTransportation()
        {
            Debug.WriteLine("A Car's mode of transportation is Wheels");
        }

        public override void NumberOfSeats()
        {
            Debug.WriteLine("A Car has four seats");
        }
    }
}
```

22. Before we get ahead of ourselves, let's open MainPage.xaml.cs and instantiate a Car. Notice, in the following code, that I declare c as a Vehicle. I could have declared it as a Car using Car c = new Car();. But because Vehicle is the superclass for Car, I can do it either way:

```
namespace InterfaceProject
{
    public partial class Page : UserControl
    {
        public Page()
        {
            InitializeComponent();
            Vehicle c = new Car();
        }
    }
}
```

23. Now, we can fire the methods of our newly created object:

```
namespace InterfaceProject
{
    public partial class Page : UserControl
    {
        public Page()
        {
            InitializeComponent();
            Vehicle c = new Car();
            c.ModeOfTransportation();
            c.NumberOfSeats();
        }
    }
}
```

239

24. If you press F5 to compile and run the application, you can see in Visual Studio's Output window the Debug statements (see Figure 10-7).

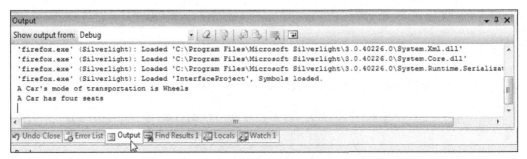

Figure 10-7. You can see the Debug statements in Visual Studio's Output window.

Thus far, all we have done is to create an abstract superclass that implements two interfaces, IModeOfTransportation and INumberOfSeats. The superclass implements the first interface as an abstract method with no method body. This requires that children implement the method themselves. The superclass implements the second interface as a virtual method and defines a default method body that the children can inherit. The children may also choose to override this method. We then create a Car class that extends the Vehicle class, and we chose to override both methods and put in some Debug statements. So, you may be asking, "How does this make for polymorphic classes?" Well, let's stop the running project and add another class called Airplane, and I will show you how.

25. Right-click the project in Visual Studio's Solution Explorer, and click Add ➤ Class.

26. Name the new Class Airplane, and click Add.

27. Have the new class extend the Vehicle class, and implement both interfaces so that your code looks like the following:

```
namespace InterfaceProject
{
    public class Airplane : Vehicle
    {

        public override void ModeOfTransportation()
        {
            throw new NotImplementedException();
        }
        public override void NumberOfSeats()
        {

        }
    }
}
```

28. Now, put in some Debug statements like the ones that follow. You will have to resolve the Debug namespace.

```
namespace InterfaceProject
{
    public class Airplane : Vehicle
    {

        public override void ModeOfTransportation()
        {
            Debug.WriteLine("An airplane's mode of transportation
is Wings");
        }
        public override void NumberOfSeats()
        {
            Debug.WriteLine("A plane has hundreds of seats");
        }
    }
}
```

29. Now, go into Page1.xaml.cs, and create a new Plane object:

```
namespace InterfaceProject
{
    public partial class Page : UserControl
    {
        public Page()
        {
            InitializeComponent();
            Vehicle c = new Car();
            c.ModeOfTransportation();
            c.NumberOfSeats();
            Vehicle a = new Airplane();
            a.ModeOfTransportation();
            a.NumberOfSeats();
        }
    }
}
```

If you press F5 to compile and run the application, your Output window should look like the one shown in Figure 10-8.

Figure 10-8. Your Output window should now look like this.

Now, you have two polymorphic classes, Car and Airplane, because they both implement their parents' methods differently. Let's go ahead now and create a new class called Skateboard that extends Vehicle and only overrides the required ModeOfTransportation method. The code for your new class should look like this:

```
namespace InterfaceProject
{
    public class Skateboard : Vehicle
    {

        public override void ModeOfTransportation()
        {
            throw new NotImplementedException();
        }
    }
}
```

30. Now, remove the default Throw new... code, and add a Debug statement like so:

```
namespace InterfaceProject
{
    public class Skateboard : Vehicle
    {

        public override void ModeOfTransportation()
        {
            Debug.WriteLine("A skateboard's mode of transportation
is legs");
        }
    }
}
```

31. Next, in Page.xaml.cs, instantiate a new Skateboard:

```
namespace InterfaceProject
{
    public partial class Page : UserControl
    {
        public Page()
        {
            InitializeComponent();
            Vehicle c = new Car();
            c.ModeOfTransportation();
            c.NumberOfSeats();
            Vehicle a = new Airplane();
            a.ModeOfTransportation();
            a.NumberOfSeats();
            Skateboard s = new Skateboard();
        }
    }
}
```

32. Now, fire the ModeOfTransportation and NumberOfSeats methods for your newly created object:

```
namespace InterfaceProject
{
    public partial class Page : UserControl
    {
        public Page()
        {
            InitializeComponent();
            Vehicle c = new Car();
            c.ModeOfTransportation();
            c.NumberOfSeats();
            Vehicle a = new Airplane();
            a.ModeOfTransportation();
            a.NumberOfSeats();
            Skateboard s = new Skateboard();
            s.ModeOfTransportation();
            s.NumberOfSeats();
        }
    }
}
```

If you again press F5 to compile and run the application, Visual Studio's Output window should look like the one shown in Figure 10-9.

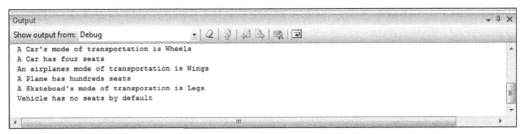

Figure 10-9. Your Output window should write out the mode of transportation and number of seats for a Car, an Airplane, and a Skateboard..

Notice that Skateboard inherited its parent's implementation of NumberOfSeats? This is because we chose not to override the method. Now, I challenge you to create two more classes that derive from Vehicle, Scooter and Motorcycle, on your own. They both have seats, so you are going to need to override both ModeOfTransportation and NumberOfSeats methods.

Summary

In this chapter, you learned about the different types of classes and when to use them. You also learned about interfaces. Next, you created a project that shows you how you can use interfaces and superclasses to create polymorphic child classes. These polymorphic classes have the ability to override the methods of their parent classes and have implementations different from other child classes.

In the next chapter, we are going to learn about a very powerful feature in Silverlight—the ability to reuse objects by making use of templatizing. This is done using `ControlTemplates`, `Styles` and custom `UserControls`.

Chapter 11

CONTROLTEMPLATES, STYLES, AND CUSTOM USERCONTROLS

What this chapter covers:

- Understanding ControlTemplates
- Understanding how Styles work with ControlTemplates
- Creating a Button ControlTemplate
- Creating Styles and using them to override Silverlight controls
- Using Styles to mandate how controls display their content
- Using ResourceDictionarys
- Applying resources to Silverlight controls
- Using Styles and ControlTemplates to create your own custom Silverlight UserControls
- Creating and using custom UserControls
- Using DependencyPropertys and custom DependencyPropertys

A very important concept in object-oriented programming is that you should be able to create something once and reuse it over and over again. Of course, this generally means you can reuse a resource in one application, but in Silverlight, you can take this concept further and reuse a resource in other applications. ControlTemplates and UserControls allow you to do just that. I have been working with Silverlight now for well over three years, and in that time, I have been able to create my own libraries of resources that I can now reuse in new applications that I create. This allows me to develop new applications faster, because I don't have to re-create new resources. I just add a reference to them in my Silverlight applications and then make use of them. In this chapter, you are going to create a Style for a Silverlight Button control that will contain a ControlTemplate, and change that ControlTemplate to have the Button show an Image control. You are then going to create a ResourceDictionary and move the Button Style to it. Finally, you are going to take everything you have learned and create a custom UserControl.

Understanding the ControlTemplate

A ControlTemplate is nothing more than a resource, usually defined in a Style, that allows you to specify the way a control is displayed in the visual tree. It literally allows you to build a template for a Silverlight control, hence the name ControlTemplate. You can create ControlTemplates for a host of Silverlight controls such as Buttons, ListBoxes, and so on. Further, once you create a ControlTemplate, say, for a Button, you are then able to make use of that resource throughout your application. Let's move forward and create a new Silverlight project, create a ControlTemplate, and then apply that ControlTemplate to other controls.

> *ControlTemplates can be defined right in the control's XAML (called inline inside the XAML node), but it is best practice to define them in a resource.*

Creating a Button ControlTemplate

You'll start off by creating a new Silverlight application project in Visual Studio 2008:

1. Open Visual Studio 2008.
2. Select Silverlight Application from the Visual Studio installed templates.
3. Enter a project name of ControlTemplateProject (see Figure 11-1), and click OK.
4. When the New Silverlight Application dialog box appears, leave the default settings and click OK.

In this project, you are going to create a ControlTemplate for a Silverlight Button control. You are then going to create a few Silverlight Buttons and apply your new ControlTemplate to them to see how simple it is to reuse a ControlTemplate resource. So, let's get started:

5. Open your project in Visual Studio, if it's not still open. Open Blend 3 and navigate to where you saved your project, and then open the .sln (solution) file.

Now you should have your project open in both Visual Studio 2008 and Blend 3. As you probably know by now, this is the typical workflow for me, as I like to do my design work in Blend 3 and then use Visual Studio to create my functionality (EventHandlers, etc.). With that in mind, you'll use Blend 3 to design your new Button ControlTemplate.

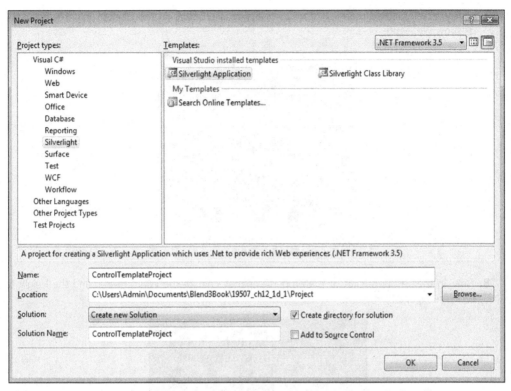

Figure 11-1. Create a new Silverlight application called ControlTemplateProject in Visual Studio.

6. In the Projects panel, double-click Page.xaml, as shown in Figure 11-2.

Figure 11-2. Open Page.xaml.

7. Give yourself a little breathing room by selecting UserControl in the Objects and Timeline panel, as shown in Figure 11-3.

Figure 11-3. Select UserControl in the Objects and Timeline panel.

8. Now, in the Layout bucket of the Properties panel, change the Width to 800 and the Height to 600 (see Figure 11-4).

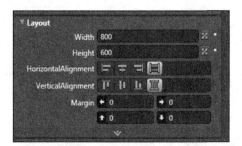

Figure 11-4. Change the height and width of the application.

9. Select the Rectangle tool in the toolbar, and draw a Rectangle control in the workspace that is roughly 100×50 display units. Use the radius handles to give your new Rectangle rounded edges (see Figure 11-5).

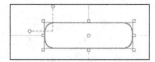

Figure 11-5. Draw a Rectangle with rounded edges in the workspace.

10. Make sure the Rectangle is selected, and in the Brushes section of the Properties panel, click Fill, and select the Gradient brush option (see Figure 11-6).

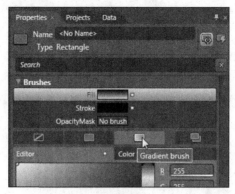

Figure 11-6. Give your Rectangle a gradient brush fill in the Brushes section of the Properties panel.

Go ahead and play with the gradient fill colors as well as the Brush Transform tool until you have something you are pleased with. Your button should look something like the one shown in Figure 11-7.

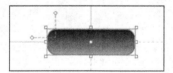

Figure 11-7. I created this gradient fill by adjusting the colors in the Brushes section of the Properties panel, and by adjusting the gradient with the Brush Transform tool.

Now that you have a Rectangle that you are happy with, you need to tell Blend that you want to use this as a ControlTemplate for a Button. The easiest way to do this is by using Blend's Make Into Control feature as follows:.

11. Make sure your Rectangle is selected, and then click Tools ➤ Make Into Control.

12. When Blend's Make Into Control dialog box appears, select Button as the Control type: name it BlueButtonControl, as shown in Figure 11-8; and click OK.

Figure 11-8. Make the Rectangle into a Button control using Blend's new Make Into Control feature.

Figure 11-9. This tells you that you are editing the BlueButtonControl ControlTemplate.

Figure 11-10. The Rectangle has been turned into a Silverlight Button control.

Blend 3 now wraps your Rectangle into a Grid with a ContentPresenter (which is what displays the Button's text). While you are still in Page.xaml, you are now only editing the BlueButtonControl's ControlTemplate. You can see this visually by looking at the top of your visual tree in the Objects and Timeline panel where it says BlueButtonControl (Button Template) (see Figure 11-9).

If you want to stop editing this ControlTemplate, you can click the button with an arrow icon just to the left of the words BlueButtonControl in the Objects and Timeline panel. Go ahead and click that button now to stop editing BlueButtonControl.

Now if you look at the Objects and Timeline panel, you will see that what was formerly your Rectangle has now been replaced with an actual Silverlight Button control (see Figure 11-10).

Now, the newly created Button control, formerly a Rectangle, has all of the capabilities of a normal Silverlight Button control, but the difference is that instead of using Silverlight's basic Button ControlTemplate, it uses yours. Pretty cool, huh? You'll give your new Button a little functionality to prove it is just like any other Silverlight standard Button control, but before you do, I think it would be good to delve into the XAML and see exactly what Blend 3 did for you under the hood.

13. Before you take a look at the XAML, give the new Button control a name. Name your Button myButton in the Name field of the Properties panel, as shown in Figure 11-11.

Figure 11-11. Name the new Silverlight Button control MyButton.

14. Now click the XAML tab (see Figure 11-12) to see the XAML that Blend 3 has created for your myButton control.

Figure 11-12. Click the XAML tab in Blend 3.

Once you click the button, you will see something very similar to, if not exactly like, the following:

```
<UserControl
    xmlns="http://schemas.microsoft.com/winfx/2006/xaml/presentation"
    xmlns:x="http://schemas.microsoft.com/winfx/2006/xaml"
    xmlns:vsm="clr-namespace:System.Windows;assembly=System.Windows"
x:Class="ControlTemplateProject.Page"
    Width="800" Height="600">
    <UserControl.Resources>
        <Style x:Key="BlueButtonControl" TargetType="Button">
            <Setter Property="Template">
                <Setter.Value>
                    <ControlTemplate TargetType="Button">
                        <Grid>
                            <vsm:VisualStateManager.VisualStateGroups>
                                <vsm:VisualStateGroup x:Name=
"FocusStates">

                                    <vsm:VisualState x:Name="Focused"/>
                                    <vsm:VisualState x:Name=
"Unfocused"/>

                                </vsm:VisualStateGroup>
```

```xml
                                    <vsm:VisualStateGroup x:Name=
"CommonStates">

                                        <vsm:VisualState x:Name="Normal"/>
                                        <vsm:VisualState x:Name=
"MouseOver"/>

                                        <vsm:VisualState x:Name="Pressed"/>
                                        <vsm:VisualState x:Name=
"Disabled"/>

                                    </vsm:VisualStateGroup>
                                </vsm:VisualStateManager.VisualStateGroups>
                                <Rectangle Stroke="#FF000000" RadiusX=
"13" RadiusY="13">

                                    <Rectangle.Fill>
                                        <LinearGradientBrush EndPoint=
"0.5,1"
StartPoint="0.5,0">

                                            <LinearGradientBrush
.RelativeTransform>

                                                <TransformGroup>
                                                    <ScaleTransform CenterX
="0.5"
CenterY="0.5"/>

                                                    <SkewTransform CenterX=
"0.5"
CenterY="0.5"/>

                                                    <RotateTransform Center
X="0.5"
CenterY="0.5"/>

                                                    <TranslateTransform X=
"0.013" Y="0.026"/>

                                                </TransformGroup>
                                            </LinearGradientBrush
.RelativeTransform>

                                            <GradientStop Color=
"#FF050066"/>

                                            <GradientStop Color=
"#FFB3AFF6" Offset="1"/>
                                        </LinearGradientBrush>
                                    </Rectangle.Fill>
                                </Rectangle>
                                <ContentPresenter HorizontalAlignment=
"{TemplateBinding HorizontalContentAlignment}" VerticalAlignment=
"{TemplateBinding VerticalContentAlignment}"/>
                            </Grid>
                        </ControlTemplate>
                    </Setter.Value>
                </Setter>
            </Style>
        </UserControl.Resources>
        <Grid x:Name="LayoutRoot" Background="White">
```

```
<Button x:Name="myButton" Height="39" HorizontalAlignment=
"Left" Margin="229,230,0,0" Style="{StaticResource BlueButtonControl}"
VerticalAlignment="Top" Width="141" Content="Button"/>

    </Grid>
</UserControl>
```

Notice that, in the main Grid (named LayoutRoot by default), there is only one UI FrameWork element: a Button control with the x:Name of myButton.

> For easier-to-read XAML, I like to reformat my code with line breaks, as I've done here:
>
> ```
> <Button
>  x:Name="myButton"
>  Height="39"
>  HorizontalAlignment="Left"
>  Margin="229,230,0,0"
>  Style="{StaticResource BlueButtonControl}"
>  VerticalAlignment="Top"
>  Width="141"
>  Content="Button"/>
> ```

Let's break down exactly what Blend 3 did:

1. It created a UserControl.Resources section.
2. In the UserControl.Resources section, it created a Style for you called BlueButtonControl (the name you provided in the Make Into Control dialog box).
3. Blend then created a setter that defines a Template. Setters are how ControlTemplates set properties for the object they are defining.
4. In that Template, Blend created a ControlTemplate with the TargetType of Button.
5. In that ControlTemplate, Blend defined how the Button will be displayed by creating the following:
   - A Grid
   - A Rectangle
   - A Rectangle.Fill
   - A ContentPresenter (this contains a TextBlock that says Button)
   - A ControlTemplate.VisualStateManager to define how interaction is handled
6. Blend then bound the Style of your Button control to the StaticResource of your BlueButtonControl Style.

Because you just created a Style that holds your ControlTemplate, I feel this would be a good time to take a closer look at Styles.

Creating Styles

Styles allow you to set properties for controls. In a project, say you have a lot of ListBoxes that have to look very different from an ordinary ListBox (with the default style). You could create a Style that defines how a ListBox should look and then apply that Style to any other ListBox you wish. However, what if you want to reuse your Style in another XAML file other than Page.xaml? To reuse a Style in another XAML file, you can define it in a file called a ResourceDictionary that is accessible to your entire application, not just Page.xaml. In fact, it is best practice to put all of your Styles in a ResourceDictionary. I'll walk you through the steps for creating a ResourceDictionary for your ControlTemplateProject project now:

1. Click the Design button located just above the XAML button to switch back to Design view. Then, on the toolbar, click the Asset Library button and do a search for listbox.

2. When you see the ListBox control appear, click it.

3. Draw a ListBox in the workspace with a width of about 200 and a height of about 400 display units.

4. Right-click the ListBox and select Edit Control Parts (Template) ➤ Edit a Copy. This will create a Style for the ListBox that we can edit.

5. In the Create Style Resource dialog box, give the new Style resource a name of MyListBoxStyle.

6. In the Define in section of the dialog box, find where it says Resource Dictionary. Notice that Resource Dictionary is grayed out, because there is no ResourceDictionary yet. To create one, click the New button.

7. Blend then opens a Resource Dictionary dialog box and asks what name you want to give to your new ResourceDictionary. Name the ResourceDictionary applicationResourceDict, and click OK.

8. Notice now that the Resource Dictionary option is no longer gray. Blend has also selected it for you and entered the name of the newly created ResourceDictionary, applicationResource-Dict. Click OK.

Blend opens the newly created applicationResourceDict.xaml file. Here you can edit the Style of MyListBoxStyle to change the way the ListBox is displayed:

1. Select [Border] (a Border control) from the Objects and Timeline panel.

2. In the Properties panel under the Layout section, change the HorizontalAlignment property from the default Stretch to Center (see Figure 11-13).

Figure 11-13. Choose Center for the HorizontalAlignment option.

Notice now that the ListBox contents change to center align-ment. If you go back to Page.xaml, by clicking the Return Scope to [UserControl] button located at the very top of the visual tree (see Figure 11-14), you see . . . wait, nothing! That is because the ListBox does not have any content yet. To add items, continue with these steps:

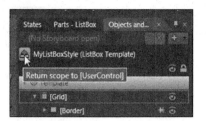

3. Right-click the ListBox and click Add ListBoxItem.

4. Repeat one time to add a total of two generic ListBoxItems.

Figure 11-14. Stop editing the Style by clicking the Return to Scope button.

Now you can see that the ListBoxItems are positioned in the center of the ListBox, as shown in Figure 11-15.

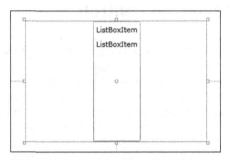

Figure 11-15. Changing the ListBox Style will affect the way your ListBox displays its content.

What if you wanted to create a new ListBox and apply your new Style to it? Here is how that is done:

5. Select the Last Used tool on the toolbar, and draw a ListBox in the workspace.

6. Right-click the new ListBox and click Add ListBox Item.

7. Repeat the previous step twice to add two more generic ListBoxItems.

8. Right-click the new ListBox, click Edit Control Parts (Template) ➤ Apply Resource ➤ MyListBoxStyle.

Notice that, right away, the new ListBox displays its content exactly the same way as the first ListBox—that is, center-justified (see Figure 11-16). This is useful because it easily allows us to modify the way a ListBox displays its content. In a large application, this can save vast amounts of time.

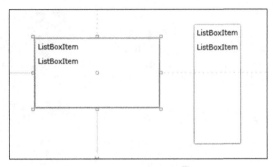

Figure 11-16. Styles can easily be applied to other controls of the same type.

Overriding default Styles for controls

You may be thinking to yourself, "Big deal!" I would not blame you, because this is a pretty boring example of applying Styles. To show you the real power of Styles, let me present you with a scenario that I recently faced. In an application I was working on, I had to populate a ListBox with PNG images. That was easy enough to do with Styles, but when one of the ListBox items (a PNG image) was selected, the background of that ListBoxItem turned blue. Turning blue when selected is the default behavior of a ListBox. If you want to see this behavior for yourself, press F5 to run the application, and click one of the ListBox items; you will see that its background will turn blue.

This default behavior presented a problem for me in my application, because the designer thought it looked horrible and said that the blue background was not what he had in mind when conceptualizing the application. So, I was tasked with getting rid of the background. After some thought, I eventually came up with the idea to use Styles to override the default behavior. This, to me, did seem like a big deal, and I feel it would be a good exercise for you to duplicate the steps I followed to override the default behavior of the ListBox:

1. In Page.xaml, select a ListBoxItem in the Objects and Timeline panel (see Figure 11-17).

2. Right-click the ListBoxItem and select Edit Control Parts (Template) ➤ Edit a Copy.

Figure 11-17. Select any ListBoxItem in the Objects and Timeline panel.

3. Leave the default name of ListBoxItemStyle1, and select the ResourceDictionary that you created earlier named applicationResourceDict. Blend 3 opens the ResourceDictionary and shows you a ListBoxItem, as you can see in Figure 11-18.

Figure 11-18. Blend allows you to visually edit your new ListBoxItem control.

4. In order to see the current states, click each state in the States panel. These are the defined states, as shown in Figure 11-19:

- Normal
- MouseOver
- Disabled
- Unfocused

- Focused
- SelectedUnfocused
- Unselected
- Selected

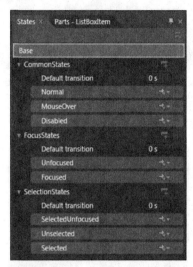

Figure 11-19. States of the ListBoxItem template

5. To change the Selected state, click the Selected state in the States panel.

6. Notice that the ListBoxItem's background becomes blue (see Figure 11-20).

7. To change this behavior, select fillColor2 in the Objects and Timeline panel, as shown in Figure 11-21.

Figure 11-20. The ListBoxItem's background becomes blue when the Selected state is selected.

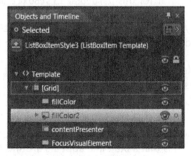

Figure 11-21. Select fillColor2 in the Objects and Timeline panel.

8. Now, click the Advanced property options button next to the Fill field in the Brushes bucket of the Properties panel (see Figure 11-22).

Figure 11-22. Click the Advanced property options button.

9. Click Reset, as shown in Figure 11-23.

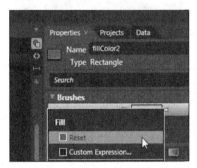

Figure 11-23. Click Reset.

Now if you look at the ListBoxItem in the workspace, you can see that it no longer has a blue background. If you were to run the application and select this particular ListBoxItem, you would see that nothing happens to the background, no matter what you do to it. Thus, we have overridden the default behavior for this particular ListBoxItem.

But now, you have to tell all of the other ListBoxItems to make use of the same Style, or they will use their default behavior.

10. Select each additional ListBoxItem, right-click it, select Edit Control Parts (Template) ➤ Apply Resource, and select ListBoxItemStyle1.

11. Recompile the application by pressing F5, and test it by selecting different ListBoxItems.

Notice that, when you click any ListBoxItem, the background stays the same color. The only thing that happens is that a blue line appears around the ListBoxItem. This is a good thing, because without it we would never know when a ListBoxItem was actually selected. However, you could remove this functionality by editing the Focused state if you wanted to.

Now you know what a Style is and how to create one. You also now know how to apply a Style to a control of the same type, and how to create a ResourceDictionary that contains your Styles that will be available to all XAML pages of your project. Finally, you have seen how Styles can be very useful in a real-world situation by giving you the ability to override a control's default behavior by using a VSM to set the control's properties, such as the Selected state of a ListBox control. Now that you understand Styles, you can get back to your Button control and do some really fun stuff.

Adding your Button Style to your ResourceDictionary

So you now understand the way that the Button control you have made is displayed inside of a Style. If you look at Page.xaml, you can see the Button control Style called BlueButtonControl defined in a section called UserControl.Resources. Earlier in this section, you learned that it is best practice to put all of your Styles in a ResourceDictionary, and you even learned how to do that. So, why did I have you create your Button control Style inside of your Page.xaml if it is not best practice to do so? Did I make a mistake? Actually, yes I did, but this mistake will allow me to show you how to fix a common error that I find many developers tend to make, and that is defining resources such as Styles in the XAML page they are working on rather than in a ResourceDictionary. So next, you'll move your BlueButtonControl resource from Page.xaml to applicationResourceDictionary.xaml:

1. Open Page.xaml in XAML view.

2. Select the following code for the BlueButtonControl Style, and cut it out of the XAML (by right-clicking and selecting Cut, pressing Ctrl+X, or selecting Edit ➤ Cut).

```xml
<Style x:Key="BlueButtonControl" TargetType="Button">
<Setter Property="Template">
        <Setter.Value>
            <ControlTemplate TargetType="Button">
                <Grid>
                    <vsm:VisualStateManager.VisualStateGroups>
                        <vsm:VisualStateGroup x:Name="FocusStates">
                            <vsm:VisualState x:Name="Focused"/>
                            <vsm:VisualState x:Name="Unfocused"/>
                        </vsm:VisualStateGroup>
                        <vsm:VisualStateGroup x:Name="CommonStates">
                            <vsm:VisualState x:Name="Normal"/>
                            <vsm:VisualState x:Name="MouseOver"/>
                            <vsm:VisualState x:Name="Pressed"/>
                            <vsm:VisualState x:Name="Disabled"/>
                        </vsm:VisualStateGroup>
                    </vsm:VisualStateManager.VisualStateGroups>
                    <Rectangle Stroke="#FF000000" RadiusX="13" RadiusY=
"13">
                        <Rectangle.Fill>
                            <LinearGradientBrush EndPoint="0.5,1"
StartPoint="0.5,0">
                                <LinearGradientBrush.RelativeTransform>
                                    <TransformGroup>
                                        <ScaleTransform CenterX="0.5"
CenterY="0.5"/>

                                        <SkewTransform CenterX="0.5"
```

```
CenterY="0.5"/>
                                            <RotateTransform CenterX="0.5"
CenterY="0.5"/>
                                            <TranslateTransform X="0.013"
Y="0.026"/>
                                        </TransformGroup>
                                    </LinearGradientBrush.
RelativeTransform>

                                    <GradientStop Color="#FF050066"/>
                                    <GradientStop Color="#FFB3AFF6"
Offset="1"/>
                                </LinearGradientBrush>
                            </Rectangle.Fill>
                        </Rectangle>
                        <ContentPresenter HorizontalAlignment=
"{TemplateBinding HorizontalContentAlignment}" VerticalAlignment=
"{TemplateBinding VerticalContentAlignment}"/>
                    </Grid>
                </ControlTemplate>
            </Setter.Value>
        </Setter>
</Style>
<Style x:Key="ListBoxItemStyle3" TargetType="ListBoxItem">
    <Setter Property="Padding" Value="3"/>
    <Setter Property="HorizontalContentAlignment" Value="Left"/>
    <Setter Property="VerticalContentAlignment" Value="Top"/>
    <Setter Property="Background" Value="Transparent"/>
    <Setter Property="BorderThickness" Value="1"/>
    <Setter Property="TabNavigation" Value="Local"/>
    <Setter Property="Template">
        <Setter.Value>
            <ControlTemplate TargetType="ListBoxItem">
                <Grid Background="{TemplateBinding Background}">
                    <vsm:VisualStateManager.VisualStateGroups>
                        <vsm:VisualStateGroup x:Name="CommonStates">
                            <vsm:VisualState x:Name="Normal"/>
                            <vsm:VisualState x:Name="MouseOver">
                                <Storyboard>
                                    <DoubleAnimationUsingKeyFrames
Storyboard.TargetName="fillColor" Storyboard.TargetProperty="Opacity">
                                        <SplineDoubleKeyFrame KeyTime=
"0" Value=".35"/>
                                    </DoubleAnimationUsingKeyFrames>
                                </Storyboard>
                            </vsm:VisualState>
                            <vsm:VisualState x:Name="Disabled">
                                <Storyboard>
                                    <DoubleAnimationUsingKeyFrames
Storyboard.TargetName="contentPresenter" Storyboard.TargetProperty=
```

```xml
"Opacity">
                                        <SplineDoubleKeyFrame KeyTime=
"0" Value=".55"/>
                                    </DoubleAnimationUsingKeyFrames>
                                </Storyboard>
                            </vsm:VisualState>
                        </vsm:VisualStateGroup>
                        <vsm:VisualStateGroup x:Name="SelectionStates">
                            <vsm:VisualState x:Name="Unselected"/>
                            <vsm:VisualState x:Name="Selected">
                                <Storyboard>
                                    <DoubleAnimationUsingKeyFrames
Storyboard.TargetName="fillColor2" Storyboard.TargetProperty="Opacity">
                                        <SplineDoubleKeyFrame KeyTime=
"0" Value=".75"/>
                                    </DoubleAnimationUsingKeyFrames>
                                </Storyboard>
                            </vsm:VisualState>
                        </vsm:VisualStateGroup>
                        <vsm:VisualStateGroup x:Name="FocusStates">
                            <vsm:VisualState x:Name="Focused">
                                <Storyboard>
                                    <ObjectAnimationUsingKeyFrames
Duration="0"
Storyboard.TargetName="FocusVisualElement" Storyboard.TargetProperty=
"Visibility">
                                        <DiscreteObjectKeyFrame
KeyTime="0">
                                            <DiscreteObjectKeyFrame.
Value>
                                                <Visibility>Collapsed
</Visibility>
                                            </DiscreteObjectKeyFrame
.Value>
                                        </DiscreteObjectKeyFrame>
                                    </ObjectAnimationUsingKeyFrames>
                                </Storyboard>
                            </vsm:VisualState>
                            <vsm:VisualState x:Name="Unfocused"/>
                        </vsm:VisualStateGroup>
                    </vsm:VisualStateManager.VisualStateGroups>
                    <Rectangle x:Name="fillColor" RadiusX="1"
RadiusY="1" IsHitTestVisible="False" Opacity="0"/>
                    <Rectangle x:Name="fillColor2" RadiusX="1"
RadiusY="1" IsHitTestVisible="False" Opacity="0"/>
                    <ContentPresenter x:Name="contentPresenter"
HorizontalAlignment="{TemplateBinding HorizontalContentAlignment}"
Margin="{TemplateBinding Padding}" Content="{TemplateBinding Content}"
ContentTemplate="{TemplateBinding ContentTemplate}"/>
```

```
                <Rectangle x:Name="FocusVisualElement" Stroke=
"#FF6DBDD1" StrokeThickness="1" RadiusX="1" RadiusY="1" Visibility=
"Collapsed"/>
                </Grid>
            </ControlTemplate>
        </Setter.Value>
    </Setter>
</Style>
```

3. Open applicationResourceDict.xaml and paste this Style right above the MyListBoxStyle Style.

4. Run the application again by pressing F5.

Notice that the Button looks exactly the way it did before, but rather than getting its Style from the Page.xaml's UserControl.Resources, it is getting it from applicationResourceDict.xaml. That was very simple indeed, but now that you have done this, you can use this Style throughout your application, which would be handy if you created an application with many different XAML pages.

Creating custom UserControls

A UserControl in Silverlight allows you to create custom controls much like the controls that ship with Blend 3, such as the Button control. You can specify how your custom controls look as well as EventHandlers for their behavior. In the preceding exercises, you used a Style with a ControlTemplate to make your Buttons look a certain way. What if you wanted to simplify that process—that is, avoid having to create a Button in the workspace and then tell that Button to use the Style resource with your ControlTemplate in it? In this exercise, I am going to show you how to create a Silverlight custom UserControl that will act much like a built-in Silverlight Button. Let's get started.

1. Go back to your ControlTemplateProject in Blend 3.

2. In the Projects panel, right-click ControlTemplateProject, and select Add New Item, as shown in Figure 11-24.

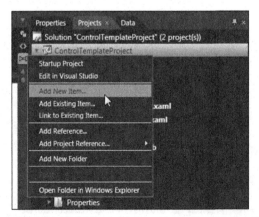

Figure 11-24. Add a new item to the ControlTemplateProject.

3. In the New Item dialog box, select UserControl and name it UC_GreenButton (see Figure 11-25).

4. Click OK.

Figure 11-25. Name the new UserControl UC_GreenButton.

5. When Blend 3 creates and opens the new UserControl, draw a green Rectangle in the top-left corner, as shown in Figure 11-26.

Figure 11-26. Draw a green Rectangle with rounded edges in the top-left corner of the new UserControl.

6. Next, click [UserControl] in the Objects and Timeline panel.

7. Use the resize handles to make the entire UserControl roughly the same size as the green Rectangle (about 100 display units wide and 50 display units tall), as shown in Figure 11-27.

Figure 11-27. Adjust the size of the UserControl to be the same size as the green Rectangle.

8. Next, copy (Ctrl+C) the green Rectangle and paste (Ctrl+V) a new one.

9. Remove the stroke from the new Rectangle.

10. Change the fill to be a gradient that goes from white to white.

11. Change the bottom gradient to have an alpha of 0% so that the Brushes panel for your new Rectangle looks like the one shown in Figure 11-28.

Figure 11-28. The Brushes panel for the new Rectangle should look like this.

12. Next, make both of the new Rectangles smaller, so each looks like the one shown in Figure 11-29.

Go ahead and add a TextBlock with a font size of 14 on top of both Rectangles, and set its Text property to read Click Me, as shown in Figure 11-30.

Figure 11-29. Your two Rectangles should look like this.

Figure 11-30. Add a TextBlock to the UserControl.

Now that we have our UserControl looking like a cool button, let's go in and add some mouse states to it—namely, MouseEnter and MouseLeave.

13. In the States panel, click the Add state group button, as shown in Figure 11-31.

Figure 11-31. Add a new state group.

14. Name the new state group MouseStates and set the default transition time to .3 seconds, as shown in Figure 11-32.

15. Click the Add state button, as shown in Figure 11-33.

Figure 11-32. Name the new state group MouseStates and give it a default transition time of .3 seconds.

Figure 11-33. Add a new state.

16. Name the new state Enter.

17. Click the Add State button again, and name the state Leave so that your States panel looks like the one shown in Figure 11-34.

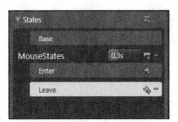

Figure 11-34. Add two states named Enter and Leave.

18. Next, click the Enter state, and notice the red line that appears around the workspace, indicating that changes are being recorded into that state.

19. Click the bottom, green Rectangle, and change it to red in the Brushes bucket of the Properties panel.

20. Now press Ctrl+Shift+B to compile the application, and switch back to Page.xaml.

21. Click the Asset Library, and then click the Custom Controls tab, as shown in Figure 11-35.

Figure 11-35. The Custom Controls tab in the Asset Library.

22. Click the UC_GreenButton UserControl. Now the very last tool on your toolbar will be a UC_GreenButton UserControl (see Figure 11-36).

23. Simply double-click this tool, and a UC_GreenButton UserControl will appear in your workspace (see Figure 11-37).

Figure 11-36. The last tool on your toolbar is now in Page.xaml.

Figure 11-37. A UC_GreenButton UserControl will now be the UC_GreenButton UserControl.

At this point, we need to first wire up the states, and then create a custom DependencyProperty so that the UC_GreenButton control will display the desired text for the button we are creating (e.g., Home or About Us). First, let's wire up the states:

24. Press Ctrl+Shift+B to compile the application, and then switch back over to Visual Studio. If the project is already open in Visual Studio, allow Visual Studio to reload it. If it is not open, then open it.

25. Open UC_GreenButton.xaml.cs and raise and handle the events for MouseEnter and MouseLeave as follows:

```
namespace ControlTemplateProject
{
    public partial class UC_GreenButton : UserControl
    {
        public UC_GreenButton()
```

```
    {
        // Required to initialize variables
        InitializeComponent();
        this.MouseEnter += new MouseEventHandler
(UC_GreenButton_MouseEnter);
        this.MouseLeave += new MouseEventHandler
(UC_GreenButton_MouseLeave);
    }

    void UC_GreenButton_MouseLeave(object sender, MouseEventArgs e)
    {
        throw new NotImplementedException();
    }

    void UC_GreenButton_MouseEnter(object sender, MouseEventArgs e)
    {
        throw new NotImplementedException();
    }
}
}
```

26. Next, remove the default throw new... code, and wire up the VisualStates as follows:

```
namespace ControlTemplateProject{

    public partial class UC_GreenButton : UserControl
    {
        public UC_GreenButton()
        {
            // Required to initialize variables
            InitializeComponent();
            this.MouseEnter += new MouseEventHandler
(UC_GreenButton_MouseEnter);
            this.MouseLeave += new MouseEventHandler
(UC_GreenButton_MouseLeave);
        }

        void UC_GreenButton_MouseLeave(object sender, MouseEventArgs e)
        {
            VisualStateManager.GoToState(this, "Leave", true);
        }

        void UC_GreenButton_MouseEnter(object sender, MouseEventArgs e)
        {
            VisualStateManager.GoToState(this, "Enter", true);
        }
    }
}
```

If you press F5 to compile and run the application, and you place your mouse over the UC_GreenButton control, you should see that it does in fact turn red.

So, what do we need to do to be able to give our UC_GreenButton the correct text to display, as we don't always want this UserControl to read Click Me? This brings us to something called a DependencyProperty.

Demystifying the DependencyProperty

Throughout this book, you have worked with many Silverlight controls such as Buttons, Rectangles, and MediaElements. Because you have worked with these controls and did things such as set the Source property of a MediaElement or the Fill property of a Rectangle, you already have experience in working with DependencyPropertys, because Fill and Source are DependencyPropertys. So, in their simplest form—and trust me, they can get much more complicated—DependencyPropertys are properties that allow you to manage in C# or XAML how controls look and behave. Let's take a look at a simple Button with a Background DependencyProperty set to Blue and a Content DependencyProperty set to "Dependency Properties Rock!":

```
<Button Background="Blue" Content="Dependency Properties Rock!"/>
```

When you set the Background property to Blue, the XAML loader type converter converts it into a Silverlight Color using the SolidColorBrush. Silverlight provides a variety of ways syntactically for setting these properties in both XAML and C#. If you give the Button a Name, like this:

```
<Button x:Name="MyButton" Background="Blue"
Content="Dependency Properties Rock!"/>
```

you can go into the code-behind file and set the Background property with code like this:

```
// create a variable of the type SolidColorBrush
// and set it to a new Red SolidColorBrush
SolidColorBrush myBrush = new SolidColorBrush(Colors.Red);
// apply the new variable to the Background of MyButton
MyButton.Background = myBrush;
```

This is all fine, and I am sure you understand DependencyPropertys, but what if you have a situation where there is no DependencyProperty that meets your needs? Say, for example, you want to be able to set the text on a custom UserControl. Sounds a lot like the issue we are having right now, doesn't it? Well, for times like this, Silverlight allows us to register your very own custom DependencyPropertys. So, with that, let's go back to UC_GreenButton.xaml.cs and register our own custom DependencyProperty called GreenButtonsText:

```
namespace ControlTemplateProject
{
    public partial class UC_GreenButton : UserControl
    {

        #region GreenButtonsText (DependencyProperty)
```

```csharp
public string  GreenButtonsText
{
    get { return (string)GetValue(GreenButtonsTextProperty); }
    set { SetValue(GreenButtonsTextProperty, value); }
}
public static readonly DependencyProperty
GreenButtonsTextProperty =
        DependencyProperty.Register("GreenButtonsText",
typeof(string), typeof(UC_GreenButton),
        new PropertyMetadata(string.Empty, new
PropertyChangedCallback(OnGreenButtonsTextChanged)));

private static void OnGreenButtonsTextChanged(DependencyObject
d, DependencyPropertyChangedEventArgs e)
{
    ((UC_GreenButton)d).OnGreenButtonsTextChanged(e);
}

protected virtual void
OnGreenButtonsTextChanged(DependencyPropertyChangedEventArgs e)
{
}

#endregion

public UC_GreenButton()
{
    // Required to initialize variables
    InitializeComponent();
    this.MouseEnter += new MouseEventHandler
(UC_GreenButton_MouseEnter);
    this.MouseLeave += new MouseEventHandler
(UC_GreenButton_MouseLeave);
}

void UC_GreenButton_MouseLeave(object sender, MouseEventArgs e)
{
    VisualStateManager.GoToState(this, "Leave", true);
}

void UC_GreenButton_MouseEnter(object sender, MouseEventArgs e)
{
    VisualStateManager.GoToState(this, "Enter", true);
}
    }
}
```

Now that we have registered the DependencyProperty, we need to go into Page.xaml and add a value to the GreenButtonsText property:

```
<Grid x:Name="LayoutRoot" Background="White">
        <local:UC_GreenButton HorizontalAlignment="Left"
VerticalAlignment="Top" GreenButtonsText="I am a Custom UC"/>
    </Grid>
```

Now that we have given the GreenButtonsText DependencyProperty a value, we need to actually do something with that value. We are now going to raise and handle a UC_GreenButton Loaded event. In that event handler, we are going to set the TextBlock's Text property to the value of GreenButtonsText value. Before we do that, though, we need to provide the TextBlock with a name so we can code against it in the code-behind.

1. In UC_GreenButton.xaml, give the TextBlock an x:Name of GreenButtonTextBlock:

```
<TextBlock
    x:Name="GreenButtonTextBlock"
    Margin="49,13,45,16"
    FontSize="14"
    Text="Click Me"
    TextWrapping="Wrap"
    d:LayoutOverrides="Height" />
```

2. Now go into UC_GreenButton.xaml.cs and raise and handle the Loaded event:

```
namespace ControlTemplateProject
{
    // Removed code for GreenButtonsText Dependency Property to make it
 easier to read

        public UC_GreenButton()
        {
            // Required to initialize variables
            InitializeComponent();
            this.MouseEnter += new MouseEventHandler
(UC_GreenButton_MouseEnter);
            this.MouseLeave += new MouseEventHandler
(UC_GreenButton_MouseLeave);
            this.Loaded += new RoutedEventHandler
(UC_GreenButton_Loaded);
        }

        void UC_GreenButton_Loaded(object sender, RoutedEventArgs e)
        {
            throw new NotImplementedException();
        }
```

```
void UC_GreenButton_MouseLeave(object sender, MouseEventArgs e)
{
    VisualStateManager.GoToState(this, "Leave", true);
}

void UC_GreenButton_MouseEnter(object sender, MouseEventArgs e)
{
    VisualStateManager.GoToState(this, "Enter", true);
}
    }
}
```

> *A Loaded event is raised when an object is loaded.*

3. Remove the throw new... default code and set the GreenButtonTextBlock's Text property to the value of the GreenButtonsText DependencyProperty:

```
void UC_GreenButton_Loaded(object sender, RoutedEventArgs e)
{
    GreenButtonTextBlock.Text = GreenButtonsText;
}
```

> *When we registered the GreenButtonsText DependencyProperty, we created an event handler for whenever the property changes. We could have just as easily set the GreenButtonTextBlock in this changed handler instead of the loaded event for the UserControl_GreenButton like this:*

```
protected virtual void OnGreenButtonsTextChanged
(DependencyPropertyChangedEventArgs e)
        {
            GreenButtonTextBlock.Text = GreenButtonsText;
        }
```

If you were to compile and run the application now, you would see something similar to what's shown in Figure 11-38, because the TextBlock is set to left-justified by default.

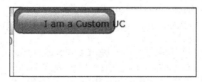

Figure 11-38. The GreenButtonTextBlock
is set by default to be left-justified.

4. In UC_GreenButton.xaml, change the GreenButtonTextBlock to be center-justified:

```
<TextBlock
    x:Name="GreenButtonTextBlock"
    Margin="9,13,7,16"
    FontSize="14"
    Text="Click Me"
    TextWrapping="Wrap"
    d:LayoutOverrides="Height"
    TextAlignment="Center" />
```

Now, if you press F5 to compile and run the application, you will see that it does in fact look correct, and the GreenTextBlock's Text property is correctly being set in the Loaded event handler to the value of our custom DependencyProperty GreenButtonsText value.

Figure 11-39. The UC_GreenButton's text now appears correctly.

My challenge to you now is to try the following steps:

1. In Page.xaml, give the UC_GreenButton an x:Name value so you can code against it in code-behind.

2. Raise and handle a MouseLeftButtonDown event.

3. In the MouseLeftButtonDown event handler, show a MessageBox that reads UC_GreenButton has been Clicked!.

You can download my ControlTemplateProject project here: http://windowspresentationfoundation.com/Blend3Book/ControlTemplateProject.zip.

Summary

In this chapter, you learned about ControlTemplates and how they work with Styles. You also learned that you can overwrite Silverlight controls such as ListBoxes using Styles. You then learned how easy it is to apply resources to controls is in Silverlight, as well as the value of keeping your resources, such as Styles, in a ResourceDictionary. You learned how to create your very own Silverlight custom UserControl, complete with mouse states. You then learned about DependencyPropertys and even how to register and make use of your own custom DependencyProperty, which then becomes an additional property of the object just like built-in properties such as Background, Width, and Height.

Thus far, we have been using only built-in Silverlight panels such as StackPanel, Grid, and Canvas. Each of these panels lays out its children in a different way. What if none of these panels meet our requirements? In that case, we would need a custom panel. In the next chapter, I am going to show you how to build just such a custom Silverlight panel.

Chapter 12

WRITING A CUSTOM CONTENT PANEL

What this chapter covers:

- How to write a custom Silverlight panel

Recently, I was tasked with creating an image viewer that held thumbnails of lots of images. The problem was that I had to at least partially show all of the thumbnail images that were all held in an ObservableCollection. Further, because the images were held in an ObservableCollection of data, I could never know how many images would be in the collection at any one time. For this reason, it was an obvious choice to put the thumbnails into a StackPanel and let the StackPanel arrange its children. The catch with this is that a StackPanel can only arrange its children vertically or horizontally and with a lot of thumbnail images that would just take up too much space. So, I decided to arrange the thumbnails in z space (one on top of the other) rather than in x or y space (left/right or top/bottom space). The problem is that no panel currently existing in Silverlight can arrange its children in z space, so my final answer was to create a brand-new Silverlight panel that does, in fact, arrange its children in z space. That is what I am going to show you how to do now.

Creating the Project

The first thing we are going to do is open Visual Studio and create a new Silverlight project called CustomZStackPanelProject. Use the settings shown in Figure 12-1.

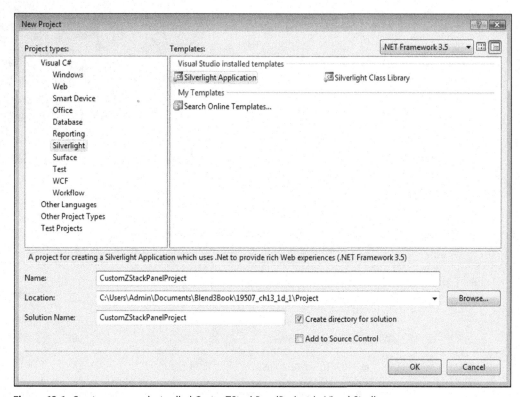

Figure 12-1. *Create a new project called CustonZStackPanelProject in Visual Studio.*

The next thing we have to do is set the settings for the new Silverlight application. Basically, Visual Studio is asking us if we want to create an ASP.NET intranet site. This means that Silverlight will simulate a web site when the application is run. Otherwise, when the application is run, Silverlight will just open the file location on the hard drive. For the purposes of this exercise, hosting a ASP.NET web site would be overkill.

1. When the New Silverlight Application dialog box appears, uncheck Host the Silverlight application in a new Web site, and click OK (see Figure 12-2).

> *If you check the* Host the Silverlight application in a new Web site *box, Visual Studio will create a server web site that acts as an intranet site. If this box is unchecked, Visual Studio will run the application directly off of your hard drive.*

Figure 12-2. Uncheck "Host the Silverlight application in a new Web site" check box

2. Next, right-click the project in Solution Explorer, and click Add ➤ Class as shown in Figure 12-3.

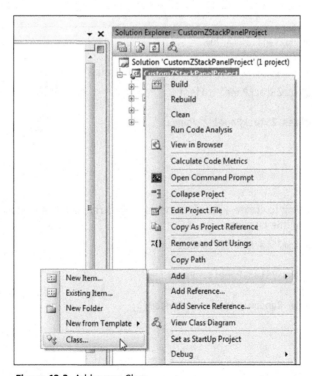

Figure 12-3. Add a new Class.

3. In the Add New Item dialog box, name the new class ZStackPanel, and click Add, as shown in Figure 12-4.

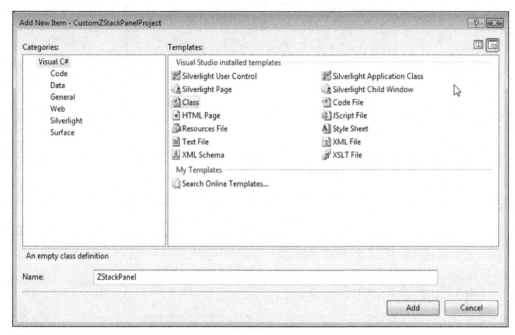

Figure 12-4. Name the new class ZStackPanel.

4. When the new class opens, have it extend the Panel class as follows:

```
namespace CustomZStackPanelProject
{
    public class ZStackPanel : Panel
    {

    }
}
```

5. Next, we are going to create a private property called rnd, which will allow us to generate random numbers a little later on:

```
namespace CustomZStackPanelProject
{
    public class ZStackPanel : Panel
    {
        private Random rnd = new Random();
    }
}
```

6. Next, we need to have each child item slightly offset and rotated from the one behind it. This way, when they are all stacked on top of each other, they will all be visible. To do that, we need two custom DependencyProperty instances for MaxOffset and MaxRotation. We will then have each child slightly offset in the x and/or y position and rotated with a random number no higher than the MaxOffset for x or y offset and no higher than the MaxRotation for the angle of rotation. Let's create those DependencyProperty instances now:

```
namespace CustomZStackPanelProject
{
    public class ZStackPanel : Panel
    {
        private Random rnd = new Random();

        #region MaxRotation (DependencyProperty)

        public double MaxRotation
        {
            get { return (double)GetValue(MaxRotationProperty); }
            set { SetValue(MaxRotationProperty, value); }
        }
        public static readonly DependencyProperty MaxRotationProperty =
            DependencyProperty.Register("MaxRotation",
typeof(double),
 typeof(ZStackPanel),
            new PropertyMetadata(0.0, new PropertyChangedCallback
(OnMaxRotationChanged)));

        private static void OnMaxRotationChanged
(DependencyObject d,
DependencyPropertyChangedEventArgs e)
        {
            ((ZStackPanel)d).OnMaxRotationChanged(e);
        }

        protected virtual void OnMaxRotationChanged
(DependencyPropertyChangedEventArgs e)
        {
        }

        #endregion MaxRotation (DependencyProperty)


        #region MaxOffset (DependencyProperty)

        public double MaxOffset
        {
            get { return (double)GetValue(MaxOffsetProperty); }
            set { SetValue(MaxOffsetProperty, value); }
        }
```

```
        public static readonly DependencyProperty MaxOffsetProperty =
            DependencyProperty.Register
("MaxOffset", typeof(double),
typeof(ZStackPanel),
            new PropertyMetadata(0.0, new PropertyChangedCallback
(OnMaxOffsetChanged)));

        private static void OnMaxOffsetChanged(DependencyObject d,
DependencyPropertyChangedEventArgs e)
        {
            ((ZStackPanel)d).OnMaxOffsetChanged(e);
        }

        protected virtual void OnMaxOffsetChanged
(DependencyPropertyChangedEventArgs e)
        {
        }

        #endregion MaxOffset (DependencyProperty)

    }
}
```

7. The next thing we need to do is declare a constructor below the DependencyProperty instances that first will run the constructor of the base class (of Panel):

```
using System;
using System.Net;
using System.Windows;
using System.Windows.Controls;
using System.Windows.Documents;
using System.Windows.Ink;
using System.Windows.Input;
using System.Windows.Media;
using System.Windows.Media.Animation;
using System.Windows.Shapes;

namespace CustomZStackPanelProject
{
    public class ZStackPanel : Panel
    {
        private Random rnd = new Random();

        // DependencyProperties not shown

        public ZStackPanel()
            : base()
        {
```

```
        }

    }

}
```

8. Next, we need to override two abstract panel classes called `MeasureOverride` and `ArrangeOverride`. These are the two methods that position children in a panel. This detail is a little out of scope for this book, but basically, `MeasureOverride` measures each child and the space available in the panel and then returns how much space there is and how big each child can be. `ArrangeOverride` then arranges the children in the panel. Let's override those two methods now:

```
namespace CustomZStackPanelProject
{
    public class ZStackPanel : Panel
    {
        private Random rnd = new Random();
// DependencyProperties not shown

public ZStackPanel()
            : base()
        {

        }

        protected override Size MeasureOverride(Size availableSize)
        {

        }

        protected override Size ArrangeOverride(Size finalSize)
        {

        }

    }
}
```

9. After the `MeasureOverride` method, the next thing we need to do is to create a `Size` variable named `resultSize`. We need to do this because, as you can see from the method signature, it expects a `Size` to be returned. Let's create the `resultSize` variable now:

```
protected override Size MeasureOverride(Size availableSize)
{
    Size resultSize = new Size(0, 0);
}
```

10. The next thing we need to do is to cycle through all of the children and measure them. The method then measures the available size of the panel and returns how much space that child will be allocated and then returns the `resultSize` variable. Add the following code to measure the children:

```
protected override Size MeasureOverride(Size availableSize)
{
    Size resultSize = new Size(0, 0);
    foreach (UIElement child in Children)
    {
        child.Measure(availableSize);
        resultSize.Width = Math.Max(resultSize.Width,
child.DesiredSize.Width);
        resultSize.Height = Math.Max(resultSize.Height,
child.DesiredSize.Height);
    }

    resultSize.Width = double.IsPositiveInfinity(availableSize.Width) ?
 resultSize.Width : availableSize.Width;
    resultSize.Height = double.IsPositiveInfinity(availableSize.Height)
 ? resultSize.Height : availableSize.Height;

    return resultSize;

}
```

11. We can now move on to the ArrangeOverride method. This method is going to cycle through each of the children and center them in the panel by setting each child's x position to be the entire width of the panel divided by two minus the width of the child divided by two. Conversely, it will set the y position of the child to the height of the panel divided by two minus the height of the child divided by two. It will then return finalSize.

```
protected override Size ArrangeOverride(Size finalSize)
{
    foreach (UIElement child in Children)
    {
        double childX = finalSize.Width / 2 - child.DesiredSize.Width
 / 2;
        double childY = finalSize.Height / 2 - child.DesiredSize.Height
 / 2;
        child.Arrange(new Rect(childX, childY,
child.DesiredSize.Width, child.DesiredSize.Height));
    }
return finalSize;

}
```

12. Now that all of the children are centered in the panel, we need to rotate them slightly and offset their x and y positions. We can encapsulate that behavior into its own method called RotateAndOffsetChild and call that for each child in the ArrangeOverride method, as shown in the following code:

```
protected override Size ArrangeOverride(Size finalSize)
{
    foreach (UIElement child in Children)
    {
```

```
        double childX = finalSize.Width / 2 - child.DesiredSize.Width
    / 2;
        double childY = finalSize.Height / 2 - child.DesiredSize.Height
    / 2;
        child.Arrange(new Rect(childX, childY,
    child.DesiredSize.Width, child.DesiredSize.Height));
        RotateAndOffsetChild(child);
    }
    return finalSize;

}

        private void RotateAndOffsetChild(UIElement child)
        {
            throw new NotImplementedException();
        }


    }
```

Now, as you probably already ascertained, we are going to rotate each child in the RotateAndOffsetChild method. To do this, we are going to need a few variables:

- xOffset: The amount the child will be offset in the x coordinate
- yOffset: The amount the child will be offset in the y coordinate
- angle: The angle the child will be rotate to

Next, we need to create x and y offset variables as well as the angle. We will use a random number so that each child will, theoretically, have slightly different values and thus have a unique position. The following code implements these variables:

```
private void RotateAndOffsetChild(UIElement child)
{

    double xOffset = MaxOffset * (2 * rnd.NextDouble() - 1);
    double yOffset = MaxOffset * (2 * rnd.NextDouble() - 1);
    double angle = MaxRotation * (2 * rnd.NextDouble() - 1);
}
```

Let's look at what the preceding calculations are doing. The xOffset is being set equal to MaxOffset multiplied by rnd (a random number) multiplied by two minus one. This calculation will ensure that, at times, we will get negative numbers, and at other times, we will get positive numbers.

> The Random.NextDouble() method returns a number greater than or equal to zero and less than (but not equal to) one.

13. Now that we have our numbers, we need to create two transforms, one for the x and y coordinates and another for the rotation:

```
private void RotateAndOffsetChild(UIElement child)
{
    double randomNumber = rnd.NextDouble();

    double xOffset = MaxOffset * (2 * rnd.NextDouble() - 1);
    double yOffset = MaxOffset * (2 * rnd.NextDouble() - 1);
    double angle = MaxRotation * (2 * rnd.NextDouble() - 1);

    TranslateTransform offsetTF = new TranslateTransform();
    offsetTF.X = xOffset;
    offsetTF.Y = yOffset;

    RotateTransform rotateRT = new RotateTransform();
    rotateRT.Angle = angle;
    rotateRT.CenterX = child.DesiredSize.Width / 2;
    rotateRT.CenterY = child.DesiredSize.Height / 2;
}
```

14. The last thing we need to do is to create a `TransformGroup` and add the transforms we create to it:

```
private void RotateAndOffsetChild(UIElement child)
{
    double randomNumber = rnd.NextDouble();

    double xOffset = MaxOffset * (2 * rnd.NextDouble() - 1);
    double yOffset = MaxOffset * (2 * rnd.NextDouble() - 1);
    double angle = MaxRotation * (2 * rnd.NextDouble() - 1);

    TranslateTransform offsetTF = new TranslateTransform();
    offsetTF.X = xOffset;
    offsetTF.Y = yOffset;

    RotateTransform rotateRT = new RotateTransform();
    rotateRT.Angle = angle;
    rotateRT.CenterX = child.DesiredSize.Width / 2;
    rotateRT.CenterY = child.DesiredSize.Height / 2;

    TransformGroup tfg = new TransformGroup();
    tfg.Children.Add(offsetTF);
    tfg.Children.Add(rotateRT);
    child.RenderTransform = tfg;
}
```

Now, the panel is complete. The next thing we need to do is implement it, that is, use it in the application. We can start to set this up in Blend. So press Ctrl+Shift+B to compile the application and switch over to Blend. Here are the steps to implement the panel:

1. In Blend, open the project.

2. Next, select [UserControl] from the Objects and Timeline panel, and in the Layout bucket of the Properties panel, change the Width to 800 and the Height to 600, as shown in Figure 12-5.

3. Next, click and hold the Button tool on the toolbar, and when it appears, select ListBox (see Figure 12-6).

Figure 12-5. Set the Height and Width of the UserControl to 800×600.

Figure 12-6. Select the ListBox tool.

4. Next, on the Workspace, draw a ListBox that is roughly 200 display units wide and 400 display units tall (see Figure 12-7).

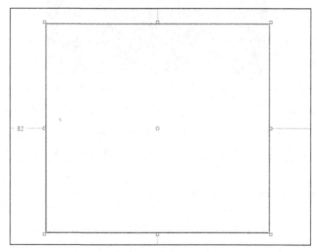

Figure 12-7. Draw a ListBox on the Workspace.

> *Next, you are going to add images to your project. I suggest you edit the images you wish to use so they are roughly 200×200 pixels.*

5. Next, right-click the project, and click Add ➤ Existing Item.

6. Locate the images you would like to use on your hard drive, and select them.

7. Your Projects panel should look something like the one shown in Figure 12-8.

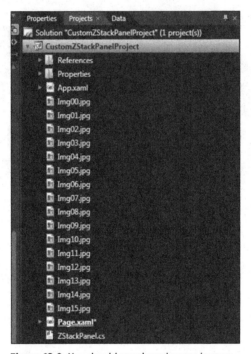

Figure 12-8. You should now have images in your Projects panel.

8. Hold down Ctrl, and click each image to select them all.

9. Drag the images onto the ListBox, and Blend should populate your list box as shown in Figure 12-9.

You can also verify that the images are in the list box by looking at the Objects and Timeline panel (see Figure 12-10).

Figure 12-9. The images are now in the ListBox.

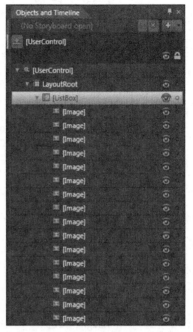

Figure 12-10. You can see the images are in your ListBox in the Objects and Timeline panel.

As you can see in Figure 12-10, this list box is not good for our purposes, as we want to take up as little real estate as possible and not have the user have to use the list box's scroll functionality. So, it's now time to use our ZStackPanel:

1. Press Ctrl+Shift+B to compile the application and switch back to Visual Studio.

2. Then, create a UserControl.Resources node in MainWindow.xaml.

3. In this new node, add a ItemsPanelTemplate resource to describe to the list box how to display its items.

4. Inside the ItemsPanelTemplate, add the following ZStackPanel (be sure to include the namespace for the ZStackPanel, which is in bold):

```
<UserControl x:Class="CustomZStackPanelProject.Page"
    xmlns="http://schemas.microsoft.com/winfx/2006/xaml/presentation"
    xmlns:x="http://schemas.microsoft.com/winfx/2006/xaml"
    xmlns:CustomZStackPanelProject="clr-namespace:
CustomZStackPanelProject"
    Width="800" Height="600">
    <UserControl.Resources>
```

289

```
<ItemsPanelTemplate
    x:Key="ZItemsPanelTemplate">

    <CustomZStackPanelProject:ZStackPanel
        MaxOffset="20"
        MaxRotation="11" />
</ItemsPanelTemplate>
</UserControl.Resources>
```

5. Now, all you need to do is to tell your list box to use your new ItemsPanelTemplate named ZItemsPanelTemplate:

```
<ListBox
        ItemsPanel="{StaticResource ZItemsPanelTemplate}"
        Margin="218,66,197,-270">
        <Image
            Height="205"
            Width="300"
            Source="Img00.jpg"
            Stretch="Fill" />
        <Image
            Height="205"
            Width="300"
            Source="Img01.jpg"
            Stretch="Fill" />
        <Image
            Height="205"
            Width="300"
            Source="Img02.jpg"
            Stretch="Fill" />
        <Image
            Height="205"
            Width="300"
            Source="Img03.jpg"
            Stretch="Fill" />
        <Image
            Height="205"
            Width="300"
            Source="Img04.jpg"
            Stretch="Fill" />
</ListBox>
```

> *In my project, I actually have 15 images. The ZItemsPanelTemplate code has only five to save space.*

Now, if you press F5 to compile and run the application, you will see that our `ListBoxItems` all stack on top of each other with x and y offsets and at slightly different angles, so we can see that we have more than one image (see Figure 12-11).

Figure 12-11. The ListBoxItems all stack on top of each other with different rotation angles as well as x and y offsets.

At this point, our application is pretty cool but not very interactive. What we would like to move the top item go to the bottom of the stack when it's clicked. Let's stop the running application and switch back to Blend to wire this up visually:

1. In Blend, open `MainPage.xaml`, and resize your list box so that it is roughly the same size as your stack of images, as shown in Figure 12-12.

Figure 12-12. Resize your list box to be about the same size as the collection of images in it.

2. Now, draw a rectangle that completely covers the list box, as shown in Figure 12-13.

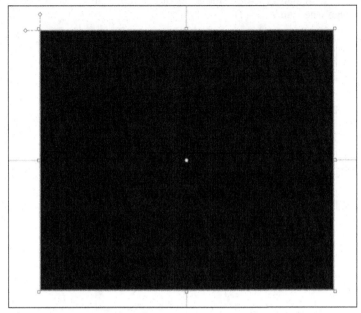

Figure 12-13. Draw a rectangle that completely covers your list box.

3. In the Appearance bucket of the Properties panel, set the Opacity of the Rectangle to 0.

4. Now, give the new Rectangle a Name of ImageSelector.

5. Press Ctrl+Shift+B to compile the application and switch back to Visual Studio.

Now, we need to go into MainPage.xaml.cs and wire up the selection functionality:

1. In MainPage.xaml.cs, raise and handle a MouseLeftButtonDown event for ImageSelector, as shown in the following code:

```
namespace CustomZStackPanelProject
{
    public partial class Page : UserControl
    {
        public Page()
        {
            InitializeComponent();
            ImageSelector.MouseLeftButtonDown += new MouseButtonEventHandler
(ImageSelector_MouseLeftButtonDown);
        }

        void ImageSelector_MouseLeftButtonDown(object sender,
    MouseButtonEventArgs e)
        {
            throw new NotImplementedException();
        }
```

```
        }
    }
```

2. Now, all you need to do is to remove the topmost item and add it back to the collection (this will put it at the end). Here is the code:

```
void ImageSelector_MouseLeftButtonDown(object sender, MouseButtonEventArgs e)
{
    // create a generic object and make it equal to the very first item
    // in ZStackLB ListBox.
    object o = ZStackLB.Items.ElementAt(ZStackLB.Items.Count - 1);
    // Make certain the o actually exists and is not null
    if (o != null)
    {
        // Remove o (the first image in the ZStackLB ListBox
        ZStackLB.Items.RemoveAt(ZStackLB.Items.Count - 1);
        // Add o back to the ZStackLB ListBox at the 0 position
        //(the last item in the ListBox)
        ZStackLB.Items.Insert(0, o);
    }
}
```

You can see the result of clicking an item in Figure 12-14.

Figure 12-14. The images will now cycle through when clicked.

You can download a copy of my project here:

http://windowspresentationfoundation.com/Blend3Book/
CustomZStackPanelProject.zip

Summary

In this chapter, you learned that you are not limited by the functionality of the existing panels in Silverlight. You learned that if a particular panel does not fit your needs, you can create your own, as long as you extend the Panel class to do so. You then learned how to build a custom panel that arranges its children in z space, rather than using (x, y) coordinates.

In the next chapter, you are going to take what you have learned up until this point and create a sample Silverlight web site, complete with custom user controls and a paging system that will load pages on demand to reduce upload time and save memory.

Chapter 13

BUILDING A SKETCHFLOW PROTOTYPE

What this chapter covers:

- Sketchflow prototyping
- Creating sample data

Blend 3 has some very exciting and innovative new features that can greatly improve rich Internet application development. In this chapter, we are going to discuss some of these features, including the very innovative and powerful sketchflow and the creation of sample data.

Sketchflow prototyping

A very new and innovative feature to Blend 3 and Silverlight is sketchflow prototyping. There are three major goals of sketchflow prototyping:

1. Quickly experimenting with a dynamic UI
2. Communicating design intent
3. Delivering compelling proposals to clients quickly and cost effectively

So, you may be asking what exactly is sketchflow prototyping? Basically, sketchflow prototyping is a way for you to create an interactive, non-designed version of an application. This sketchflow prototype can then be delivered to the client for immediate feedback that can be integrated directly into the prototype and seen by the developer. This prototype can be made very quickly and easily in Blend 3 and thus is cost effective. This prototype is then used by the designers and developers as a roadmap for the application. Further, assets and/or functionality created in the prototype can be used in the actual application. To better illustrate what sketchflow prototyping is, I am going to lead you through an exercise that will show you how to build an application prototype. I am going to show you how to create a WPF sketchflow prototype, but the Silverlight version is almost exactly the same. With that, let's fire up Blend 3 and create a new sketchflow prototype for a web application for a shopping website.

The Star Wars shopping application

Because I am a Star Wars fan, we are going to make a sketchflow prototype for an application where you can purchase Star Wars merchandise—specifically, Star Wars action figures, costumes, and books. It is going to be a simple application with a homepage, an action figure shopping page, a costume shopping page, a book shopping page, a view cart page, a checkout page, and finally a thank you page. Let's jump into Blend 3 and start now:

1. In Blend 3, click File ➤ New Project.

2. Select WPF Sketchflow Prototype.

3. Name the application StarWarsShoppingApp, and click OK, as shown in Figure 13-1.

Figure 13-1. Create a new WPF Sketchflow Prototype project in Blend 3.

4. Open the Application Flow panel, as shown in Figure 13-2.

Figure 13-2. Open the Application Flow panel.

The Application Flow panel allows you to model the flow, navigation, and composition of an application in a visual manner. The navigation screen named Start (shown in Figure 13-2) is where users will enter your application. Let's change it to say Homepage.

> *A navigation screen is represented by a blue icon and represents a page that a user can navigate to.*

5. Right-click the node and left-click Rename, as shown in Figure 13-3.

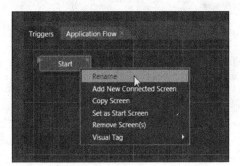

Figure 13-3. Rename the node.

6. Rename the node Homepage.

7. Now place your mouse over the Homepage navigation screen until a drawer slides out.

8. Place your mouse over the little square in the drawer and drag out a new navigation screen, as shown in Figures 13-4 and 13-5.

Figure 13-4. Place your mouse over the navigation screen until the utilities drawer slides out.

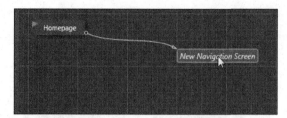

Figure 13-5. Drag out a new navigation screen.

9. Rename the new navigation screen Shop for Action Figures, as shown in Figure 13-6.

Figure 13-6. Rename the new navigation screen Shop for
Action Figures.

10. Repeat this process to add two more navigation screens named Shop for Costumes and Shop for
Books, so that you have what is shown in Figure 13-7.

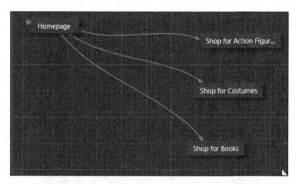

Figure 13-7. Your Application Flow panel should now look like this.

11. Next, we want our users to be able to navigate from each of the shopping pages to a View Cart
page. So, from the Shop for Action navigation screen, drag out a new navigation screen and
name it View Cart, so that you now have what is shown in Figure 13-8.

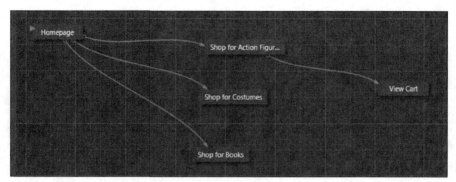

Figure 13-8. Add a View Cart navigation screen that originates from Shop For Action Figures.

12. Now use the same utility drawer for Shop for Costumes and Shop for Books to draw a connection to the View Cart navigation screen, as shown in Figure 13-9.

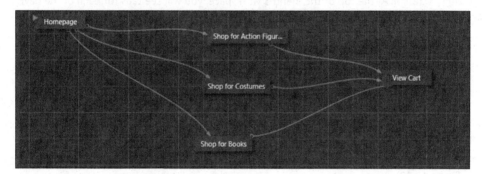

Figure 13-9. Make connections for all shopping pages to the View Cart page.

13. Now drag a new navigation screen from View Cart to create a navigation screen named Checkout, as shown in Figure 13-10.

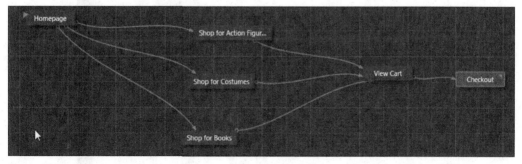

Figure 13-10. Add a new navigation screen named Checkout that originates at the View Cart navigation screen.

14. Finally, add a new navigation screen named Thank You that originates from the Checkout page, as shown in Figure 13-11.

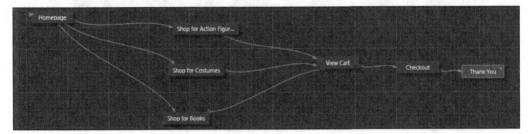

Figure 13-11. Add a new navigation screen named Thank You that originates from the Checkout navigation screen.

At this point, we are ready to start putting in placeholder objects that will represent our individual pages without design. At the top of the Blend 3 workspace, you will see tabs for each of the navigation screens you have created (see Figure 13-12).

Figure 13-12. The navigation screens that you have created

15. Click the Homepage screen and select the Pencil tool.

16. Draw out some Star Wars merchandise items (I have drawn two ships and the Death Star. See Figure 13-13).

Figure 13-13. Draw out some visuals for the homepage. Keep in mind that prototypes don't have design.

17. Next, draw a title TextBlock that reads "Welcome to the Star Wars Shop" with a font size of 36, as shown in Figure 13-14.

Figure 13-14. Draw a TextBlock that will represent the title.

18. Now we need to add some navigation buttons. In the Asset Library, located at the bottom of Blend's toolbar on the very left, select WigglyStyles, and then select WButtonStyle, as shown in Figure 13-15.

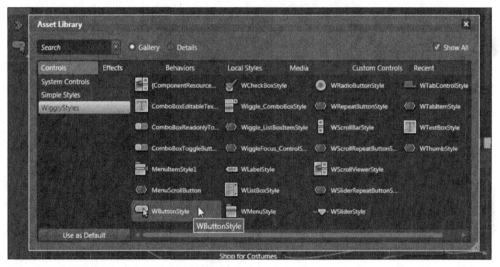

Figure 13-15. Select the WigglyStyles WButtonStyle.

What are **wiggly styles**, you ask? Good question. They are styles that are made to represent an object that is devoid of design. They are meant to look like someone has sketched them out on a cocktail napkin.

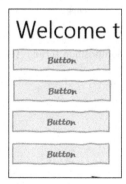

19. Now that you know what wiggly styles are, draw four wiggly buttons in the workspace, as shown in Figure 13-16.

Figure 13-16. Draw four wiggly buttons.

20. Rename the buttons to Shop for Action Figures, Shop for Costumes, Shop for Books, and Checkout (see Figure 13-17).

Now we want to be able to have this navigation on every page. Sketchflow prototyping allows us to easily make this a composition screen that can be reused. Let's turn the buttons into a composition screen now.

> A **composition screen** is meant to be added to a navigation screen and cannot be navigated to directly.

Figure 13-17. Rename the buttons.

21. Select all four buttons, right-click to bring up the context menu, and then click Make Into Composition Screen, as shown in Figure 13-18.

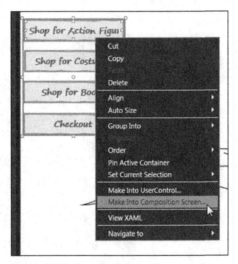

Figure 13-18. Turn the buttons into a composition screen.

22. In the Make Into Composition Screen dialog box, name the composition screen Navigation and click OK.

Now if you take a look at your Application Flow panel, you will see a new green icon that represents the composition screen (see Figure 13-19).

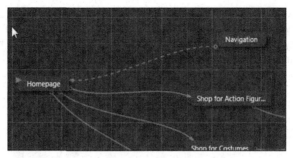

Figure 13-19. The new Navigation composition screen is represented by a green icon in the Application Flow panel.

23. In the workspace, select the composition screen, press Ctrl+C to copy it, click each of the navigation screens (Shop for Action Figures, Checkout, etc.), and press Ctrl+V to paste an instance of the composition screen. Now each navigation screen will have the Navigation composition screen.

Next, we'll add some items to the Shop for Action Figures navigation screen.

24. Click the Shop for Action Figures navigation screen.

25. Grab the Pencil tool from the Blend toolbar, and draw a stick figure, as shown in Figure 13-20.

26. Next, add a wiggly button underneath the stick figure that reads Add to Shopping Cart, as shown in Figure 13-21.

Figure 13-20. Draw a stick figure on the Shop for Action Figures navigation screen.

Figure 13-21. Add a wiggly button that reads Add to Shopping Cart.

27. Now hit the V key to select the Selection tool, hold down the Ctrl key, and select both the stick figure and the wiggly button. Press Ctrl+C and then Ctrl+V to copy and paste them, and then move the newly pasted figure and button to the right of the first. Do this again so that you have three figures and buttons, as shown in Figure 13-22.

Figure 13-22. Copy and paste so you have three figures and buttons.

28. Next, we are going to mimic an Item Added dialog box by adding a Rectangle with a gray fill, a TextBlock that reads "This item has been added to your shopping cart," and a wiggly button that says OK (see Figure 13-23).

Figure 13-23. Create a Item Added dialog box by adding a Rectangle, a TextBlock, and a wiggly button.

29. Now hold down the Ctrl key and select all three items (Rectangle, TextBlock, and wiggly button), right-click the selection, and then select Group Into ➤ Grid from the context menu, as shown in Figure 13-24.

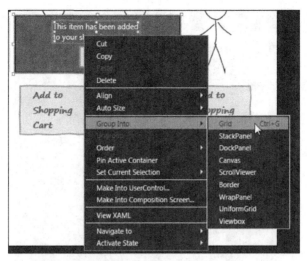

Figure 13-24. Group the three elements into a Grid.

30. Now, with the newly created Grid selected, set its opacity to 0% in the Properties panel's Appearance bucket, as shown in Figure 13-25.

Figure 13-25. Set the newly created Grid's opacity to 0%.

At this point, we could go on and add objects to the other navigation screens, but let's first wire up the Navigation composition screen, and then the objects in the Shop for Action Figures navigation screen.

31. Click the Navigation composition screen tab so you are viewing all of the navigation buttons.

32. Right-click the first Shop for Action Figures button, and then select Navigate to ➤ Shop for Action Figures from the context menu, as shown in Figure 13-26.

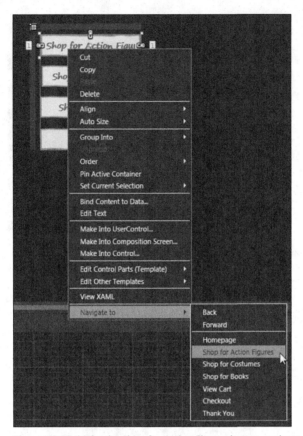

Figure 13-26. Make the Shop for Action Figures button navigate
to the Shop for Action Figures navigation screen.

33. Repeat this process to make each navigation button go to its corresponding navigation screen.

At this point, you can go ahead and press F5 to compile and run the application. Then click the Shop for Action Figures navigation button, and you will see that your prototype does actually navigate to the correct page. After you do this, close the application, and let's wire up the objects in the Shop for Action Figures page.

34. Click the Shop for Action Figures tab so you are viewing the corresponding navigation screen. We want the Add Item to Shopping Cart dialog box to appear when the user clicks the Add Item to Shopping Cart button. To accomplish this, we are going to use **states**.

35. Click the States tab (located next to the Objects and Timeline tab), as shown in Figure 13-27.

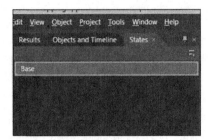

Figure 13-27. The States panel

36. Click the Add state group button, as shown in Figure 13-28.

Figure 13-28. Add a state group.

37. Name the new state group AddItemStateGroup and give it a default transition time of 0.5s, as shown in Figure 13-29.

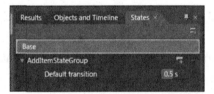

Figure 13-29. Name the new state group and give it a default transition time.

38. Now click the Add state button, as shown in Figure 13-30.

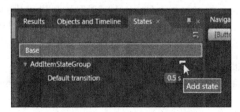

Figure 13-30. Add a new state.

39. Name the state Default, as shown in Figure 13-31.

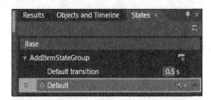

Figure 13-31. Name the new state Default.

40. Next, create a new state named ShowDialogBox, as shown in Figure 13-32.

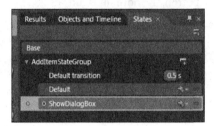

Figure 13-32. Create a new state named ShowDialogBox.

Notice that there is now a red line around the workspace to indicate that everything you do will be recorded into the state.

41. Select the Grid that contains the Item Added dialog box (currently with an opacity of 0%).

42. With the ShowDialogBox state still selected, change the opacity of the Grid to 100%.

43. Click Base in the States panel to select the Base state and stop recording. The Base state is the application when it is not in any state.

44. Next, click the Add to Shopping Cart button.

45. Right-click the add to shopping cart button, and then select Activate State ➤ Shop for Action Figures / ShowDialogBox, as shown in Figure 13-33. This will tell the application to switch to the ShowDialogBox state when the Add to Shopping Cart button is clicked.

46. Do this for each of the three Add to Shopping Cart buttons.

47. Now click the OK button in the Item Added dialog box (it's a little difficult as it has an opacity of 0%, but you can do it). Then, as before, have it activate a state—but this time have it activate the Default state.

Press F5 to run the application again. Navigate to the Shop for Action Figures navigation screen and click Add to Shopping Cart, and you will see the Item Added dialog box. You can also click the OK button in the dialog box to make it disappear. Pretty cool, huh? We have a functioning interactive prototype, and we have not written one line of code. Let's move on to the Shop for Costumes page.

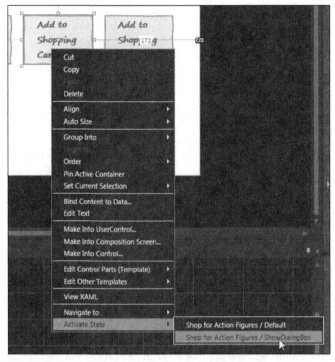

Figure 13-33. Have the Add to Shopping Cart button activate the ShowDialogBox state.

48. Switch over to the Shop for Costumes navigation screen, and draw a Jedi robe and Luke Skywalker's Bespin jacket using the Pencil tool (I told you I was a Star Wars fan).

49. Copy the Item Added dialog box and Add Item button from the Shop for Action Figures navigation screen, and paste them into the Shop for Costumes navigation screen, as shown in Figure 13-34.

50. In the States panel, add a state group named AddItemStateGroup with a default transition of 0.5 seconds.

51. Add a new state called Default.

52. Add a new state called ShowItemAddedDialogBox.

53. Give the dialog box an opacity of 100%.

54. Right-click each Add button and have it activate the ShowItemAddedDialogBox state.

55. Click the dialog OK button and have it activate the Default state.

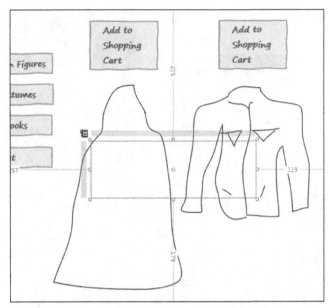

Figure 13-34. Draw a robe and jacket, and then copy and paste the dialog box and two wiggly buttons.

Now if you run the application, you will see that you can navigate to the Shop for Costumes navigation screen and click the Add Item dialog box. Let's move on to the Shop for Books navigation screen.

56. Click the Shop for Books navigation screen and draw a book with the Pencil tool.

57. Copy one Add to Shopping Cart button and the dialog box Grid from the Shop for Costumes page, and paste them into the Shop for Books navigation screen, as shown in Figure 13-35.

58. In the States panel, add a state group named AddItemStateGroup with a default transition of 0.5 seconds.

59. Add a new state called Default.

60. Add a new state called ShowItemAddedDialogBox.

61. Give the dialog box an opacity of 100%.

62. Right-click each Add button and have it activate the ShowItemAddedDialogBox state.

63. Click the dialog OK button and have it activate the Default state.

Figure 13-35. Draw a book and copy/paste the dialog box and a wiggly button.

Press F5 to run the application again. You should be able to navigate to the Shop for Books navigation screen, and click the Add an Item button to show the Item Added dialog box. You can also click OK to make the dialog box disappear. Let's now move on to the View Cart navigation screen.

64. Click the View Cart navigation screen to view it.

65. Add TextBlocks for subtotal, tax, total, items, and a title (each with a font size of 36).

66. Add a wiggly button that reads Proceed to Checkout, as shown in Figure 13-36.

Figure 13-36. Add TextBlocks that have dummy shopping cart information.

67. Right-click the Proceed to Checkout button and have it navigate to the Checkout navigation screen.

68. Now move on to the Checkout navigation screen and add some dummy information and a Buy button, as shown in Figure 13-37.

Figure 13-37. Add a TextBlock with dummy information and a Buy button.

69. Right-click the Buy button and have it navigate to the Thank You navigation screen.

70. Click the Thank You navigation screen, and add a TextBlock that reads Thank You and a Continue Shopping button, as shown in Figure 13-38.

Figure 13-38. Add a Thank You TextBlock and a Continue Shopping button.

71. Now right-click the Continue Shopping button and have it navigate to the homepage.

Now if you press F5 to compile and run the application, you can see the entire flow of the application in action:

1. Enter at the homepage.
2. Click Shop for Action Figures.
3. Add an action figure.
4. Close the Item Added dialog box. .
5. Click Shop for Costumes.
6. Add an item.
7. Close the Item Added dialog box.
8. Click the Shop for Books button.
9. Add an item.
10. Close the Item Added dialog box.
11. Click Checkout.
12. Review your order and charges.
13. Click Proceed to Checkout.
14. Click Buy.

On the Thank You page, click Continue Shopping. This sketchflow prototype can show a client quickly and efficiently how users will navigate through their new shopping application or website. And you were able to create it in a very short amount of time, thus saving money.

Summary

In this chapter, you learned about some exciting new features of Blend 3 and Silverlight. Namely, you learned about a powerful new feature in Blend 3 called sketchflow prototyping. This feature allows you to quickly create application prototypes that have working navigation and functionality, and even have storyboards. These prototypes can be shown to clients so that they can see the interaction of their new, designless application.

In the next chapter, you are going to take what you have learned up until this point and create a sample Silverlight web site, complete with custom user controls and a paging system that will load pages on demand to reduce upload time and save memory.

Chapter 14

PUTTING EVERYTHING TOGETHER TO BUILD A SAMPLE SILVERLIGHT WEBSITE

What this chapter covers:

- Building a sample website
  - Creating a Silverlight paging system
  - Creating a navigation UserControl
  - Creating a custom Silverlight Button to serve as navigation buttons
  - Creating a content holder UserControl
  - Creating content pages (Home, About Us, Contact Us, etc.)
  - Creating a method that switches out content pages
  - Wiring up the navigation buttons to switch content pages when clicked

Now that you have come this far, it is a good time to put everything you have learned together into a real-world application and build a Silverlight website. With that said, let's get right to it!

The problem

The problem is that up until now, we have put all of our UserControls right into the main LayoutRoot Grid. Because our applications have been relatively light regarding content, this has not been a problem. But what if we were to create a rich Internet application with a lot of content such as video and images? Well, we could put all of the content into UserControls, and then have each navigation button show its UserControl and hide all others. The problem with this approach is that *all* of that content would have to be loaded as soon as the website was accessed, and this would take quite a long time if every UserControl had a lot of content. Further, each UserControl, whether visible or collapsed, would take up precious memory and thus be very taxing on the CPU. For this reason, this approach just will not work.

The solution

What will work is a Silverlight paging system that loads the appropriate UserControl on demand (on the click of a navigation button, to be more precise) and also sets the previous content up to be cleared from memory via garbage collection (for a refresher on garbage collection, refer to Chapter 3). This will make it so all content will be loaded when requested and also keep memory usage as low as possible. So, in this chapter, we are going to create a sample website for a fictitious (I hope) company called GENX Furniture. We are then going to do the following:

1. Create a custom styled button.
2. Create a navigation UserControl that will hold the navigation buttons that can be shared across all pages.
3. Create page UserControls for Home, AboutUs, ContactUs, and Portfolio.
4. Create a content holder page that the content pages will be loaded into. This will be the only page that is shown in the application.
5. Create a method that will switch content in the content holder page.

Creating the GENX Furniture website

Open Blend 3 and create a new Silverlight 3 application and website called GenXFurniture, as shown in Figure 14-1.

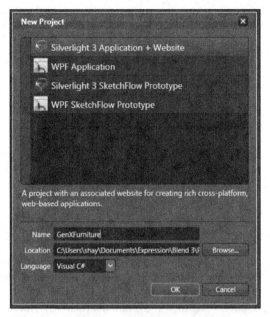

Figure 14-1. Create a new Silverlight 3 application and website called GenXFurniture.

The first thing we need to do is create the content holder and tell the application that this is the default UserControl to show when the application starts. Let's tackle that now:

1. In the Project panel, right-click the GenXFurniture project and click Add New Item, as shown in Figure 14-2.

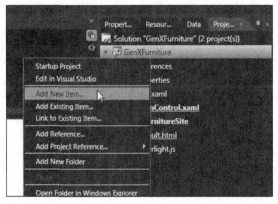

Figure 14-2. Add a new item to the project.

2. In the New Item dialog box, select UserControl, name it ContentHolder, and click OK, as shown in Figure 14-3.

Figure 14-3. Name the UserControl ContentHolder.

3. For testing purposes, put a TextBlock in the new UserControl. Have it read ContentHolder, and give it a white foreground and a font size of 22, as shown in Figure 14-4.

Figure 14-4. Add a TextBlock
that reads ContentHolder.

4. Now set the LayoutRoot Grid to be a solid color of black.

5. Next, in the Project panel, open App.xaml.cs and change this.RootVisual to be a new instance of ContentHolder, as shown in Figure 14-5. This will make ContentHeader.xaml the UserControl that is displayed when the application starts (it was previously MainControl. xaml).

```
private void OnStartup(object sender, StartupEventArgs e)
{
    // Load the main control here
    this.RootVisual = new ContentHolder();
}
```

Figure 14-5. In app.xaml.cs, set this.RootVisual to be a new
instance of ContentHolder.

Now press F5 to compile and run the application, and the ContentHolder will be shown when the application starts (see Figure 14-6).

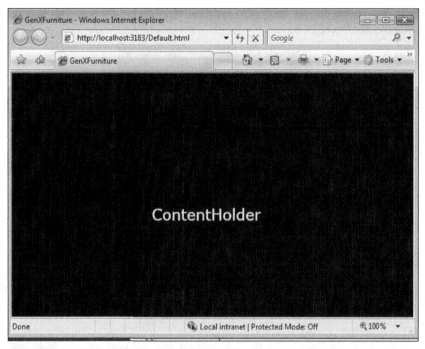

Figure 14-6. The ContentHolder is now the UserControl that is shown when the application starts.

At this point, we can delete MainControl.xaml from the Project panel, as we are never going to use it. It's not really necessary, but to be neat, I like to delete objects that will not be used in the application. Now we need to make our pages.

6. In the Project panel, right-click the project and click Add New Item.

7. In the New Item dialog box, select UserControl and name it Homepage, as shown in Figure 14-7.

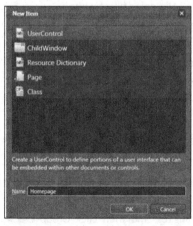

Figure 14-7. Add a new UserControl called Homepage.

8. Repeat this process for the AboutUs, ContactUs, and Portfolio pages, so that your Project panel looks like Figure 14-8.

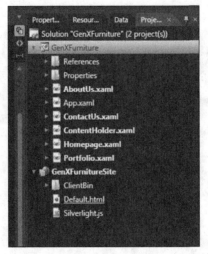

Figure 14-8. Your Project panel should now look like this.

Now we have our ContentHolder set at the UserControl that will load when the application loads, and we have our pages. However, we have no way to navigate to any of these pages. Before we make this happen, let's create a custom Silverlight button that all of the navigation buttons will use:

9. In ContentHolder, draw a Rectangle in the workspace and then use the radius handles to give it rounded edges, as shown in Figure 14-9.

10. Give the Rectangle a solid color fill of blue.

11. Copy and paste the Rectangle.

12. Give the new Rectangle a solid color fill of white.

13. Make it a bit smaller than the original Rectangle so you have something like that shown in Figure 14-10.

14. Now remove the white Rectangle's stroke and give it a gradient fill that goes from white to white.

15. Make the bottom color stop have an alpha of 0 so you have something that looks like Figure 14-11.

At this point, we are ready to group these two Rectangles into a Grid and then let Blend 3 turn them into a button for us. Let's do exactly that now.

16. In the Objects and Timeline panel, hold down Ctrl and click the two Rectangles.

17. Right-click the two Rectangles, and then click Group Into ➤ Grid, as shown in Figure 14-12.

Figure 14-9. Draw a Rectangle with rounded edges in ContentHolder.

Figure 14-10. Draw a new white Rectangle and make it slightly smaller than the original one.

Figure 14-11. Set the top Rectangle to have no stroke, a gradient fill that goes from white to white, and a bottom color stop with an alpha of 0.

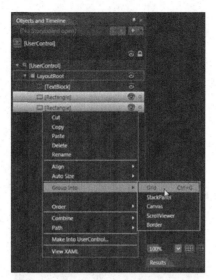

Figure 14-12. Group the two Rectangles into a Grid.

18. With the newly created Grid selected, click Tools ➤ Make Into Control, as shown in Figure 14-13.

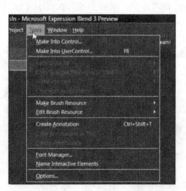

Figure 14-13. Make the Grid into a control.

19. When the Make Into Control dialog box appears, select Button, and name it Style_BlueButton. Then, in the Define in section, click the New button to create a new ResourceDictionary, as shown in Figure 14-14.

Figure 14-14. Click the New button to
create a new ResourceDictionary.

20. In the New Item dialog box, name the new ResourceDictionary RD_MainResourceDictionary,
and click OK, as shown in Figure 14-15.

Figure 14-15. Name the new ResourceDictionary
RD_MainResourceDictionary.

21. Click OK in the Make Into Control dialog box.

Switch back to ContentHolder.xaml, and your Button control should look like
Figure 14-16.

22. In the Common Properties bucket of the Properties panel, change Content
to read Home.

Figure 14-16.
Your Button should
now look like this
in ContentHolder.
xaml.

23. Copy and paste the Button three times so that you have a total of four Buttons.

24. Change the content of the Buttons so that they read Home, About Us, Contact Us, and Portfolio, as shown in Figure 14-17.

Figure 14-17. Your navigation buttons should now have the correct content.

25. In the Properties panel, change the names of the Buttons to HomeBtn, AboutBtn, ContactBtn, and PortfolioBtn, respectively.

Now that we have our navigation buttons, we need to create a navigation UserControl that will hold them. We need to do this because ContentHolder will have its content set dynamically. Let's do this now.

26. In the Project panel, right-click the project and click Add New Item.

27. In the New Item dialog box, select UserControl, name it Navigation, and click OK, as shown in Figure 14-18.

Figure 14-18. Name the new UserControl Navigation.

28. Switch back to ContentHolder.xaml and select all of the navigation buttons.

29. Switch over to Navigation.xaml and paste the buttons.

30. In the Objects and Timeline panel, select [UserControl] and make the UserControl only big enough so that it won't overlap other UserControls in the application (see Figure 14-19).

Figure 14-19. Add the buttons to Navigation.xaml.

Now that we have the navigation, we need to go into every page and add the UserControl. For this, I like to switch over to Visual Studio because IntelliSense makes it much easier.

31. To do that, right-click the project in the Project panel and click Edit in Visual Studio, as shown in Figure 14-20.

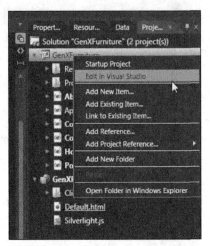

Figure 14-20. Tell Blend to open the project in Visual Studio.

If Visual Studio gives you a security warning, click Load the Project Normally.

32. Open Homepage.xaml and add a namespace called local, as in the following code:

```
<UserControl
 xmlns="http://schemas.microsoft.com/winfx/2006/xaml/presentation"
 xmlns:x="http://schemas.microsoft.com/winfx/2006/xaml"
 xmlns:d="http://schemas.microsoft.com/expression/blend/2008"
 xmlns:mc="http://schemas.openxmlformats.org/markup-compatibility/2006"
 mc:Ignorable="d"
 x:Class="GenXFurniture.Homepage"
 d:DesignWidth="640" d:DesignHeight="480"
    xmlns:local="clr-namespace:GenXFurniture">
```

33. Now we can use the new local namespace to add a Navigation control in the LayoutRoot Grid. See the following code:

```
    <Grid x:Name="LayoutRoot">

        <local:Navigation/>
    </Grid>
</UserControl>
```

Now press Ctrl+Shift+B to compile the application, switch back to Blend 3, and reload the project when prompted. If you now open Homepage.xaml, you will see the Navigation control. Way to go! Now we need to copy and paste this control from Homepage.xaml into all of the other pages (AboutUs, ContactUs, and Portfolio).

Press Ctrl+Shift+B to compile the application in Blend 3, and you can switch back to Visual Studio to set the content initially and then add the functionality to the navigation buttons to have them load the appropriate content into ContentHolder.xaml. Let's switch over to Visual Studio and do this now.

34. In Visual Studio, open the ContentHolder.xaml.cs code-behind file and raise and handle a Loaded event, as shown in the following code:

```
namespace GenXFurniture
{
public partial class ContentHolder : UserControl
{
public ContentHolder()
{
// Required to initialize variables
InitializeComponent();
}

        void ContentHolder_Loaded(object sender, RoutedEventArgs e)
        {
            throw new NotImplementedException();
        }
}
}
```

35. In the new Loaded handler, remove the default throw new... code, and then set the content to be a new instance of Homepage, as shown here:

```
        void HomeBtn_Click(object sender, RoutedEventArgs e)
        {
            ContentHolder ch = Application.Current.RootVisual
as ContentHolder;
            ch.SwitchContent(new Homepage());
        }
```

Now if you press F5 to run the application, you will see the navigation buttons. However, how do we know that we have loaded Homepage.xaml into ContentHolder? We don't. So, add a TextBlock with a black foreground and a font size of, say, 20, for each page that says the name of the page. Run the application and you should see that Homepage.xaml is loaded into ContentHolder (see Figure 14-21).

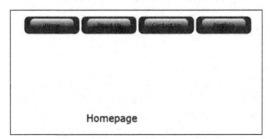

Figure 14-21. Now you can tell that Homepage.xaml has been loaded into ContentHolder.xaml.

The last thing we need to do is have each navigation button load its content into ContentHolder.xaml. So switch over to Visual Studio, and let's do that now.

36. Open Navigation.xaml.cs and raise and handle the Click event for each button, as in the following code:

```
namespace GenXFurniture
{
public partial class Navigation : UserControl
{
public Navigation()
{
// Required to initialize variables
InitializeComponent();
            HomeBtn.Click += new RoutedEventHandler(HomeBtn_Click);
            AboutBtn.Click += new RoutedEventHandler(AboutBtn_Click);
            ContactBtn.Click += new RoutedEventHandler
(ContactBtn_Click);
            PortfolioBtn.Click += new RoutedEventHandler
(PortfolioBtn_Click);
 }

        void PortfolioBtn_Click(object sender, RoutedEventArgs e)
        {
            throw new NotImplementedException();
        }

        void ContactBtn_Click(object sender, RoutedEventArgs e)
        {
            throw new NotImplementedException();
        }

        void AboutBtn_Click(object sender, RoutedEventArgs e)
        {
            throw new NotImplementedException();
        }

        void HomeBtn_Click(object sender, RoutedEventArgs e)
        {
            throw new NotImplementedException();
        }
    }
}
```

37. Now we need to create a SwitchContentHandler method in ContentHolder.cs. This method will accept a UserControl (Homepage, AboutUs, etc.) as an argument and then set the content of ContentHolder to that UserControl. See the following code:

```
namespace GenXFurniture
{
    public partial class ContentHolder : UserControl
```

```
    {
        public ContentHolder()
        {
            // Required to initialize variables
            InitializeComponent();
            this.Loaded += new RoutedEventHandler
(ContentHolder_Loaded);
        }

        void ContentHolder_Loaded(object sender, RoutedEventArgs e)
        {
            this.Content = new Homepage();
        }

        public void SwitchContent(UserControl requestedPage)
        {
            this.Content = requestedPage;
        }
    }
}
```

38. Now all we need to do is to go back to Navigation.xaml.cs and load the appropriate content into ContentHolder in the event handlers. We do this by creating a new ContentHolder object called ch that will act as the application's RootVisual. We can then access the SwitchContent method and pass in a new instance of the appropriate UserControl. See the following code.

> In Silverlight, RootVisual is a property that sets the application's main UI.

```
public partial class Navigation : UserControl
{
public Navigation()
{
// Required to initialize variables
InitializeComponent();
        HomeBtn.Click += new RoutedEventHandler(HomeBtn_Click);
        AboutBtn.Click += new RoutedEventHandler(AboutBtn_Click);
        ContactBtn.Click += new RoutedEventHandler
(ContactBtn_Click);
        PortfolioBtn.Click += new RoutedEventHandler
(PortfolioBtn_Click);
}

        void PortfolioBtn_Click(object sender, RoutedEventArgs e)
        {
            ContentHolder ch = Application.Current.RootVisual
as ContentHolder;
            ch.SwitchContent(new Portfolio());
        }
```

```
        void ContactBtn_Click(object sender, RoutedEventArgs e)
        {
            ContentHolder ch = Application.Current.RootVisual
as ContentHolder;
            ch.SwitchContent(new ContactUs());
        }

        void AboutBtn_Click(object sender, RoutedEventArgs e)
        {
            ContentHolder ch = Application.Current.RootVisual
as ContentHolder;
            ch.SwitchContent(new AboutUs());
        }

        void HomeBtn_Click(object sender, RoutedEventArgs e)
        {
            ContentHolder ch = Application.Current.RootVisual
as ContentHolder;
            ch.SwitchContent(new Homepage());
        }
    }
}
```

Now if you run the application, you will see that you can click the navigation buttons to switch to the correct UserControl. As for content, you can go ahead and add that in yourself. I've taught you how to build a simple sample site that loads content on demand to save on download time and memory. My challenge to you is to go ahead and add dummy content and maybe some cool storyboards. Feel free to send me links to your projects; I'd love to see them.

You can download this project here: http://www.windowspresentationfoundation.com/Blend3Book/ GenXFurniture.zip.

Summary

In this chapter, you have put what you have learned in this book to practical use by creating a simple sample Silverlight website. The site loads its content on demand to save on download time and memory usage. Further, you made a custom Silverlight Button control and placed it into a navigation UserControl that can be used in all of the website pages. Doing this arms you with the knowledge you need to go out into the real world and create a Silverlight website application. Of course, it is up to you to come up with the content, but you already know how to do that. The pages could include media players, image viewers, a ListBox bound to a collection of data, a custom panel, and so on. The possibilities are endless, and you now know how to accomplish all of it. Now go out there and build something cool. Be sure and send me an e-mail so I can see what I have helped you to create!

INDEX